The Family
BIBLE
ENCYCLOPEDIA

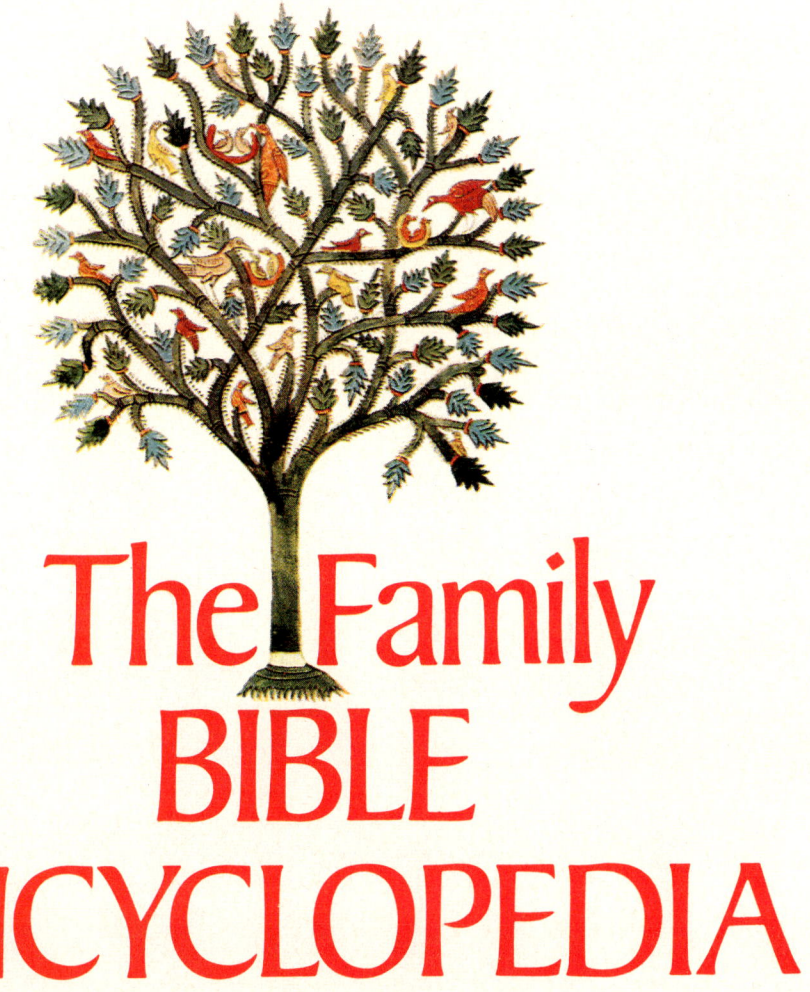

The Family
BIBLE
ENCYCLOPEDIA

Published in New York by Curtis Books, Inc.
and simultaneously in Toronto, Canada, by
Curtis Distributing Company, Ltd.

CREATED AND PRODUCED BY
COPYLAB PUBLISHING COUNSEL, INC., NEW YORK

Copyright © 1972
by
Copylab Publishing Counsel, Inc.

All rights reserved, including, without limitation, the right to reproduce this book or portions thereof in any form. Library of Congress Card Catalog Number 79-187552.

Printed in the United States of America

19th-century lithograph showing Jerusalem from the east (*New York Public Library*).

JEROHAM (Heb., *yeroham,* "cherished" or "pitied of the Lord"), a name borne by a number of OLD TESTAMENT personages: a member of the LEVITES who was the paternal grandfather of the Judge-Prophet SAMUEL (I Sam. 1:1; I Chron. 6:27); two men of the TRIBE OF BENJAMIN who lived in JERUSALEM (I Chron. 8:27; 9:8 [the two may have been one and the same person]); the ancestor of one of the Levites who flourished in Jerusalem during the royal governorship of NEHEMIAH (Neh. 11:12 [and probably the Jeroham mentioned in I Chron. 9:12]); the father of two Benjaminites who joined DAVID at ZIKLAG during the future monarch's period of outlawry (I Chron. 12:7); the father of AZAREEL who was chief of the TRIBE OF DAN during King David's reign (I Chron. 27:22); and the father of AZARIAH, one of the "captains of hundreds" who assisted JEHOIADA in deposing the usurper queen ATHALIAH and putting her grandson JOASH on the throne of the Southern KINGDOM OF JUDAH (II Chron. 23:1).

JERUBBAAL (Heb., *yeruv baal,* "contender with Baal"), the surname of GIDEON, one of the major JUDGES OF ISRAEL, so-called by his father when he destroyed an altar to BAAL (Judg. 6:32).

JERUBBESHETH (Heb., *yeruvvesheth,* "strife with the idol [BAAL is probably intended here]"), a surname for GIDEON as it appears in the Second Book of SAMUEL (11:21).

JERUEL (Heb., *yeruel,* "founded by God"), a battlefield ("wilderness" in the text), probably in the vicinity of EN-GEDI but otherwise unidentifiable, at which place JAHAZIEL predicted that the armies of King JEHOSHAPHAT should encounter the armies of the MOABITES and AMMONITES (II Chron. 20:16).

JERUSALEM (from the Amorite *Urushalimmu,* "Shalim [an Amorite god] has founded"), the capital of modern-day Israel and indisputably the most important city, religiously, militarily, and politically, of the BIBLE; it was and continued to be of central importance in three of the world's major religions, JUDAISM, CHRISTIANITY, and Islam. Known as The City of DAVID, after the Israelite king who conquered it at the beginning of the first millennium B.C. and established his political and religious capital there, Jerusalem continued, with brief interruptions, as the political center of Judaism for more than a thousand years and as the religious and spiritual center of worldwide Jewry for nearly three millennia. As the scene of the CRUCIFIXION and RESURRECTION of JESUS CHRIST, it became the most sacred city of Christendom, and, though overshadowed by the city of ROME administratively, it remains the sacred focal point of all the various Christian sects throughout the world. To the adherents of Islam, which adopted and adapted many of Judaism's traditions, it ranks as the third holiest city—after Mecca and Medina—for nearly half a billion Moslems. Since in the broadest sense the history of Jerusalem is almost identical with the latter portion of OLD TESTAMENT history in general, this article will consider Jerusalem in its geographical sense and will refer to the wider historical events only insofar as they impinge on the history of the city of Jerusalem itself.

The most striking feature in the history of Jerusalem is that were it not for the arbitrary selection of the city by David as The Holy City of GOD and the events that unfolded therefrom, Jerusalem would doubtless have been of little importance to the world at large and would have played no part in the emergence of Western civilization. This sweeping statement seems supportable from the nature of the site of Jerusalem: Unlike virtually all other capital cities, ancient and modern, Jerusalem is neither on the sea nor easily accessible from the sea, stands on no major river or canal, and is not even a convergence point for trade routes, ancient or modern. Hence, it could never have derived importance as a mercantile center or as a strategic military position. Located 2,500 feet above sea level in mountainous country thirty-seven miles from the Mediterranean Sea and fourteen miles from the northern end of the DEAD SEA, the site seems unattractive even from the local point of view, since it lacks an adequate supply of water, is surrounded by relatively infertile land, and is hemmed in by deep valleys and tortuous trails which tend to make even a short cross-country journey an arduous affair.

Though all these considerations attest by implication to the importance of the religious element in the city's primacy in Western civilization, it remains to be asked why, in the absence of the religious factor, a city was ever built on the site. Ironically, the answer lies in the very disadvantages of the site, for its commercial unimportance and natural inaccessibility rendered it a natural and easily defensible fortress, a factor which in the turbulent and insecure conditions obtaining in the third and second millennia B.C., sufficed to make it attractive to local inhabitants. In addition, though its water supply was far from adequate, it did—unlike neighboring and equally defensible hills—have access to a natural water supply, the Spring of GIHON (also known as the Virgin's Fountain) which skirts the eastern edge of the site. Thus, by ancient standards, Jerusalem was suitable only as a citadel on a limited tribal scale.

Topographically, the biblical city of Jerusalem was constructed on two roughly triangular-shaped ridges which converge toward the south. On the east lay the deep ravine, known as the Valley of KIDRON, which rendered the site virtually invulnerable to attack from the east. On the west lay the deep gorge known as the Valley of HINNOM which ran first southward and then turned eastward until it met the Valley of Kidron. The hilly plateau bounded by these two valleys was bisected by the Tyropoeon Valley (now filled in with debris and appearing only as a slight depression) which separated the two ridges from one another and which ran into the Kidron Valley at a point just north of the confluence of the valleys of Hinnom and Kidron. Each of the ridges therefore was protected on both east and west by deep ravines, and, since each formed a promontory pointing southward, each was naturally protected in this direction as well. Only on the northern side, where each of the ridges broadened out to join the central mountain ridge of JUDAH, was the city vulnerable to military attack.

According to an erroneous tradition, the first of the two ridges to be settled was the higher and more spacious western spur, the natural advantages of which would seem to make it easier to defend than the far less lofty eastern spur. But the absence of an easily accessible water supply on the western ridge (since the Spring of Gihon flows through the Valley of Kidron)

Copy of a mosaic map of Jerusalem dating from Byzantine times (*Counsel Collection*).

JERUSALEM 1545

Panoramic view of Jerusalem showing recent reconstruction of the Holy Sepulchre Basilica, built over the traditional site where Jesus was crucified (*Counsel Collection*).

has led modern scholars to postulate that the eastern ridge was the first to be settled, a hypothesis that ARCHAEOLOGY has borne out. In addition, further investigation has revealed that both sites were equally defendable: for while in modern warfare the lower eastern ridge would be seriously menaced by the higher western ridge, the absence of highly developed missile weapons in prebiblical and early biblical times nullified this seeming advantage, since the two ridges were separated by the precipitous Tyropoeon ravine. Thus the relative availability of water on the eastern ridge must have been crucial in making it more attractive to the earliest settlers.

To secure this water supply, the early settlers of Jerusalem seem to have gone to considerable lengths—since the Spring of Gihon flowed beneath the natural ramparts formed by the Valley of Kidron, it was necessary to bring the water upward and inside the natural fortress.

According to archaeological evidence, an ingenious and sophisticated tunnel was constructed, shaped like a letter "Z" except that the crossbar was vertical instead of diagonal. Since the upper horizontal tunnel ran eastward into the ridge, buckets could be lowered down the vertical tunnel to draw up the water which had been made to flow westward into the lower horizontal tunnel from the Spring of Gihon. The magnitude of such an engineering feat in Bronze Age society is alone sufficient to indicate the importance of the water supply in the choice of Jerusalem as a site for a city. But the engineers who accomplished the feat seem not to have realized that their Z-shaped tunnel was, in effect, a double-edged sword. At the beginning of the first millennium B.C., when David's army besieged Jerusalem, it is probable that his commander JOAB first gained access to the heart of the city by shinnying up the walls of the Z-shaped tunnel (II Sam. 5:8).

The earliest inhabitants of Jerusalem were most probably Semitic herdsmen who clustered around the Spring of Gihon in the Kidron Valley toward the end of the fourth millennium B.C., at a time contemporaneous with the rise of urban civilization throughout SYRIA and PALESTINE. What little is known of these early settlers—and indeed of their successors for the next two millennia—is largely the product of archaeological excavations, the earliest finds of which have been pottery remains from tombs cut into the rock of the easternmost slope. During the third millennium B.C., as these herdsmen prospered, it appears that they established themselves on the eastern ridge where the precipitous ravines provided natural defenses on all sides but the north. In this direction an artificial defense was constructed no later than 2200 B.C., in the form of a trench which ran in an east-west direction between the Kidron and Tyropoeon valleys. Over succeeding centuries, the city expanded northward beyond this trench, and by 1500 B.C., a city wall more than a yard thick had been constructed. Three centuries later a new, stronger wall was erected, twenty feet thick with towers more than twenty feet in height. The course of this wall was almost a quarter-mile long, four hundred feet in width, and enclosed an area of nearly twelve acres, making Jerusalem one of the largest cities of CANAAN at the time.

The earliest mention of Jerusalem in written documents is to be found in Egyptian Execration Texts dating to the middle of the nineteenth century B.C., in which two chiefs of *Urushalimmu* (the Egyptian designation for Jerusalem), *Yaquir-'ammu* and *Shayznu,* are numbered among the enemies of the Egyptian PHARAOH. Both names are AMORITE in origin and their hostile stance toward EGYPT confirms evidence, derived from independent sources, that an imperialistic Egypt was, during the first three centuries of the second millennium B.C., attempting to gain hegemony over the Amorite city-states that had been established throughout Palestine and Syria. It is to this period as well that the biblical encounter between MELCHIZEDEC, the "king of Salem" (undoubtedly Jerusalem) and ABRAHAM (Gen. 14:18-20) may be dated. Abraham's deference to Melchizedec may indictate that the seminomadic Patriarch was, at the time, a retainer of this early Jerusalemite king.

During the period of HYKSOS domination of Egypt and Palestine which followed, Jerusalem probably received an influx of Hurrian (the biblical HORITES) and Indo-Aryan migrants and was governed by a Hyksos overlord. Though the Amorite inhabitants of Jerusalem were culturally influenced by the invaders (particularly with the introduction of new military techniques such as the horse-drawn war chariot), the next historical mention of Jerusalem, in the TEL EL-AMARNA Letters of the fourteenth century B.C., indicates that a hereditary Amorite king had been reinstalled on the throne. At this time, Egypt enjoyed a hegemony in Palestine, and the Letters contain the lamentations of the Jerusalemite king *Abdi-Khiba,* whose territory was being overrun by freebooting mercenaries, and an appeal to the Egyptian pharaoh for military aid against the outlaws.

Nothing further is known of Jerusalem until its biblical period commences with the Israelites' invasion of Canaan under their commander JOSHUA. According to the Book of JOSHUA (10:1), ADONI-ZEDEK was king of Jerusalem at the time. Fearing the power of the Israelites, who had recently scored victories over JERICHO and AI, Adoni-zedek headed a coalition of five kings, but was defeated by the Israelites with "a very great slaughter," taken prisoner, and hanged. From the narrative in Joshua, it would appear that the Israelites captured the city-state of Jerusalem at that time (10:42), and assigned the conquered territory to the TRIBE OF BENJAMIN (18:28). But the narrative of the Book of JUDGES indicates that though the Israelites had scored a victory against Jerusalem (1:8), they did not occupy the city (1:21), and that it remained in the hands of the JEBUSITES (the popular name for the combined Canaanite-Hurrian-Indo-Aryan population of Jerusalem) well into the PERIOD OF THE CONQUEST AND JUDGES (19:11). The apparent contradiction may be resolved, however, by passages in Joshua, in which the border of the lands occupied by the TRIBE OF JUDAH are said to have extended as far north as "the south side of . . . Jerusalem" (Josh. 15:8), but that as concerned "the in-

JERUSALEM 1547

habitants of Jerusalem, the children of Judah could not drive them out" (15:63)—in other words, the lands of the city-state of Jerusalem were occupied by the Israelites, but the Jebusites retained control of the city itself.

It remained, then, for David to bring the city of Jerusalem finally under Israelite control. By the time of his campaign, Jerusalem's local significance had increased enormously. During the period (1225-1025 B.C.) in which the JUDGES OF ISRAEL flourished, and early in the subsequent PERIOD OF THE MONARCHY, disunity had been endemic and enervating among the Israelites. The existence of a Canaanite stronghold such as Jerusalem in the midst of Israelite territory

Tomb of the Virgin Mary, at the foot of the Garden of Gethsemane. The traditional site of Mary's burial place lies within one of the oldest churches in the world, 47 steps below the church's entrance (*Counsel Collection*).

contributed largely to this disunity, and its continued occupation by the Jebusites would effectually prevent any permanent union between the northern and southern portions of the Israelites' territory. In addition, jealousies among the TWELVE TRIBES OF ISRAEL required that a capital for a united monarchy be established on hitherto neutral territory, and the central position of Jerusalem led David to select it as his future capital.

The campaign against Jerusalem may have been conducted on two fronts. After investing the city in the face of the jeering Jebusites, who were overconfident in the defenses of their city, David called for volunteers to "getteth up to the gutter" (the Z-shaped tunnel) and thereby gain entry into the city. And though Joab won the position of "chief and captain" of David's forces for accomplishing the exploit, it may actually have amounted to no more than the distraction that enabled the main body of David's force to make a breach in the northern wall and thereby capture the city (c.f., II Sam. 5:6-8, I Kings 11:27).

Almost immediately after its capture by David, Jerusalem began to assume the character that it would present to the world for the next three millenia. Since Jerusalem had been conquered by David and his army of personal retainers, the city became, in the literal sense, The City of David (i.e., a crown possession) as well as the capital of a united ISRAEL. Thus the destiny of the city became identified with the fortunes of its founder and his hereditary dynasty, which, in turn, became inseparably linked to the fate of the Israelites and, later, of the Jewish people. Since the basic factor that linked the various Israelite tribes was their common worship of YAHWEH at an amphictyonic shrine (SHILOH), David completed the charismatic-religious-political unity by bringing the TABERNACLE, after several vicissitudes, from its former site at Shiloh to the new capital at Jerusalem.

Among David's first actions after conquering Jerusalem was perforce the refortification of the city. These new works centered about a *millo* (or tower) and were "built round about from Millo and inward" (II Sam. 5:9). In addition, after concluding an alliance with the prosperous Phoenician king HIRAM of TYRE, David used highly skilled Phoenician craftsmen and materials in construction of a royal palace, which also served as a stronghold. Since remains of this work have not yet been discovered through excavation, it is not certain that David expanded the city walls northward beyond the former Jebusite fortifications, though it is highly probable that he contemplated such an expansion since the THRESHING FLOOR of ARAUNAH, the site chosen for the future TEMPLE, lay outside the walls of the former Canaanite enclave.

If the character of Jerusalem was first fixed by David, it remained for his son and successor SOLOMON to accomplish the physical glorification of the city. The most important, if not the most magnificent, of the works constructed by Solomon during a prosperous and relatively peaceful forty-year reign was the Temple, which lay at one end of a vast complex of buildings that formed a citadel within the city. This complex was constructed on a rise somewhat to the north of the Davidic city and became known thereafter as the Temple Mount. The northernmost and highest edifice was the Temple itself, which measured about 125 feet in length, fifty-five in width and fifty in height, not including a porch that flanked the eastern side and rectangular chambers on each of the other three sides. Immediately to the south of the Temple was a courtyard which enclosed the Royal Palace, with which was connected a special palace built for the most prominent of Solomon's wives. In addition, there were three other important buildings within the citadel complex: a Hall of Justice, a Hall of Pillars, and a House of the Forest of Lebanon. Though no remains of these buildings have been excavated, it is known that the dimensions of each, with the possible exception of the Hall of Justice (the extent of which is unknown), exceeded the area of the Temple. Since the Israelites had no adequate architectural style of their own, it is probable that these buildings were based either on Phoenician or Egyptian models. (*See also* ARCHITECTURE.)

These works formed only one part of Solomon's glorification of Jerusalem, for it was probably during his reign that the city was expanded to include the hitherto extramural western ridge. According to the Second Book of the CHRONICLES (8:11), this expansion may have arisen from the necessity of housing Solomon's heathen wives—in particular, the daughter of the Egyptian Pharaoh—as far as possible from the sacred precincts of the Temple, though it is likely that prosperity and a concomitant increase in population may have been more important factors in the enlargement. Though archaeologists are in disagreement over the exact course of the new Solomonic walls, it is probable that they extended westward from the Temple across the Tyropoeon Valley to the Valley of Hin-

Street view in the ancient walled town of the Old City of Jerusalem (*left*), and (*below*) view of the Via Dolorosa, the route followed by Jesus on the way to his Crucifixion (*Counsel Collection*).

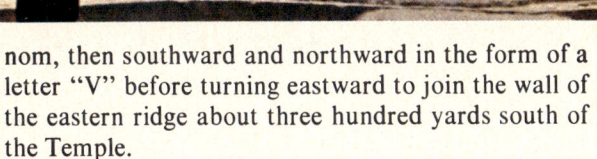

nom, then southward and northward in the form of a letter "V" before turning eastward to join the wall of the eastern ridge about three hundred yards south of the Temple.

Ironically, this initial period of splendor for Jerusalem came to an end with the death of Solomon about 922 B.C., for with the partition of the Hebrew monarchy that followed, Jerusalem relapsed into what politically might be termed provincial status. (*See* ISRAEL, KINGDOM OF; JUDAH, KINGDOM OF.) During

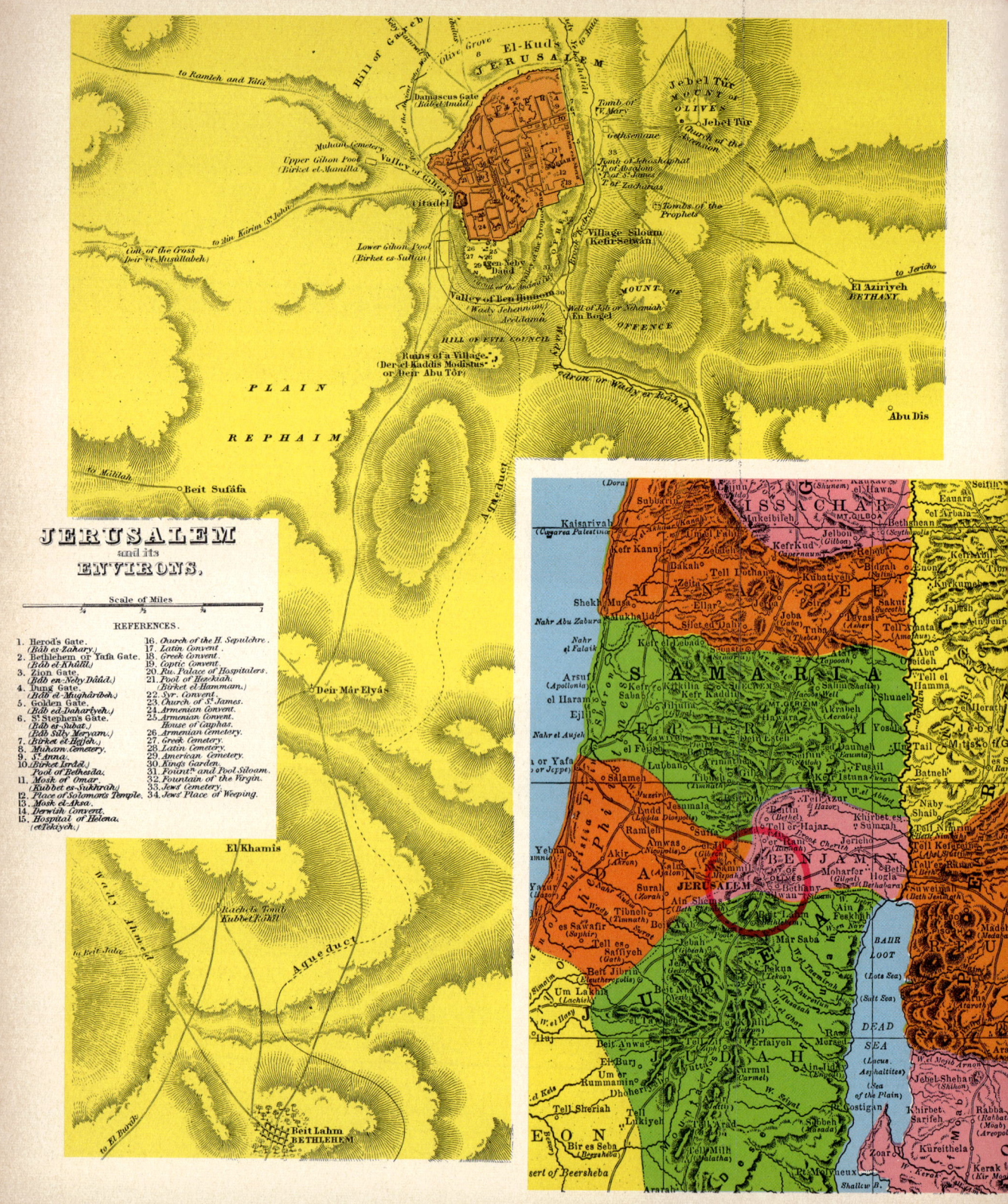

the succeeding three centuries its very geographical obscurity militated in its favor, for as capital of the less prosperous and less strategic Southern Kingdom of Judah, it was left relatively untouched by the international political struggles that consumed the energies of the Northern Kingdom of Israel, which lay astride the trade routes and military roads of the ancient Near East. In effect then, it did not become an adjunct of its richer and more powerful neighbor to the north only because of the Northern Kingdom's preoccupation with politically more powerful neighbors, and it was thereby permitted to develop for three centuries the tradition of loyalty to the Davidic line and the character as a sacred city that were to form the basis of its reputation forever after.

Nonetheless, the city endured occasional vicissitudes. Shortly after the partition, the hostile stance of the Northern Kingdom led Solomon's son and successor REHOBOAM to seek aid from the Egyptian pharaoh SHISHAK. The latter provided support but at great cost, and Rehoboam was forced to strip the Temple that his father had built of much of its treasure in order to satisfy the oppressive demands of his erstwhile protector. Greater depredations occurred seventy-five years later during the reign of JEHORAM. Apparently this coincided with a period of religious dissension within Jerusalem and military weakness without, for the Second Book of the Chronicles speaks of the erection of HIGH PLACES (pagan shrines) in the hill country around Jerusalem, and of the successful revolt of the Southern Kingdom's vassals, EDOM and LIBNAH (21:8-11). Encouraged apparently by Jerusalem's unpreparedness, a combination of Philistine and Arabian tribes conducted extensive raids in the countryside around Jerusalem "and brake into it, and carried away all the substance that was found in the king's house, and his sons also, and his wives; so that there was never a son left him, save Jehoahaz, the youngest of his sons" (21:17).

Internal strife, for both religious and political reasons, apparently continued in Jerusalem for about half a century until the accession (c. 800 B.C.) of AMAZIAH, who was able to attack and reconquer Edom. Flushed with victory, Amaziah seems to have assumed an arrogant stance toward the Northern Kingdom's monarch JEHOASH, who, after jeering at Amaziah's presumptuousness, "came to Jerusalem, and brake down the wall of Jerusalem from the gate of Ephraim unto the corner gate, four hundred cubits. And he took all the gold and silver, and all the vessels that were found in the house of the Lord, and in the treasures of the king's house, and hostages, and returned to Samaria" (II Kings 14:13-14; see SAMARIA). The portion of the city wall herein referred to was probably a two-hundred-yard section of the defenses that Solomon had built across the northern boundary of the western ridge, though the successive refortifications that must have taken place during this period make the identification uncertain.

Once again, the insignificance of Jerusalem worked in its favor, and the victorious king Jehoash made no attempt to annex Jerusalem to the Northern Kingdom. This reprieve provided Amaziah's successor UZZIAH with the opportunity to refortify the city. In addition to successful raids against the Philistines and the Arabians, Uzziah, according to the Second Book of the Chronicles, "built towers in Jerusalem at the corner gate, and at the valley gate, and at the turning of the wall, and fortified them . . . And he made in Jerusalem engines, invented by cunning men, to be on the towers and upon the bulwarks, to shoot arrows and great stones withal" (26:9, 15).

Apparently these new fortifications stood Jerusalem in good stead, for about 730 B.C., when King AHAZ refused to join a local coalition against the threat of an Assyrian invasion, he was attacked by the alliance's leaders REZIN, king of DAMASCUS, and PEKAH, king of Israel. According to the Second Book of the Kings, they "came up to Jerusalem to war: and they besieged Ahaz, but could not overcome him" (16:5). Ahaz thereupon sent messengers to the Assyrian monarch TIGLATH-PILESER, saying, "I am thy servant" (16:7), and thereby avoided the Assyrian reprisals that brought a catastrophic end to both the Northern Kingdom of Israel and the Kingdom of Damascus.

But the establishment of an ASSYRIAN EMPIRE hegemony throughout Palestine and Syria did little to bring stability to the area, as the various vassal states continually contemplated and occasionally committed rebellion against their irresistible and often brutal overlords. Ahaz' successor in Jerusalem, HEZEKIAH, wisely rejected the overtures of nearby ASHDOD, which was crushed by Assyria in 711 B.C., and spent his time instead in preparing the city for the Assyrian onslaught that appeared increasingly inevitable. His most notable endeavor was the construction of the famous Tunnel and Pool of SILOAM, which replaced the ancient Z-shaped tunnel that had by then gone out of use owing to the construction of cisterns within the city walls. The twofold purpose of this new work was to divert the waters of the Spring of GIHON from their former course to within the walls of the city and to deny a prospective besieger of Jerusalem access to this precious spring. According to II Chronicles, "Hezekiah . . . stopped the upper watercourse of Gihon, and brought it straight down to the west side of the city of David" (32:30).

To do this, access to the entrance of the Z-shaped tunnel was sealed off, and, from within, a new underground aqueduct was quarried which ran southward under the eastern ridge and then westward until it opened out into the Pool of Siloam in the Tyropoeon Valley between the eastern and western ridges. Altogether, the subterranean aqueduct measured 1,700 feet in length, a major engineering feat for the period. Since the southern portion of the Tyropoeon Valley lay outside the Solomonic walls of Jerusalem, Hezekiah brought the Pool of Siloam within the city's boundaries by constructing a line of fortifications that joined the southern extremity of the western ridge with that of the eastern. Since the defensive works of the preceding two centuries had consisted largely of repairs to the Solomonic walls, this marked the first extension of the city's area since Solomon's days.

Hezekiah's new wall and aqueducts were barely completed before the threatened Assyrian invasion occurred. Fearing the reprisals of the neighboring states more than those of the overlords, Hezekiah joined in the anti-Assyrian coalition that was formed upon the death of the Assyrian monarch SARGON II in 705 B.C. Within four years, Sargon's successor SENNACHERIB had crushed the rebellion and had laid siege to Jerusalem. According to II Kings, however, with Jerusalem in straitened circumstances, a miracle occurred that mysteriously decimated the invaders, and

Tower built over the traditional burial site of King David, atop Mount Zion in Jerusalem (*Counsel Collection*).

JERUSALEM 1553

A holy site revered by Jews, Christians, and Moslems alike: the Dome of the Rock. It is the traditional site of Abraham's sacrifice of Isaac, of the Holy of Holies in the Temple built by Solomon, and of Mohammed's ascent to heaven (*Counsel Collection*).

"Sennacherib king of Assyria departed, and went and returned" to his capital at NINEVEH (19:36). Though the biblical account speaks of an ANGEL OF THE LORD who killed 185,000 Assyrians, the fifth-century B.C. Greek historian Herodotus reports that a plague raged through the camp of the Assyrian besiegers and forced their withdrawal. This latter account may gibe with the nature of Hezekiah's defensive preparations, for the absence of adequate water supplies in the Assyrian camp may have brought about unsanitary conditions that led to an outbreak of plague.

The eventual acceptance of Assyrian overlordship by Hezekiah brought about relatively peaceful conditions during the forty-five-year reign of his successor MANASSEH, who took the opportunity to extend Jerusalem's boundaries northward. To this end, he extended the western wall of the eastern ridge about five hundred yards northward and then ran it in a southwesterly direction across the Tyropoeon Valley and hence southward until it met with the western wall that Solomon had constructed on the western ridge, thus adding a rectangle of about seventy acres to the city's area.

These new walls constructed by Manasseh stood for less than a century before they and the rest of Jerusalem along with them were destroyed. The Jerusalem kingdom had been able to remain relatively secure throughout the seventh century B.C., as the vassal of the Assyrian Empire. But with the disintegration of Assyria toward the end of the century, Jerusalem found itself poised precariously between the rising NEO-BABYLONIAN EMPIRE, which had succeeded to the Assyrian Empire, and an imperialistic Egypt, which with the decline of Assyria attempted to reassert its influence in Asia. Jerusalem unfortunately chose the latter as an ally, and in 597 B.C., the city was assaulted by the Neo-Babylonian monarch NEBUCHADNEZZAR and captured after a three-month siege. Though ten thousand of Jerusalem's most prominent citizens were taken prisoner and deported, the city itself was left intact. Ten years later, when Jerusalem renewed its alliance with Egypt, the city was again successfully besieged, and on its capitulation in 586 B.C., more captives were deported, the city's walls were torn down, the Temple was razed to the ground, and most of the rest of the city's buildings were utterly destroyed. (*See also* JEREMIAH; ZEDEKIAH.)

Though Jerusalem lay in ruins throughout the half-century of the ensuing PERIOD OF THE BABYLO-

NIAN CAPTIVITY, it was most probably not entirely uninhabited, for some of the houses that were not entirely destroyed are likely to have been occupied by remnants of the decimated population. In addition, the Book of BARUCH in the APOCRYPHA speaks of money and sacred vessels sent by captive Jews in Babylonia so that ritual observances in the ruins of the temple might be carried on (1:6-8).

But when, with the decree of the Persian emperor CYRUS that the Jews might return to Jerusalem and rebuild their ruined Temple, the Exile came to an end (538 B.C.), there seems to have been little enthusiasm felt by Jews of the Captivity for a Return to The City of David. Though the biblical accounts of the Return (the books of EZRA and NEHEMIAH) are extremely confused, it appears most plausible that only a relatively small contingent returned with ZERUBBABEL, and that this group, in the face of hostile neighbors (some of whom were descendants of Jews of the Northern Kingdom who had not been deported in 722 B.C.), made little headway toward reconstruction of the city and the Temple. (*See also* "TEN LOST TRIBES OF ISRAEL.") About fifteen years later, however, a new and more determined group returned, and within five more years the Temple had been restored and the city made habitable. But again, perhaps because the unwalled status of Jerusalem forced the returnees to occupy themselves fully in repelling the attacks of hostile neighbors, work toward reconstruction seems to have come to a halt, and a hiatus of sixty years of virtual stagnation followed.

This period came to an end and a new period of reconstruction commenced about 445 B.C., with the arrival of NEHEMIAH, an influential Jew at the imperial court who had persuaded the Persian monarch ARTAXERXES to appoint him governor of Jerusalem for the expressed purpose of rebuilding the city's walls. According to the detailed account contained in the Book of Nehemiah, the walls of the city had been so broken down that the new governor, on his initial inspection tour, was unable to make his way among the debris that littered the course of the former walls. Nehemiah's superintendence was apparently a marvel of organization and administration, for with various groups assigned to specific sections of the wall, the entire undertaking was completed in a mere fifty-two days (Neh. 6:15). According to the references in chapters three and twelve of the Book of Nehemiah, the rebuilt walls followed essentially the same course as the fortification that had been destroyed by Nebuchadnezzar nearly a century and a half before. The sole exception seems to have been on the eastern wall of the eastern ridge, where erosion of the cliff face seems to have forced the new governor to shift the boundary westward by approximately a hundred yards.

Nehemiah's physical reconstruction of Jerusalem was followed by the religious reconstruction of EZRA in which the nationalistic elements of the Jewish religion were deemphasized in favor of its more purely spiritual and moral elements. The two restorations viewed together seem to form an organic whole which reflected the altered state of the Jewish people at the time. For whereas the nationalistic features of the Solomonic city—the Royal Palace and its various appendages—had in size and splendor far overshadowed the religious—the Temple—now the religious element was preeminent, since the Royal Palace residential complex had not been restored. And where the king had been the city's most important personage prior to the Babylonian Captivity, the HIGH PRIEST of the Temple was, in practice, supremely influential after the restorations of Nehemiah and Ezra.

During the succeeding century of PERSIAN EMPIRE domination, Jerusalem seems to have enjoyed peace and prosperity, if not independence. The general satisfaction of Jerusalem's inhabitants with their status under Persia may be reflected in an apocryphal anecdote related by the historian FLAVIUS JOSEPHUS concerning the conquest of Persia by ALEXANDER THE GREAT. According to Josephus, Jerusalem remained loyal to the Persian monarch even after his main army had been routed by Alexander at Issus in 333 B.C.; when Alexander marched on Jerusalem, seemingly determined to take reprisals, the Jews remained firm and, with the High Priest at their head, met Alexander en masse outside the walls of Jerusalem. The anecdote concludes by noting that it was only by a gracious and tactful deference to the religion and privileges of the Jews that Alexander was able to win their sympathy.

During the wars of the Diadochi (the successors of Alexander) that followed Alexander's death in 323 B.C., the countryside about Jerusalem was the frequent scene of clashes between contending armies.

The "Wailing Wall" (*right*)—according to tradition the last remaining wall of the Temple built by King Solomon (*New York Public Library*).

On at least one occasion, in 320 B.C., the city itself was captured by PTOLEMY I SOTER. According to the Apocryphal book ECCLESIASTICUS (50:1-4), the High Priest SIMON ("the Just") repaired the Temple and the city walls and built new cisterns about 300 B.C. Thereafter, for the century-long period of Ptolemaic domination by the Egyptian PTOLEMAIC DYNASTY, Jerusalem enjoyed stability and virtually the same privileges that had been granted under Persian rule. Outwardly these felicitous conditions continued even after Jerusalem passed under control of the Syrian SELEUCID DYNASTY with the defeat of the Ptolemies at Panion in 198 B.C., but inwardly, the subtle and increasingly irresistible encroachment of Hellenistic culture began to create tension among various groups in the city. While much of Hellenistic culture was genuinely attractive and could be considered merely as "progress" or "modernity," virtually all facets of Greek civilization were ultimately bound to an acceptance of pagan deities, and it was this underlying feature that was ultimately unacceptable to Judaism.

Initially, HELLENISM was most popular among the richer and ruling classes in Jerusalem; as a result, Greek customs became fashionable and a typically Greek building, a gymnasium, was erected. Ironically, the petty internecine political squabbles that characterized the city-states of GREECE were also adopted by the ruling class in Jerusalem, so that during the first thirty years of the second century B.C., the city was the scene of incessant internal strife that occasionally broke out into bloodshed. The pro-Hellenistic Seleucid monarch ANTIOCHUS IV EPIPHANES mistook these struggles for wholehearted anti-Hellenistic demonstrations and accordingly resolved to abolish entirely the Jewish religion as a means of removing the major obstacle to the acceptance of Hellenistic culture. In 167 B.C., he found a pretext to occupy the city and savagely attacked it, slaughtering many of its inhabitants, pulling down its walls and houses, and plundering the Temple, in which he erected an altar to the pagan god Zeus Olympios. Thus he implemented the decree he had issued which outlawed the practice of the Jewish religion. In addition, to the north of the Temple Mount, he fortified a strong citadel in which he garrisoned the occupying troops and stored the treasures he had plundered from the Temple.

Though many Jews apostasized, a large number of Jerusalem's inhabitants fled the city and took refuge in the surrounding countryside where the resistance movement coalesced under the leadership of JUDAS MACCABEUS. Operating initially as a leader of a guerrilla band against isolated Seleucid detachments, Judas extended his power so rapidly that by the end of 164 B.C., he was able to capture Jerusalem and rededicate the Temple. This victory bore permanent fruit, for even though Judas was eventually defeated and killed by the Seleucids, the ban on the Jewish religion remained a dead letter. In the following two decades, under the leadership of Judas' brothers JONATHAN and SIMON, and aided by the rapid disintegration of the Seleucid power, the MACCABEES were able to establish Jerusalem as the political capital of a newly independent JUDAEA, a position that it had not enjoyed since its catastrophic defeat at the hands of Nebuchadnezzar more than four centuries before. The last vestige of Seleucid overlordship was eliminated in 142 B.C., when the Akra, the citadel that Antiochus IV Epiphanes erected, was captured and its Seleucid garrison expelled. Ten years later the Seleucid monarch ANTIOCHUS VII SIDETES took revenge by besieging the city and starving it into submission, but with the death of Antiochus four years later, Jerusalem was rid finally of the Seleucid threat.

Over the next sixty years, Jerusalem enjoyed outward prosperity and suffered from inner turmoil as the HASMONAEAN DYNASTY (the descendants and successors of the Maccabees) deteriorated into a petty despotism. The restorations of Nehemiah and Ezra had made the religious element supreme among the Jews and had left them unable and unwilling to accept the monarchical principle that the Hasmonaeans increasingly embodied. The situation produced a civil war during the reign of Simon Maccabeus' grandson ALEXANDER JANNAEUS, and probably would have resulted in further civil strife had not the Roman power arrived on the scene and entirely altered the complexion of affairs.

Reduced at a stroke from the position of capital of an independent nation to a Roman client city-state through the intervention of POMPEY, who by 63 B.C. had successfully completed the conquest of what had formerly been the Seleucid realm, Jerusalem became the scene of struggle between various factions, each of which sought to curry favor with the new overlords. On Pompey's appearance he was met with appeals by two contending Hasmonaean brothers, HYRCANUS II and ARISTOBULUS II. But when Pompey temporized, Aristobulus fortified himself in Jerusalem and was ousted only after a three-month siege. Though Pom-

Sheep grazing on the Mount of Olives, looking toward Jerusalem (*Counsel Collection*).

pey did pull down the walls of the city and did, through what appears to have been wanton curiosity, violate the Holy of Holies, he refrained, unlike previous conquerors, from plundering the Temple of its treasures.

Over the following two decades, as the Romans engaged in a civil war of their own, Jerusalem was again the battleground between opposing factions until HEROD THE GREAT, who rose to influence as the protegé of Hyrcanus II and then dispensed with his patron, emerging as the favorite of the Romans and the king of Judaea. Herod conducted his regime along the same despotic lines—though more efficiently—than had his Hasmonaean predecessors, so that Jerusalem

1558 THE FAMILY BIBLE ENCYCLOPEDIA

Painting, on paper, of Jerusalem by the 17th-century Persian Hayrapit (*Counsel Collection*).

underwent a four-decade period of peace and prosperity, if not contentment, during Herod's tenure on the throne. Architecturally, the city was adorned with unpredecedented magnificence, though in a Greco-Roman style that in all likelihood was not especially appealing to its inhabitants. Herod's first work was the construction of the ANTONIA, a palace-fortress situated to the north of and dominating the Temple Mount. Notable features of this edifice, from an architectural and military point of view, were the three great towers, named Phaesel, Mariamme, and Hippicus, two of which survive in part today. Other Herodian constructions included a theater, a hippodrome, a *xystus* (or assembly place), and a new Royal Palace which was built about 25 B.C., on the northwestern corner of the western ridge. In addition, Herodian engineers greatly improved the water supply of Jerusalem by constructing the large reservoirs (known erroneously as Solomon's Pools) located seven miles south of the city, and by erecting the aqueducts that brought the water thence to Jerusalem.

But the crowning achievement of Herod's reign was the reconstruction, on an incredibly lavish scale, of the Temple built half a millennium earlier by Zerubbabel. In its entirety, the Herodian Temple measured nearly four hundred yards in length and more than 350 in breadth, and was not finished until about 64 A.D., more than eighty years after work had commenced and only six years before it and the city that housed it were destroyed. The Temple building itself, because of its sacred character, was constructed by a team of a thousand priests, and was completed within eighteen months after work was begun. In front was an entrance porch facing east and measuring 150 feet in width and about 155 feet in height; behind lay the building proper, measuring ninety feet in width, the whole measuring 150 feet in length. In addition, there were numerous courtyards, the outermost of which was flanked on all four sides by magnificent colonnades.

But for the majority of Jerusalem's population, behind the magnificence of the Herodian facade there lay a deep discontent which came to the surface only upon the ruthless tyrant's death in 4 B.C. A large delegation of Jews petitioned the Roman emperor AUGUSTUS for an end to the monarchy and the establishment of direct Roman rule, and after ten years of riotous misgovernment by Herod's son ARCHELAUS, their wishes were granted. The reality of Roman government proved quite different than had been foreseen, however, and Roman governors, none too competent at best, committed numerous outrages against the Jews, who, in turn, completed the vicious circle by assuming an oversensitive stance and thereby provoking the Roman governors to even greater excesses.

At the same time, and partly in consequence of Jerusalem's humiliation at Roman hands, many Jews rejected specifically political solutions and hearkened back to the OLD TESTAMENT prophecies which predicted the appearance of a MESSIAH who would, with miracles and wonders, lead the Chosen People of Israel to victory for the greater glory of YAHWEH. Accordingly, there arose many, like JESUS CHRIST, who were believed by their followers to be the promised Messiah. And like Jesus, nearly all met with death at the hands of the ROMAN EMPIRE overlords, if not in circumstances so dramatic or so significant for the course of Western civilization as did the inspirer of Christianity. As concerns the identification of the sacred sites connected with the Passion of Jesus Christ—GOLGOTHA, GETHSEMANE, the PRAETORIUM—the disagreements among archaeologists are so extensive that a highly respected authority on Jerusalem has termed the problems unsolved and destined to remain insoluble.

About a decade after the Crucifixion, Jerusalem enjoyed a three-year respite from Roman rule before resuming its headlong career to destruction. This occurred through the appointment of the Jewish prince HEROD AGRIPPA I, a grandson of Herod the Great and a friend of the Roman emperor CLAUDIUS, as king of Judaea. Equally as capable as his grandfather, but less brutal and more tactful, Herod Agrippa won the approbation of virtually all classes within Jerusalem, and gave his subjects good reason to regard his rule, in retrospect, as a period of unparalleled felicity for Jerusalem. So rapidly had the city expanded and so promising was the prospect of future expansion, that Agrippa embarked upon the construction of a new northern wall that virtually doubled the area of Jerusalem. Known as the Third Wall, this new fortification extended the old easternmost wall more than 1,100 yards northward, and then followed a westward course for a thousand yards before turning southward to join up with the westernmost wall built by King Manasseh. Some modern archaeologists question the authenticity of this wall, suggesting instead that the wall built by Agrippa followed the considerably more modest course described by the present-day walls of Jerusalem. But their objections seem to rest largely on an inability to believe that the Agrippan city could have covered so vast an area. Apparently the Roman Emperor Claudius was equally awed by the magnitude of this work—which, according to Josephus, would have been impregnable had Agrippa been permitted to finish it—for he ordered Agrippa to cease construction before the fortification had reached the projected height lest it be used to defend successfully against Roman besiegers.

Upon Agrippa's death in 44 A.D., after a three-year reign, Jerusalem again felt the oppressiveness of direct Roman rule as a series of increasingly incompetent governors—Cuspius Fadus, Tiberius Alexander, Ventidius Cumanus, Antonius Claudius FELIX, Porcius FESTUS, and L. Lucceius Albinus—exacerbated the resentment the Jews felt at the loss of the independence they had enjoyed briefly under Agrippa. The extreme anti-Roman party of the ZEALOTS gained numerous adherents, particularly in reaction to the excesses of the last governor, Gessius Florus, whose illegal confiscations from the Temple treasury were so notorious that the inhabitants of Jerusalem resorted to sarcasm—they publicly collected alms for the presumably impoverished governor—as a means of protest. When Gessius responded by setting a cohort of soldiers loose to plunder the city, open rebellion was declared, the Roman troops expelled, and the city fortified. In the initial stages of the rebellion, Jerusalem gained an unexpected victory which fanned the flames of revolt throughout Judaea and Galilee. The Roman governor of Syria, Cestius Gallus, marched on Jerusalem with one complete Roman legion and detachments from others, and encamped before the city. But when, fearing an attack on his flank, he attempted to withdraw to winter quarters, the inhabitants of Jerusalem regarded the withdrawal as a miraculous deliverance—paralleling the retreat of the Assyrian armies of Sennacherib nearly eight centuries before—and attacked the Romans, turning the withdrawal into a rout.

Cestius was replaced as commander by the future Roman emperor VESPASIAN, who embarked on a carefully planned series of campaigns designed to level the entire countryside around Jerusalem before attacking the city itself. This gave the rebels in the city a two-year reprieve which was consumed largely in suicidal intramural warfare as moderate elements within Jerusalem battled with extremist factions and various splinter groups in what amounted to a Reign of Terror. Toward the end of 69 A.D., Jerusalem was invested, and when, in the spring of 70 A.D., under Vespasian's son and eventual successor Flavius Vespasianus TITUS, the Romans began their large-scale siege operations, defeat was inevitable. By May, the northern wall that Agrippa had built less than four decades earlier was breached, and five days later, the second of the three walls fell into Roman hands. By June, the Antonia was taken, and after a two-month siege, Roman soldiers broke into the Temple and amid fire and bloodshed destroyed it. Still, the defenders continued to resist, taking refuge on the southern portion of the eastern ridge in what had once been the city of the Jebusites. By September, however, amid renewed massacre and the nearly complete destruction of the city, resistance was finally ended. (See JEWISH REVOLT.)

Jerusalem emerged from the calamitous war as a heap of charred and bloodstained ruins destined never to regain its former splendor. With its Temple destroyed and the High Priesthood and SANHEDRIN abolished, it ceased to act as the administrative center of worldwide Jewry, even though a number of Jews filtered back into the city, taking up their abode among the ruins. The anticlimactic coup de grace did not come until sixty years later when the proposal of the emperor Hadrian to turn Jerusalem into a pagan city, Aelia Capitolina, touched off a new rebellion. This revolt, which lasted from 132 to 135 A.D., ended in a complete Roman victory, and the Roman city that was erected on the site of Jerusalem was thenceforth regarded as forbidden ground for Jews.

The break in religious continuity that the construction of Aelia Capitolina represented was reflected also in the topography of the city. Henceforth for about four centuries the city had no defensive walls, and even its old orientation—with the main street running from north to south—was changed; the new main street ran east to west in accordance with Roman ideas of city planning.

With the triumph of Christianity throughout the Roman Empire and the construction of the Church of the Holy Sepulchre (on what was assumed to be the site of the Crucifixion) in the fourth century A.D., Jerusalem became the Holy City of Christendom par excellence. Toward the end of the same century, the pagan emperor Julian the Apostate contemplated rebuilding the Temple as a counterweight to Christianity, but with his death several years later the plan was abandoned. During the Byzantine period, Jerusalem prospered and new defensive walls were built, but

JERUSALEM, GATES OF

A section of the Via Dolorosa in the Old City of Jerusalem (*Counsel Collection*).

with the temporary decline of Byzantine power in the seventh century A.D., the city was conquered and sacked by Persian invaders (614 A.D.). Sixteen years later the Byzantine emperor Heraclius recaptured the city, but in 638 A.D., the rising tide of Islam engulfed Jerusalem, and it was to remain a Moslem metropolis for nearly half a millennium. The most prominent existing remains of this first period of Moslem occupation is the Dome of the Rock, a huge mosque completed in 691 A.D., on the site of the old Temple.

During the Middle Ages, Jerusalem became the supreme object of crusading zeal, and on July 15, 1099, it fell to the Christian soldiers of the First Crusade and remained in Christian hands as the capital of the Latin Kingdom of Jerusalem until 1187, when it was retaken by the Moslem armies of Salah-ad-Din (Saladin). Over the next three centuries Jerusalem was controlled by the Mameluke sultans of Egypt, but in 1516, with the defeat of the Mamelukes by the Ottoman Turks, Jerusalem passed under Turkish control. It was at the beginning of this period (1537-1542) that the Ottoman emperor Suleiman the Magnificent constructed the walls of the old city that are still standing today. But over the succeeding centuries Jerusalem declined into a political, cultural, and economic backwater until, with the establishment of the British Mandate in Palestine in 1919, Jerusalem regained its status as a capital city.

Two years earlier, the Balfour Declaration, which announced the intention of establishing a National Homeland for the Jews in Palestine, had been issued, and over the following three decades numerous Jews, whose ancestors had for the most part been barred from their Holy City for nearly two millennia, settled in and around Jerusalem. A new city whose population was predominantly Jewish was constructed to the west of the old city, and in the truce that followed the Arab-Israeli War of 1948-1949 and marked the birth of modern-day Israel, the new city was allotted to Israel while the old remained in Moslem hands. Less than two decades later, as a result of what has become known as the Six-Day War, the old city and the surrounding countryside was captured by Israel; it has remained occupied by the descendants of the biblical Israelites until the present day. *V.J.G.*

JERUSALEM, GATES OF (Heb., *shaar*, "gate"); traditionally assumed to have been twelve in number, corresponding to the TWELVE TRIBES OF ISRAEL, the gates of JERUSALEM were probably massive wooden

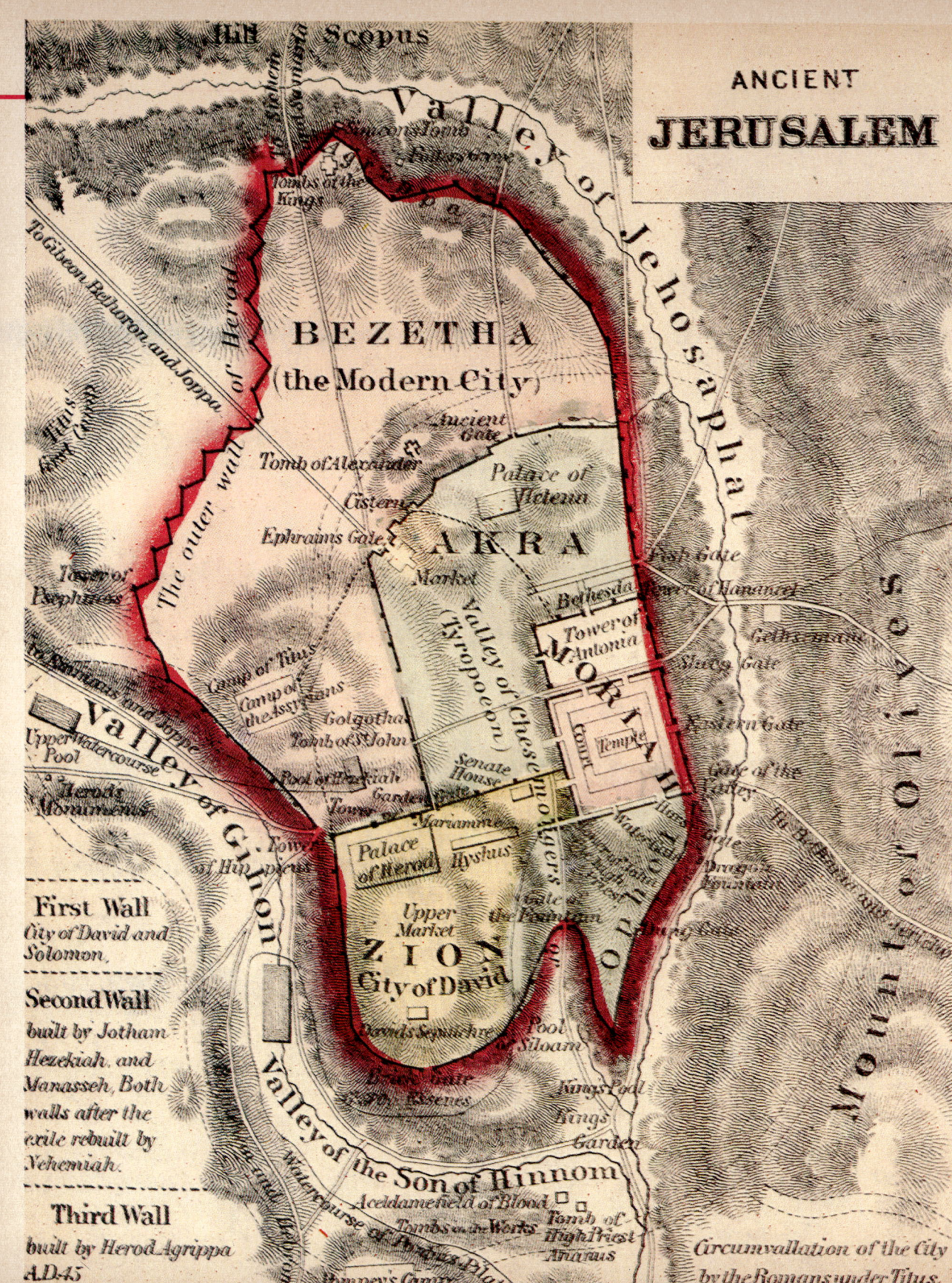

JERUSALEM, GATES OF 1563

double doors plated with iron. Biblically the names of only ten gates are mentioned up until the time that SOLOMON built the TEMPLE, and in the report of the reconstruction of the walls in the Book of NEHEMIAH, fifteen separate gates are listed. Whether new gates were added or whether some of the gates simply had two names, a formal name and a popular, descriptive name, is unclear. Following are all the gates of Jerusalem mentioned in the KING JAMES VERSION:

Benjamin Gate (Heb., *shaar binyamin*) was named after the TRIBE OF BENJAMIN. When the Prophet JEREMIAH warned that God would destroy Jerusalem, PASHUR, the chief governor in the TEMPLE, was so angered that he had the Prophet put in the stocks near the Benjamin portal (Jer. 20:2). Later, after Jeremiah had been freed and had continued, despite his imprisonment, to warn the people of their impending doom, he was placed in a dungeon by the princes of the Southern KINGDOM OF JUDAH. EBEDMELECH, an Ethiopian servant in the palace of King ZEDEKIAH, concerned that the prophet might starve to death in the dungeon, went to the Benjamin Gate to look for his master and plead with him to order the princes to release Jeremiah (38:7), a request which was granted. Despite this, Jeremiah's warning came to pass—Jerusalem was destroyed by the Babylonian forces of NEBUCHADNEZZAR. Subsequently, when the Jews returned following the PERIOD OF THE BABYLONIAN CAPTIVITY, the Prophet ZECHARIAH foretold of a day of peace when Jerusalem would be inhabited from the Benjamin Gate to the Tower of Hananeel (named after HANANEL) and no enemies would try to enter and destroy the city again (Zech. 14:10.)

Gate Between the Two Walls (Heb., *shaar bayn hachomotayim*), the gate through which King Zedekiah tried unsuccessfully to elude the CHALDEAN

The Lion's Gate of the Old City of Jerusalem, facing Gethsemane and the Mount of Olives. It is also known at St. Stephen's Gate (*Counsel Collection*).

forces of Nebuchadnezzar (II Kings 25:4); pursued, he was eventually captured and slain (25:5,7).

Corner Gate (Heb., *shaar hapinah*), one of the two gates, the other being the Ephraim Gate, through which King JEHOASH of the Northern KINGDOM OF ISRAEL entered Jerusalem in his barbarous quest for plunder in the Temple and the palace of King AMAZIAH of the Southern Kingdom of Judah (II Kings 14:13; II Chron. 25:23). Similar conduct on the part of many other Jewish monarchs of both kingdoms (see CHRONOLOGY OF THE OLD TESTAMENT) caused the PROPHETS to warn the people that the Lord would have to punish both Jewish nations if they did not keep the Law of MOSES; the Prophet Jeremiah, while castigating the evil deeds of many of these monarchs, also reassured the people and promised them that the Lord would not allow the permanent destruction of the Corner Gate: "the city shall be built . . . from the tower of Hananeel unto the gate of the corner" (Jer. 31:38).

Dung Gate (Heb., *shaar haashpot*), one of the gates rebuilt under the direction of NEHEMIAH upon his return to Jerusalem as Royal Governor from the court of the Persian monarch ARTAXERXES; an account of this reconstruction of the walls and gates of Jerusalem is contained in chapter three of the Book of NEHEMIAH. The Dung Gate was repaired and rebuilt by MALCHIAH: "he built it, and set up the doors thereof, the locks thereof, and the bars thereof" (3:14).

East Gate, the gate where the Prophet Jeremiah preached while holding a potter's earthen bottle which he subsequently broke to show how easily God could break the people of the Southern Kingdom of Judah if they persisted in sinning (Jer. 19:2). In the original Hebrew text of the Book of JEREMIAH the gate is called *shaar hacharsit* or "gate of the potter's bottle"; in the King James Version of the Bible, however, the sixteenth-century scholars mistakenly translated it "East Gate." Later English translations (see BIBLE, ENGLISH VERSIONS) have been more accurate—in the REVISED VERSION of the Bible, for example, it is called the "Harsith Gate"; in the REVISED STANDARD VERSION of the Bible and the NEW ENGLISH BIBLE it is rendered the "Potsherd Gate."

Ephraim Gate (Heb., *shaar ephraim*) was named after the TRIBE OF EPHRAIM. King Jehoash of the Northern Kingdom of Israel entered Jerusalem through it and the Corner Gate (II Kings 14:13; II Chron. 25:23). In the postexilic period following the Period of the Babylonian Captivity, at the time EZRA gave the Israelites back their law, the people celebrated and "made themselves booths . . . in the street of the water gate, and in the street of the gate of Ephraim" (Neh. 8:16). When the people dedicated the newly built wall around Jerusalem they celebrated at, among other places, the gate of Ephraim (12:39).

Fish Gate (Heb., *shaar hadagim*), furthest point of a fortified wall built by King MANASSEH, one of the later monarchs of the Southern Kingdom of Judah (II Chron. 33:14). During the restoration of Jerusalem under Nehemiah the Fish Gate was repaired by the sons of HASSENAAH, "who also laid the beams thereof, and set up the doors thereof, the locks thereof, and the bars thereof" (Neh. 3:3). The celebration attending the dedication of the newly built wall took place at, among other places, the Fish Gate (12:39).

Gate of the Foundation (Heb., *shaar hayisod*), one of three locations at which the High Priest JEHOIADA posted the LEVITES and priests, whom he had divided into three groups (II Chron. 23:4,5), when he overthrew Queen ATHALIAH and placed the legitimate heir, JOASH, on the throne of the Southern Kingdom of Judah.

Fountain Gate (Heb., *shaar haayin*), one of the spots visited by Nehemiah when he returned to Jerusalem from the Persian court of Artaxerxes: "Then I went on to the gate of the fountain, and to the king's pool: but there was no place for the beast that was under me to pass" (Neh. 2:14). The rebuilding of the gate was done by SHALLUN: "But the gate of the fountain repaired Shallun, . . . he built it, and covered it, and set up the doors thereof, the locks thereof, and the bars thereof, and the wall of the pool of Siloah by the king's garden and unto the stairs that go down from the city of David" (3:15). When the newly built wall around Jerusalem was finished and the people celebrated, they gathered at the Fountain Gate, among other places (12:37).

Horse Gate (Heb., *shaar hasoosim*), the spot where Queen Athaliah was slain (II Chron. 23:15). The Prophet Jeremiah promised the people that God would not allow the Horse Gate to be permanently destroyed (Jer. 31:40). In the time of Nehemiah the Horse Gate was rebuilt (Neh. 3:28).

Old Gate, one of the gates rebuilt by Jehoiada under the direction of Nehemiah: "Moreover the old gate repaired Jehoiada" (Neh. 3:6); people gathered there at the dedication of the wall (12:39).

Miphkad Gate (Heb., *shaar hamiphkad*, "gate of

JERUSALEM, GATES OF

The Gold Gate of the Old City of Jerusalem, dating to the 5th century (*Counsel Collection*).

the muster," rendered "muster gate" in the Revised Standard Version of the Bible, "gate Hammiphkad" in the Revised Version of the Bible), it was rebuilt by Malchiah under the direction of Nehemiah (Neh. 3:31).

Sheep Gate (Heb., *shaar hatzoan*), was rebuilt by the High Priest ELIASHIB "with his brethren the priests, . . . they sanctified it, and set up the doors of it" (Neh. 3:1; *also* 32). People gathered there at the dedication of the wall (12:39).

Valley Gate (Heb., *shaar hagay*), one of the places where King UZZIAH of the Southern Kingdom of Judah built fortified towers (II Chron. 26:9). When Nehemiah returned to Jerusalem it was one of the

Crowds thronging through the Damascus Gate in the Old City of Jerusalem (*Counsel Collection*).

places he visited (Neh. 2:13). HANUN was responsible for rebuilding it (3:13).

Water Gate (Heb., *shaar hamayim*), given as a site near which the NETHINIM dwelt (Neh. 3:26). The people gathered "into the street that was before the water gate" to hear Ezra read the Law (8:1,3) and celebrated there following this event (16).

Other features of the Jerusalem walls were the Broad Wall built during Nehemiah's restoration (Neh. 12:38) and the guard towers, including the Tower of the Furnace (3:11; 12:38), the Tower of Hananeel already mentioned, and the Tower of Meah (3:1; 12:39), translated "Tower of the Hundred" in other English translations of the Bible (*see* BIBLE, EN-

GLISH VERSIONS). Of course Jerusalem, like other ancient fortified cities, had walls so thick that they were topped by streets lined with shops and houses. *G.B.K.*

JERUSALEM, NEW, see NEW JERUSALEM.

JERUSALEM BIBLE, the first major Roman Catholic version of the BIBLE to be rendered in modern English. Published in 1966, it is the work of twenty-seven Roman Catholic scholars at Christ's College, Liverpool, England, under the editorship of Alexander Jones. The Jerusalem Bible is basically a translation of the French-language *Bible de Jerusalem,* which was produced by the Dominican Fathers of L'Ecole Biblique de Jerusalem in what was then the Jordanian sector of that city, in 1956. This was the first completely new Roman Catholic Bible to be translated from the original languages, rather than from the Latin VULGATE. In the English edition, the introductory articles to the various books, and the many explanatory notes accompanying the text, are translated directly from the French edition. The text itself, however, while following the French text, is not slavishly dependent upon it. The English translators also used the MASSORETIC TEXT and the SEPTUAGINT in working on the OLD TESTAMENT, and several ancient Greek versions in translating the NEW TESTAMENT.

Outmoded expressions such as "thee," "art," "thine," and "mayest," are replaced by "you," "are," "yours," and "may" in the Jerusalem Bible (and by their French equivalents in the French edition), and the name for GOD used in the Hebrew text, YAHWEH, is used rather than the traditional "the Lord." The Latinized titles of some Old Testament books, which have long mystified non-Roman Catholic readers, such as "Osee," "Abidias," and "Sophonias," are recognizable in the Jerusalem Bible as HOSEA, OBADIAH, and ZEPHANIAH. As to the notes, Father Jones defends them as necessary, observing that the Book of JONAH, without notes, "is simply a story of a whale. With the notes, it can be seen for the satire it is."

Paradoxically, Christian translators of the Bible tend to do a better job on the Old Testament than the New, since almost any verse in the latter may be important for dogmatic theology, and hence put a strain on the translator's capacity for objectivity. Thus the New Testament of the Jerusalem Bible—particularly the notes and introductory sections—reflect more conservative Roman Catholic views than does the Old Testament. Overall, however, the literary quality is excellent, owing in part to the inclusion of literary as well as biblical scholars on the translation committee, a notable member being the popular novelist J.R.R. Tolkien (*see also* BIBLE, ENGLISH VERSIONS). *G.Y.*

JERUSHA, JERUSHAH (Heb., *yerusha,* "possession" or "to possess"), the wife of UZZIAH and mother of JOTHAM, ninth and tenth monarchs, respectively, of the Southern KINGDOM OF JUDAH (II Kings 15:33, "Jerusha," II Chron. 27:1, "Jerushah").

JESAIAH (Heb., *yeshayah,* "the Lord saves"), a name borne by two OLD TESTAMENT personages who flourished during or after the PERIOD OF THE BABYLONIAN CAPTIVITY (Neh. 11:7; I Chron. 3:21); the latter was a grandson of ZERUBBABEL, and thus a lineal descendant of King DAVID).

JESHAIAH (Heb., *yeshayah,* "the Lord saves"), a name borne by four OLD TESTAMENT personages, all of whom were LEVITES: the head of the eighth musical course during the reign of King DAVID (I Chron. 25:3,15 [*see also* COURSE OF PRIESTS AND LEVITES]); the ancestor of SHELOMITH, one of King David's treasurers (I Chron. 26:25); and two who returned to JERUSALEM following the PERIOD OF THE BABYLONIAN CAPTIVITY (Ezra 8:7,19).

JESHANAH (Heb., *yeshanah,* "old"), a town, presumably in the vicinity of BETHEL in the territory of the TRIBE OF EPHRAIM but otherwise unidentifiable, which was one of the many captured by King ABIJAH, son of REHOBOAM, the first monarch of the Southern KINGDOM OF JUDAH (II Chron. 13:19).

JESHARELAH (Heb., *yesharelah,* "straight are these"), one of the LEVITES during the reign of King SOLOMON, and leader of the seventh musical course in the Temple services (I Chron. 25:14; *see also* COURSE OF PRIESTS AND LEVITES).

JESHEBEAB (Heb., *yeshevav,* "seat of the father"), leader of the fourteenth priestly course during the reign of King DAVID (I Chron. 24:13; *see also* COURSE OF PRIESTS AND LEVITES).

JESHER (Heb., *yesher,* "uprightness"), the eldest son of CALEB of the TRIBE OF JUDAH (I Chron. 2:18).

The village of En-Lissane, which some scholars identify with the biblical city of Jeshanah (*Counsel Collection*).

JESHIMON (Heb., *hayeshimon*, "a desert" or "a waste"), the arid plateau southeast of HEBRON where DAVID, during his period of outlawry, hid while in flight from King SAUL (I Sam. 23:19,24); it was in this area that Saul encamped, prior to the incident in which David spared the monarch's life (I Sam. 26:3 ff.). "Jeshimon" is not a place name per se, but rather a general term referring to the easternmost section of the Judaean hill country contiguous to the DEAD SEA. In the original Hebrew text of the OLD TESTAMENT, the word *hayeshimon* was often used to indicate a desert (e.g., Deut. 32:10; Pss. 78:40; Isa. 43:19).

JESHISHAI (Heb., *yeshishai*, "aged"), a minor member of the TRIBE OF GAD (I Chron. 5:14).

JESHOHAIAH (Heb., *yeshochayah*, "salvation lives"), an early member of the TRIBE OF SIMEON (I Chron. 4:36).

JESHUA (Heb., *yeshua*, "the Lord is salvation"; this is another form of the Heb. proper noun Joshua), a name borne by a number of OLD TESTAMENT personages, all of whom were LEVITES. With the exception of the Jeshua who headed the ninth COURSE OF PRIESTS AND LEVITES during the reign of King DAVID (I Chron. 24:11), and the Levite in charge of the distribution of tithes during the reign of King HEZEKIAH (II Chron. 31:15); all flourished in JERUSALEM following the PERIOD OF THE BABYLONIAN CAPTIVITY. These included the ancestor of a group who returned with ZERUBBABEL (Ezra 2:6; cf. Neh. 7:11); and the ancestor of a family who oversaw the workmen during the reconstruction of the TEMPLE (Ezra 2:40; 3:9; Neh. 7:43), one of the Levites who assisted EZRA in expounding the MOSAIC LAW (Neh. 8:7), a Levite who led in the worship (Neh. 9:4), and one of the Levites who assisted NEHEMIAH in sealing the COVENANT (Neh. 10:9).

Jeshua is also the alternate rendering (Neh. 8:17) of JOSHUA, the successor to MOSES, and of the JOSHUA who served as HIGH PRIEST following the Return (Ezra 2:2; Neh. 7:7; cf. Hag. 1:1; Zech. 3:1).

JESHURUN, JESURUN (Heb., *yeshurun*, "blessed" or "upright one"), a name symbolizing

JESSE 1569

ISRAEL, found only in the OLD TESTAMENT (Deut. 32:15 [where it is used in a pejorative sense]; 33:5,26; Isa. 44:2 [where, used as a title of honor, it is rendered "Jesurun"]).

JESIAH (Heb., *yishshiyah,* perhaps "the Lord loans"), one of the "mighty men" of DAVID who joined the future monarch at ZIKLAG during his period of outlawry (I Chron. 12:6); a second Jesiah was one of the LEVITES mentioned only in the genealogies of the First Book of the CHRONICLES (23:20).

JESIMIEL (Heb., *yesimiel,* "God sets up"), one of the leaders of the TRIBE OF SIMEON during the tribe's early history (I Chron. 4:36).

JESSE (Heb., *yshai,* perhaps "strong" or "wealthy"), the grandson of BOAZ and RUTH by their son OBED, and father of King DAVID. Member of a distinguished BETHLEHEM family of the TRIBE OF JUDAH, Jesse was a simple countryman who sent the youngest of his eight sons, David, out to herd sheep; in Jesse's eyes, this last-born was probably rather unimpressive. When the LORD, disenchanted with the kingship of SAUL, sent the Judge-Prophet SAMUEL to "Jesse the Bethlehemite: for I have provided me a king among his sons," Jesse did not think to call David in from the pastures until Samuel had rejected the other seven and asked, "Are here all thy children?" (I Sam. 16:1-11), whereupon the future monarch was summoned. When, subsequently, Saul sent for David, Jesse sent along "an ass laden with bread, and a bottle of wine, and a kid" (I Sam. 16:20), certainly the gifts of a country squire rather than of a courtier.

It was Jesse who set his son's feet on the road that was to lead to monarchy, when he sent David to the battlefield with food for his three eldest brothers, who had "followed Saul" (I Sam. 17:14). David's ensuing fame put his entire family in jeopardy; when he became an outlaw from Saul, his parents and "all his father's house" had to take refuge in the cave of ADULLAM. Even there David feared for their safety, and took his father and mother to King MIZPEH of MOAB (the birthplace of his ancestress Ruth), to live under his protection. Through his last son, Jesse secured fame far beyond his own accomplishments; his name is used as the symbol in the prophecy of ISAIAH regarding the coming MESSIAH: "And there shall

Jesse (*far right*) presents his eight sons to the Judge-Prophet Samuel (*seated*) (*Tissot, Brooklyn Museum*).

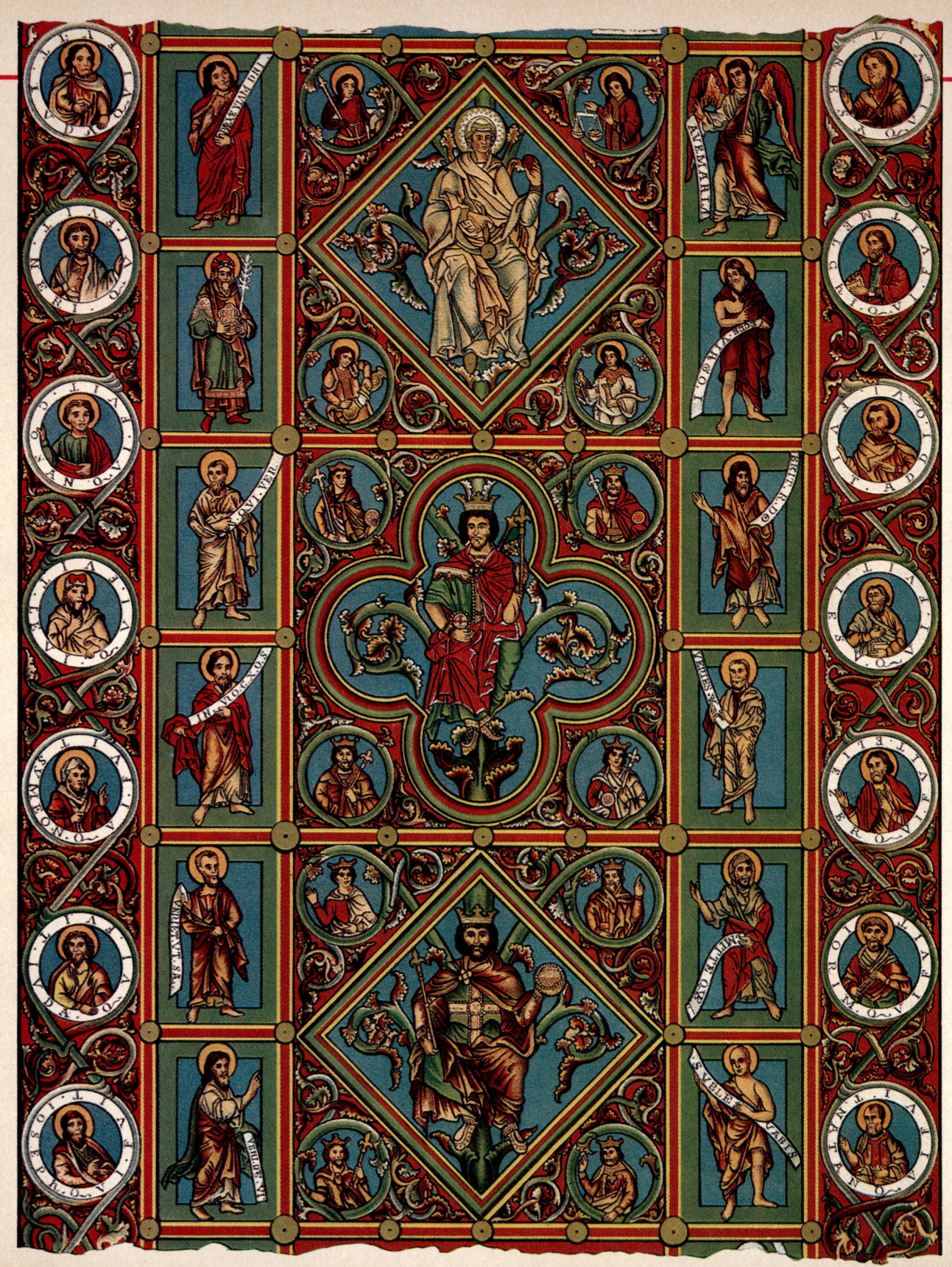

come forth a rod out of the stem of Jesse . . ." (Isa. 11:1). He is thus enshrined in the genealogies of both David and JESUS CHRIST (e.g., Matt. 1:5). (*See also* GENEALOGY OF JESUS CHRIST.) N.P.

JESSUE, JESU, in the APOCRYPHA, the ancestor of a group who returned to JERUSALEM following the PERIOD OF THE BABYLONIAN CAPTIVITY (I Esd. 5:26 ["Jessue"]; 8:63 ["Jesu"]).

JESUI (Heb., *yeshui,* "level"), the eponym of a clan within the TRIBE OF ASHER which was included in the CENSUS ordered by MOSES (Num. 26:44 [cf. Gen. 46:17 where he is named ISUI]).

JESUS BEN SIRACH (Gr. form of the Heb., *Yehoshua ben Sira,* "Joshua, the son of Sira"), author of ECCLESIASTICUS, the seventh book of the APOCRYPHA in the KING JAMES VERSION; it is part of the WISDOM LITERATURE of the ancient Israelites. The only one among OLD TESTAMENT or Apocryphal writers who signed his works, he is named in the superscription of chapter fifty-one (as well as in 50:27). The Translator's Foreword, written by his grandson, reveals that the younger man took the work to EGYPT soon after 132 B.C. and translated it into Greek for the benefit of the Jewish community in ALEXANDRIA. (*See also* SEPTUAGINT.) The author is called "Jesus the son of Sirach of Jerusalem" (or "the Jerusalemite") in the Greek text, but the translator refers to him simply as "my grandfather Jesus." The oldest manuscripts also add the name of Elazar, probably his grandfather. The sum of the evidence of all extant manuscripts seems to be that the author's full name was Jesus the son of Simon the son of Elazar ben Sirach.

Aside from the little contained in the Greek text and in quotations in later writings, our knowledge of Jesus ben Sirach is derived entirely from internal evidence in Ecclesiasticus. The supposition that he was connected with the PRIESTHOOD is probably the result of a scribal error. Neither was he a rabbi or a physician, as has sometimes been inferred from 49:1-5 and from the introduction by his grandson. All that is known about him, other than the fact that he was a Palestinian Jew and wrote in Hebrew, is that he was a scholar and one of the early SCRIBES (cf. 38:24-39:11), well versed in the MOSAIC LAW, the writings of the PROPHETS, and the Wisdom Literature of his time. He describes himself as a teacher of wisdom "for all of them that seek learning" (33:17). In one passage (51:23) he seems to be inviting young men to attend his academy, described as a *bet hamidrash* ("house of study"), the first usage in extant literature of a now widely accepted term for rabbinical schools. His portrayal of the ideal scribe (38:24-39:11) may be an idealized version of his own life.

His book is a collection of maxims and moral counsel written at various times in his life (as is evidenced by the frequent repetitions and contradictions). It is often utilitarian and mainly secular, for Ben Sirach never set forth legal restrictions in a juristic manner. The work records the practical wisdom and religious teachings of its author in his academy for Jewish boys during the first quarter of the second century B.C. His ethics are derived from both Jewish wisdom writings (particularly the Book of PROVERBS) and from his own rational reflections upon his experiences and observations. A man of culture and means, and a polished writer, he was well able to express himself in classical Hebrew. According to the Greek version of his book, he traveled extensively (34:11) and often found himself in dangerous situations (34:12). In a hymn in chapter fifty-one he speaks of many perils from which he was saved by GOD (51:1-12), but this reference may be no more than a form of stylization often seen in the Psalms.

Like other wise men of his day he may have been sent on diplomatic missions in the course of which he appeared before heads of state (39:4) and served in the courts of foreign princes (34:11-12). Some commentators see traces of Hellenic influence in his writings, possibly as a result of his travels, which brought him into contact with Greek ideas and ways, although he consciously resisted HELLENISM. He speaks of foreign poets and moralists and often describes customs taken from Greek social situations, but we cannot say with any certainty that he knew Greek, had a firsthand acquaintance with the works of Greek writers, or borrowed ideas from them. He reveals a great distrust of women, based partly on personal knowledge or observation of unhappy marriages (25:16-26), on his views of women as enticing men to wrongdoing (42:9-14), on fathers' problems with oversexed daughters (26:10-12), and partly on a metaphysical theory

13th-century fresco, "The Tree of Jesse."
According to New Testament tradition,
Jesus was descended from Jesse
(*New York Public Library*).

Initial, showing Jesus Ben Sirach, from a 12th-century Latin Bible illumination (*Bibliotheque Sainte Genevieve*).

of the origin of evil (25:24); but he held nonetheless that a man with a good wife was infinitely more blessed than a bachelor (36:18-26).

Of a philosophical turn of mind with a profound understanding of the human heart, he was witty and poetic, but always practical and prudent; he eschewed metaphysical speculations because he saw the ultimate mysteries of life as beyond the understanding of man (3:17-24). He was above all an ethical monotheist in the tradition of the Prophet AMOS and the Prophets after him. Certain of his passages anticipate talmudic developments (*see* TALMUD), but he differed from the postbiblical rabbis in that he considered ritualistic rulings secondary to the ethical. It may be significant that in his listing of great men of the past (44:1 ff.) he does not so much as mention EZRA, who is revered in pharisaic and talmudic tradition as the paragon and symbol of the scholar.

Ben Sirach was probably born some time in the latter part of the third century B.C. He must have been well into his maturity when he put his teachings into writing, presumably about 180 B.C. The dating is established in part by his eulogy of the High Priest Simon ben Johanan, which seems to be based on personal recollection. It is generally accepted that the subject of his praise was Simon II, who died shortly after 200 B.C., although the Jewish historian FLAVIUS JOSEPHUS maintained that it could only have been Simon I (300-287 B.C.), known as "Simon the Just." The theory of the later dating is supported by the fact that the author's grandson migrated to Egypt in the reign of PTOLEMY VII PHYSCON (170-117 B.C.). Ben Sirach apparently lived before the persecutions of ANTIOCHUS IV EPIPHANES reached their climax in 168 B.C. and the rebellion of the MACCABEES which they precipitated, since he indicates no awareness of anything connected with that turbulent era.

The period of his literary activity, therefore, is assumed to have been about 190-170 B.C. As JUDAEA was ruled by the Syrian SELEUCID DYNASTY at that time, Ben Sirach was resisting the effects of Hellenization and particularly the efforts to impose Greek culture and religion on the Jewish people. He marshaled all the forces of JUDAISM against the new threat: he supported the LAW and TEMPLE and its liturgy, and held the priestly office up to esteem. In general he taught the traditional doctrines and was spiritually deep in the sacred books, but his great contribution was the identifying of wisdom with the Law of MOSES (24:23-24). He integrated wisdom with the observance of the religious precepts set down in the TORAH. Wisdom, in his mind, was fear of God.

Ben Sirach is the last canonical representative of the school of Jewish wisdom in Palestine. He is a foremost example of the *chassidim* (the "pious ones," the biblical ASSIDEANS) of Judaism who were soon to defend their faith against the religious excesses of Antiochus Epiphanes. Though his book was not admitted into the CANON OF THE OLD TESTAMENT, it was widely read by the Jews of its day. Ben Sirach was highly esteemed and was quoted in rabbinical literature as if his writings were Scripture. His wide readership during the talmudic period is seen in the citation of a number of his verses in the Aramaic, indicating that it had been translated into the vernacular of the Jews of that time. It is known that an Aramaic version of Ecclesiasticus existed at the time of the Amoraim (teachers that flourished in BABYLON and PALESTINE from A.D. 219 to the completion of the Babylonian Talmud, about 500). Evidence of his great popularity with the Jewish masses is found in the *Alphabet of Ben Sirach,* a small book containing a double list of proverbs supposedly his—twenty-two in Aramaic, twenty-two in Hebrew—arranged in alphabetical order. These are enriched with commentary and legends added centuries later. *H.G.G.*

JESUS CHRIST, considered the founder of CHRISTIANITY—a major world religion that now claims nearly one billion adherents—more than any other religion in history. Although our knowledge of Jesus derives only from the FOUR GOSPELS, his historicity is beyond question. That Jesus Christ actually lived cannot be doubted, even by those who deny the accuracy or validity of the Gospels. Believed to have been born in 4 B.C., Jesus was the son of MARY and JOSEPH, the latter a carpenter by profession. During his lifetime Jesus was recognized as a preacher, miracle worker, and religious reformer within the tradition of JUDAISM. Little if anything is known of Jesus' childhood, even on the basis of the Gospels, which concern themselves with the last years of his life. He was put to death by the Roman authorities sometime between A.D. 28 and 33, for preaching what they believed to be subversion of imperial authority. Three days after his CRUCIFIXION, he was, in the Christian tradition, resurrected; to adherents of Christianity he represented the fulfillment of the OLD TESTAMENT promise of a MESSIAH, or Redeemer, and is held to be the Son of God (*see* CHRISTOLOGY).

The Annunciation: the Archangel Michael and the Virgin Mary (*Counsel Collection*).

It is probable that the emergence from his life and teachings of the dominant world religion—a religion whose central article of faith is the personal divinity of Jesus Christ—would have astounded the historical Jesus. The closest examination of the Gospels fails to reveal a single overt declaration that he intended to found a new religion (Matt. 5:17); on the contrary, he saw himself as the embodiment of his native Judaism. Admittedly, he must have scandalized many pious Jews, not only by addressing God as "Father," but by doing so in Aramaic, the language of the common people, instead of in the Hebrew of the Old Testament (Mark 14:36; cf. Matt. 6:5-15; *see also* LANGUAGES OF THE BIBLE).

Jesus always insisted that his mission was to complete the work of MOSES and the PROPHETS, not to destroy it (Matt. 5:17); he was also convinced that, in some sense, the end of the world was at hand (*see* PAROUSIA). Whether or not he foresaw the cataclysmic events of A.D. 70, when the Romans conquered JERUSALEM and destroyed all hopes of Jewish independence for nearly two thousand years, we have no good reason to believe that his outlook transcended his own time and place to any extraordinary degree. (*See also* JEWISH REVOLT.)

In Jesus' time, the most intensely religious Jews—citizens of Jesus' native JUDAEA, who were little influenced by HELLENISM—believed that, from a spiritual point of view (which was the only point of view that mattered to them), contact with GENTILES, or non-Jews, was like touching filth. Thus Jewish tax collectors ("publicans") were despised, not only because they profited from a taxation system that Jews considered a religious and patriotic insult, but because, as functionaries of the ROMAN EMPIRE administration, they had to deal with Gentiles. To enter a Gentile's house was to become polluted; to eat at the same table with one was an abomination. Sometimes this had strange consequences. Thus Jesus' accusers would not enter Roman military headquarters on the eve of the PASSOVER (John 18:28). (Later, PAUL THE APOSTLE was nearly lynched after being seen in the company of a Greek at the same time of year [Acts 21: 27-29].) Gentiles were allowed only in the outer court of the TEMPLE at Jerusalem; an inscription warned that any Gentile who went further would be killed. This was no idle threat; many Jews were prepared not only to kill but to die for their religion at a moment's notice.

The Romans, with their usual mixture of insensitivity and efficiency, had stationed a garrison of soldiers in a fort adjoining the northernmost portion of the Temple area. On major religious festivals, people flocked to Jerusalem from all over the Middle East, and the garrison, with the Jewish Temple guard, had the responsibility for keeping order. The fort overlooked the Temple courtyard. During the governorship of Ventidius Cumanus (A.D. 48-52), one of the Roman soldiers stationed on the wall made an obscene gesture at the worshippers below. According to the Jewish historian FLAVIUS JOSEPHUS, the riot that followed was put down at the cost of between twenty and thirty thousand casualties (*The Antiquities of the Jews*, XX: 105-113).

Jesus shared this horror of the Gentile presence. He is on record as having instructed his DISCIPLES not to waste their time on Gentiles (Matt. 10:5), whom he describes elsewhere as "dogs" (Mark 7:27) and "swine" (Matt. 7:6). Yet the Church that bears his name is overwhelmingly Gentile, and the approximately fourteen million Jews who have survived to worship the God that he called "Father" do not even recognize him among their Prophets. How did all this happen?

For anyone seriously interested in the truth, the first thing that has to be faced about Jesus is that almost nothing is really known about him. The German Protestant scholar Adolf Harnack (1851-1930), who wrote a history of Christian doctrine in seven volumes, was fond of remarking that all the known facts about Jesus could easily be written on one small sheet of paper. We do not even know if Jesus was ever married, though it seems rather unlikely in view of his desire to abolish divorce, which was an ancient Jewish custom (Matt. 5:31-32; cf. 22:23-30). Indeed, very little is recorded about him until he began his public ministry, at the age of thirty (Luke 3:23). The longest term that anyone has been able to assign to this ministry is about three years. The FOUR GOSPELS are virtually our only source of information on what Jesus said and did during this time (fragments of other gospels have survived but, apart from a few sayings that sound authentic, they are worthless as history; *see* APOCRYPHAL NEW TESTAMENT). Here we face the first of the many obstacles that seem to bar our way to the truth.

Modern scholarship has established beyond any reasonable doubt that the earliest surviving Christian writings are the PAULINE EPISTLES, or at least those of them that can safely be ascribed to Paul. Unfortunately, Paul was not interested in the historical facts about Jesus. Indeed, he believed that they were completely irrelevant to his faith (II Corin. 5:16). Accordingly, there is very little to be learned from Paul on this subject. The first connected account of Jesus' life and teachings—the GOSPEL ACCORDING TO ST. MARK—was probably written sometime between A.D. 63 and 67, the period of Paul's martyrdom. This, it should be noted, was at least thirty years after Jesus' death. The next two canonical gospels—the GOSPEL ACCORDING TO ST. MATTHEW and the GOSPEL ACCORDING TO ST. LUKE—can be dated at any time between about A.D. 75 and 100. Despite certain additions and alterations, both are patterned after the St. Mark Gospel. These three are the so-called SYNOPTIC GOSPELS; with their sources, written and unwritten, they constitute the synoptic tradition—and are themselves the only surviving examples of it. The synoptic tradition is our chief source of information of Jesus' life and teachings. The GOSPEL ACCORDING TO ST. JOHN, which appears to stand completely outside that tradition, contains proportionately less narrative and more teaching than any of the Synoptic Gospels.

The two longest uninterrupted statements by Jesus that we have are the so-called SERMON ON THE MOUNT and the Farewell Discourses (John 14:1-16:16, to which 17:1-26 should perhaps be added). It is obvious that the former is essentially a collection of short sayings, while the latter is more like a regular sermon, or a series of at most three sermons. Quite apart from the fact the the St. John Gospel was written last—few scholars now date it before A.D. 100, and many believe it to be a work of the second or third decade of the second century—it is most unlikely that Jesus' words were ever transmitted in any such form. At most, the discourses may be a mixture of someone's reminiscences and the teaching of the Church to which he belonged, all probably written up by someone else. (*See also* AGRAPHA.)

The Synoptists, on the other hand, seem to have drawn on a collection of Jesus' sayings that was just that—isolated sayings, preserved at first in the memories of those who happened to have heard Jesus preach, and then by Church members who learned them by heart. We can be fairly sure that there was no conscious attempt at editing or interpreting these sayings when they were first written down. The same, alas, cannot be said of the Synoptists themselves, but we can at least check them against each other. Not that the St. John Gospel should be dismissed as essentially a work of fiction; on the contrary, as we shall see, there are some areas in which it makes better historical sense than any other Gospel. But, since Jesus' life is known only in the barest outline, any detailed impression of him that is not a fantasy must depend mainly on his words. And the Synoptic Gospels probably bring us as close to Jesus' actual words as we shall ever get.

It is important to emphasize this fact because in recent years there has been a tendency among some NEW TESTAMENT scholars to declare that the Jesus of history is forever concealed from us. Certainly, we have very little to go on: four short books, the earliest dating from at least thirty years after Jesus' death, the latest from perhaps a hundred years, all of them written by authors whose identity is uncertain, and based on sources now lost. Moreover, as scholars never tire of pointing out, it is impossible to reconcile these books completely with each other—which in turn raises the possibility that none of them is reliable. Nevertheless, as generations of readers have witnessed, the Four Gospels do succeed in giving a coherent overall impression. The Jesus of the St. Matthew Gospel differs somewhat from the Jesus of the St. Luke Gospel, while both differ to a measurable degree from the Jesus of the St. John Gospel. But it is still recognizably the same Jesus, doing and saying the same kinds of things. And after every last difference between the Gospels has been explored and catalogued, there remains an irreducible core of agreement to which only the most skeptical will refuse the name of truth.

Here is how one contemporary scholar defines this core: (1) Jesus was a Jew; (2) he was brought up in NAZARETH, an unimportant town in the unimportant (and partly Gentile) region of the GALILEE; (3) his father, a carpenter by profession, was named JOSEPH, and his mother, MARY; (4) he had four brothers: JAMES, JOSES, JUDE, and SIMON (*see also* BRETHREN OF JESUS CHRIST); (5) he also had sisters (we do not know their names); (6) his mother and brothers at first strongly disapproved of his mission, but after his death they joined his followers; (7) like his fellow countrymen, he spoke Aramaic; (8) he could read the Jewish Scriptures in the original Hebrew; (9) the turning point in his life was his BAPTISM by JOHN THE BAPTIST, when he was about thirty years old; (10) not long after this, he began his own ministry in Galilee; (11) unlike the Baptist, he set out to help the poor

"The Nativity," by the Renaissance artist Master of Flemalle (*Mella, Milan*).

The Holy Family,
by the great Dutch master
Rembrandt van Rijn.
(*Mella, Milan*).

and suffering, while preaching a version of Judaism that aroused the suspicion and finally the enmity of the Jewish religious authorities; (12) he won considerable popular support; (13) he decided to carry his message—a message that could be summed up as the proclamation of the KINGDOM OF GOD—to the holy city of Jerusalem; (14) having done so, he was arrested and finally executed by crucifixion, the standard Roman method of capital punishment for those who were not Roman citizens (G. Bornkamm, *Jesus of Nazareth,* New York, 1960, pp. 52-55).

Clearly, this was no ordinary man. But it is hard to tell, from an outline like this, exactly what he stood for. On what charges was he condemned? What was this "kingdom of God" that he preached? Was it anything political? If all he did was help the poor and suffering, why was he such a controversial figure? Was he a Prophet? How did he see himself in relation to John the Baptist? And just what were the Jewish religious authorities so worried about? These, of course, are all strictly historical questions, arising out of the basic historical facts as outlined above. But most readers of the Gospels are not historians, and they are likely to have different kinds of questions. Did Jesus live again after he was crucified? Did he really work miracles? Will he ever come in glory to judge the living and the dead? These are religious questions, and historians have no business even attempting to answer them. Nevertheless, it must be admitted that the most reasonable answer to both types of question, both historical and religious, is that we do not know. Christians should not take alarm. "The just shall live by faith" (Rom. 1:17; cf. Hab. 2:4). This is as true now as when Paul wrote it. Jesus himself consistently refused to prove that he had any kind of special authority from God (Mark 8:11-12; cf. John 4:48). All he asked was that people should believe in him. Believing in a person is not at all the same as believing this or that set of facts about him, and Jesus struggled to get this point across (Mark 9:23; Luke 9:48; John 6:35-40). But no church has ever taught that Christians should ignore the facts.

One fact of which all readers of the Scriptures should be aware is the destruction of Jerusalem by the Romans in A.D. 70. In 66 the Jewish religious authorities decided to reject the customary offerings from ROME and the emperor—an action that amounted to a proclamation of Jewish independence. Four years later Jerusalem was captured by a Roman

Italian altar sculpture depicting the adoration of the infant Jesus (*Mella, Milan*).

The flight of the Holy Family into Egypt, thought by scholars to be apocryphal (*Mella, Milan*).

army under TITUS FLAVIUS VESPASIANUS, son of the recently proclaimed emperor VESPASIAN. The Temple was looted of its sacred treasures, and much of Jerusalem burned. The importance of this event to the history of Christianity cannot be exaggerated. Already, PETER (SIMON PETER) had been martyred in ROME, probably as a result of the persecution of Roman Christians by the emperor NERO in 64. JAMES, brother of Jesus and an early head of the Jerusalem Church, had, according to Josephus, been stoned to death for BLASPHEMY at the order of a Jewish HIGH PRIEST. Henceforth, little is heard of Jesus' family or of the original TWELVE APOSTLES. If the Jerusalem Church had any records, they were probably destroyed during the anti-Roman revolt; we do not know how many Church members perished along with it, but it is reasonable to assume that many of them stayed to fight the Roman invaders. All this must have produced a major break in Church tradition, and so in our knowledge of Jesus.

Another fact that has to be faced is that the Four Gospels are quite transparently pro-Roman. Indeed, if they were designed, as they seem to have been, for circulation mainly among Gentiles, they could scarcely have been anything else. There was no real freedom of worship under the Roman Empire. To be sure, the Romans tolerated an almost infinite variety of religions, but only because they were satisfied that there was nothing subversive about them. In effect, such religions operated under license from the Roman state. The "license fee" was some token of submission to the emperor, who was worshipped, at least outside Italy, as a god in his own lifetime. (*See* EMPEROR WORSHIP.) Polytheistic religions had no special difficulty in adapting to this; the emperor was just one god among many. But it was a terrible dilemma for a monotheistic religion such as Judaism. Jews had always considered it blasphemy to pay divine honors to any but the one true God (Exod. 20:3-6). The question was complicated unbearably by the fact that the Jews believed their homeland had been promised to them by God, so that, in a sense, it belonged to Him,

Famous Tissot painting of Jesus as a young boy (*Brooklyn Museum*).

and He was king over it. (*See* COVENANT.) From a strictly political point of view, this attitude was somewhat out of date by the time Jesus was born.

In the Middle East, the times had long favored large, bureaucratic kingdoms under Greek-speaking monarchs. The culture of the region as a whole was Greek; it had formerly been conquered by ALEXANDER THE GREAT, whose successors founded a great many cities after the Greek model. (*See also* HELLENISM; PTOLEMAIC DYNASTY; SELEUCID DYNASTY.) In general, they encouraged the native populations to take up what passed for a Greek way of life (today we call it "Hellenistic," meaning that it was a mixture of Greek and other elements). But somehow the Jews maintained their traditional religion and culture. There was little active interference with either until the Seleucid emperor ANTIOCHUS IV EPIPHANES, who was descended from one of Alexander's generals, made a bloody attempt to suppress the Jewish religion in the name of Hellenization. The priestly family of the MACCABEES was provoked into starting a revolt that eventually gave the Jewish people their first period of genuine political independence since the rule of the House of DAVID. Meanwhile, Rome was becoming the leading power in the Mediterranean world. When the Maccabean HASMONAEAN DYNASTY fell apart, the Romans picked up the pieces.

For a while they controlled Judaea (as the Jewish nation was then called) indirectly, through the HERODS, a dynasty that ruled over EDOM (Idumea) and was therefore identified as traditional enemies of the Jews, their forced conversion to Judaism notwithstanding. Although the Herods were quite thoroughly Hellenized, they adopted a policy of appeasing Jewish religious sentiment rather than antagonizing it. In particular, HEROD THE GREAT made a great show of observing the MOSAIC LAW, and even built the magnificent Jerusalem Temple that the Romans were later to destroy. But when he died in 4 B.C., a sizable proportion of the Jewish people decided that they had had enough of Edomites. There were armed revolts in Jerusalem and all over the country; one of them was led by a certain Judas ben Hezekiah.

Finally, Judaea was pacified by the Roman governor of SYRIA, whose army was the chief instrument of Roman security in the Middle East. Two thousand Jewish patriots were crucified. Herod's kingdom was divided between three rulers: his son ARCHELAUS, in Judaea; HEROD ANTIPAS, another son, in Galilee; and PHILIP, half-brother of Herod Antipas, in the northern Palestinian region of Iturea and Trachonitis (now in Syria, except for the portion occupied by Israel in June 1967). In A.D. 6, the emperor AUGUSTUS dismissed Archelaus for incompetence and placed Judaea under direct Roman rule. The governor was to be a PROCURATOR, or imperial official of non-senatorial rank. As a necessary first step, the governor of Syria, to whom the procurator of Judaea would normally report, was ordered to conduct a CENSUS. This provoked another revolt, led by another Judas, JUDAS OF GALILEE.

The revolt was, of course, crushed, but it was survived by an organized guerrilla movement composed of Judas' followers. Calling themselves ZEALOTS (Heb., *kanna'im,* doubtless from Num. 25:11), they enjoyed considerable support in the countryside. It was into this world that Jesus was born.

Because one tradition mentions Herod the Great as still alive (Matt. 2:13-16), the date of his birth is generally placed no later than 4 B.C. According to the same tradition, Herod (who undoubtedly followed standard practice and maintained a court astrologer) was very worried by a remarkable star that had been drawn to his attention by three magicians from Persia (Matt. 2:1-3; *see* ASTROLOGY). It is an astronomical fact that in the summer and fall of 7 B.C. the planet Jupiter, which in ancient astrological lore signified "lord of the world," crossed several times with the planet Saturn, which signified PALESTINE. Moreover, this interplanetary conjunction took place in the constellation of Pisces, which signified "the last days." Such a phenomenon occurs only once every 794 years, so it was quite enough to bring wise men from the East (E. Stauffer, *Jesus and His Story,* London, 1960, pp. 36-38).

The only other verifiable tradition about Jesus' birth is that it was in the same year as the imperial decree "that all the world should be taxed," that is, submit to a census (Luke 2:1). Since the only Judaean census even remotely near this period was in A.D. 6, the author of the St. Luke Gospel would appear to have gotten his dates wrong (*see* CHRONOLOGY OF THE NEW TESTAMENT). It is easy to see how this could

19th-century lithograph showing the young Jesus disputing in the Temple (*Counsel Collection*).

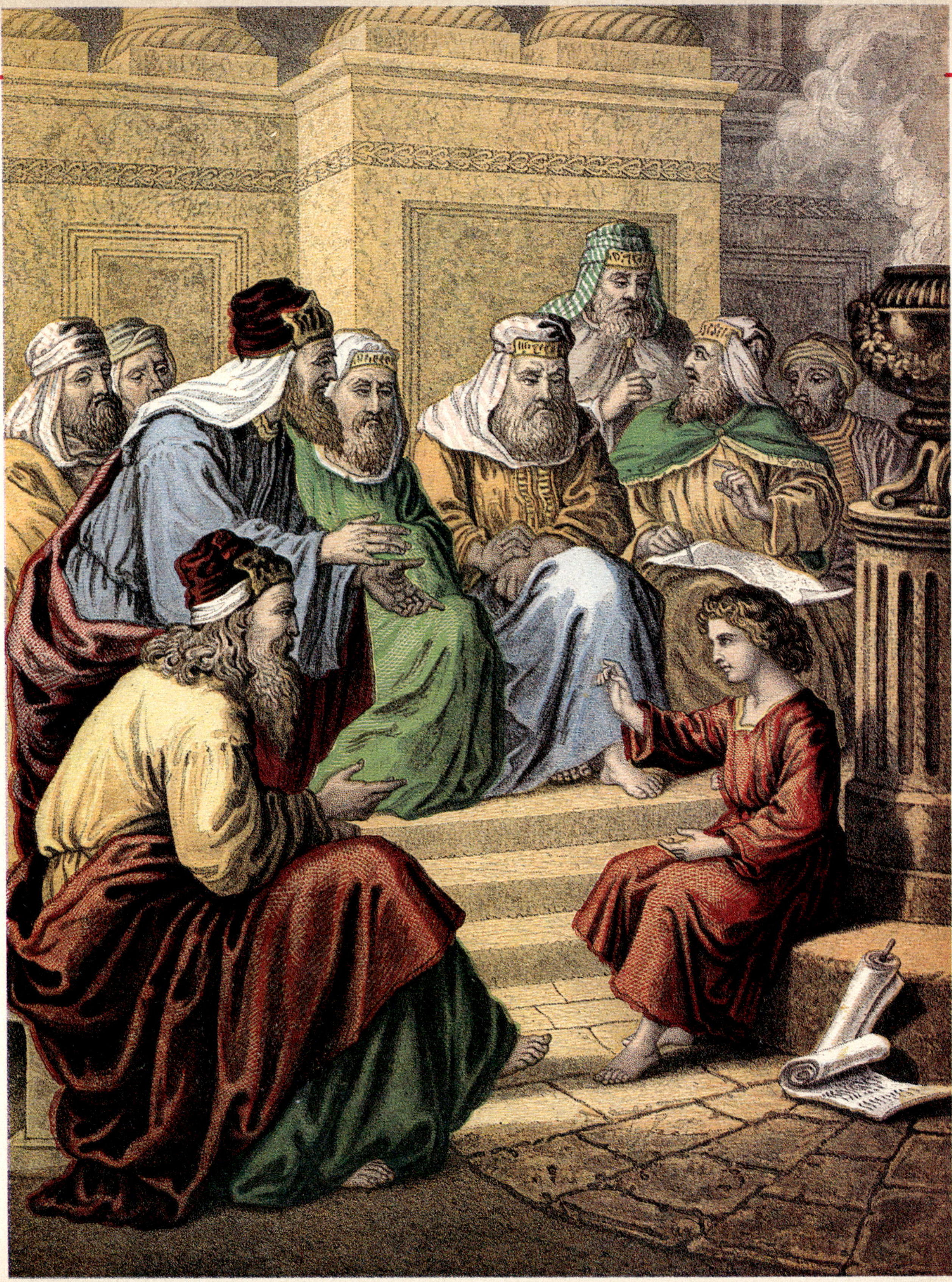

have happened: tradition said that the MESSIAH would be born in BETHLEHEM (Matt. 2:4-6; cf. Micah 5:2); and the author, at a loss why anyone should go all the way from NAZARETH to Bethlehem in order to have a baby, hit upon the explanation of the census. The rival tradition is that Joseph's home town was originally Bethlehem and that he settled in Nazareth later (Matt. 2:13-23). The same regard for tradition led to a couple of interesting attempts to reconstruct Jesus' family tree (*see* GENEALOGY OF JESUS CHRIST). Other aspects of the delightful Christmas legend need not detain us here; it should be enough to note that neither the St. Mark Gospel nor the St. John Gospel contains a single word about it.

Also worth noting is what the opening chapters of the Gospels do *not* say: they say nothing about the revolts of 4 B.C. and A.D. 6, the reduction of Judaea to a Roman province, the appointment of a Jewish High Priest (Ananus, or ANNAS) by the Roman governor of Syria, or the existence of a Jewish resistance movement in Jesus' native Galilee. And yet Jesus was a Jew who was executed by the Roman authorities on a charge of subversion. We are even told that one of his disciples, SIMON THE ZEALOT, belonged to this very resistance movement—a fact that the authors of the St. Mark and St. Matthew Gospels try to gloss over by using the Aramaic word for "Zealot" without translating it (Luke 6:15; Mark 3:18; Matt. 10:4). Nevertheless, the Gospels are clearly designed to show that Jesus, if not exactly a loyal citizen of the Roman Empire, was at any rate no danger to it.

Of course, such a view is not necessarily wrong. This topic is discussed further below; meanwhile, we enter what are generally known as Jesus' "hidden years," that is, the years not covered in the New Testament.

If it were not for the author of the St. Luke Gospel we would lack even a hint of Jesus' life when he was growing up. But the little that this author tells us sounds entirely plausible. His parents were pious Jews: every year, as the Law prescribed, they went up to Jerusalem for the Passover—at least a week's journey. When Jesus was twelve, and so approaching the age at which he would traditionally have been expected to assume the religious responsibilities of an adult, they took him with them. Ever since the late Middle Ages, most Orthodox Jews have celebrated their sons' thirteenth birthdays with a ceremony in which the young man is called upon to read aloud from the Scriptures in his local SYNAGOGUE. He is then considered *bar mitzvah* (Heb., "a son of the Law"). We do not know if this was required of Jesus (the custom cannot be traced so far back), but in any case he demonstrated his knowledge of the Hebrew Scriptures in a remarkable fashion. After spending Passover week in Jerusalem, his parents were returning homeward. On such occasions, whole communities used to travel together. Accordingly, Jesus' absence was not noticed at first. When it became clear that he was not with them, Joseph and Mary returned to Jerusalem—and according to Luke, found him listening to and questioning the learned doctors of the Law in the Temple. When Mary scolded him for causing them so much anxiety, he replied—somewhat coldly, it may seem to us—that they should have left him alone: he had his "Father's business" to attend to (Luke 2:41-49).

There is no compelling reason to disbelieve this story. Jesus could have taught himself Hebrew by regular attendance at the synagogue in Nazareth, since the Scripture of the day was always read first in Hebrew and then in Aramaic. Other twelve-year-olds have attended graduate seminars, before and since. And even if the story is not true, it points to one very important fact: Jesus' entire thought and behavior—indeed, his very being—was formed by study of the Hebrew Scriptures.

The other glimpse of Jesus' hidden years that we owe to the St. Luke Gospel is the information that Jesus was the cousin of John the Baptist (1:36, 57-79). There can be little doubt that Jesus began his religious career as one of the Baptist's disciples. According to the Synoptic Gospels, Jesus actually came to the Baptist in order to be baptized by him (Mark 1:9-11; Matt. 3:13-17; Luke 3:21-22). They add that this was the occasion when Jesus received not only the HOLY SPIRIT but the power to confer it on others. The St. John Gospel, though it mentions no baptism, describes the Baptist as bearing witness to the Spirit's descent. The next day two of the Baptist's disciples, apparently with his approval, left him to follow Jesus (1:32-37). A little later in the same Gospel we learn that Jesus went with his disciples to Judaea, where he baptized people just as the Baptist was still doing. It seems that the Baptist's disciples were concerned about Jesus' growing popularity, and that the Baptist assured them it was the will of God (3:22-30). None of this appears in the Synoptic Gospels, which all imply that one of the ways in which Jesus immediately distinguished himself from the Baptist was that he did *not* baptize. This, then, is virtually all we know about Jesus at the time he started on the road to the cross. The "hidden years" leave us with many unanswered questions. How long did he work in his father's carpentry business? What sort of impression was made on him by the revolt of Judas of Galilee? Was he, like Judas, a fully trained rabbi? If not, did his parents want him to be one? How old was he when his father died? (There is no mention in the Gospels of Joseph's death, but many scholars infer from such passages as Luke 8:19-21, where he is not mentioned, that he died before Jesus.) Did he quarrel with his brothers and sisters? At least we know his brothers' names: James, Joses, Simon, and Jude (Matt. 13:55; Mark 6:3). But we shall never know why, after he began his mission, he would have nothing to do with his family.

It is clear that Jesus was deeply impressed by the teaching of John the Baptist, and we know roughly what that teaching was. Baptism was a kind of purification ceremony; in the Jewish religion, there were many such. But John's was "the baptism of repentance for the remission of sins" (Mark 1:4). It was linked with two great themes: "he who shall come," a way of referring to the Messiah (Mal. 3:1; cf. Matt. 11:3), and the Kingdom of Heaven (Matt. 3:2) or of God (Luke 16:16). The Messiah was not only a king but a judge; if the Jews wanted to go on being God's Chosen People, they had better mend their ways. The Baptist was widely accepted as a Prophet—he even dressed like ELIJAH (Matt. 3:4; cf. 11:7-14). Under the political conditions then existing, anyone with a following might be regarded as dangerous by the authorities. The Baptist was eventually jailed for criticizing the marriage of Herod Antipas with HERODIAS (Mark 6:17-18). Soon after this, according to the St. Mark Gospel, Jesus returned to Galilee and began to preach "the gospel of the kingdom of God" (1:14). To take up the Baptist's old theme in Herod Antipas' own territory showed an extraordinary degree of courage. But it seems that Jesus had recently undergone—and surmounted—a major spiritual crisis.

After his baptism in the JORDAN RIVER (tradition places it at the ford of Hijlah, three or four miles north of the DEAD SEA), he had gone south, into the Wilderness of Judah. Directly on his route lay the religious community at QUMRAN, where a Jewish sect called the ESSENES lived an austere life in accordance with their own version of the Scriptures. A number of their books, including some purely Essene works,

John the Baptist (*left*) baptizing Jesus in the waters of the Jordan (*Tissot, Brooklyn Museum*).

were found in caves near Qumran during the period 1947-1956; they are generally known as the DEAD SEA SCROLLS and include the oldest surviving Old Testament manuscripts. We have no way of telling whether Jesus ever visited Qumran, but it seems unlikely that he would have omitted the opportunity to do so. Perhaps he rejected the Essenes as too remote from everyday life. But there is no trace of this in our only detailed accounts of the Temptation in the Wilderness, both of which seem designed to reassure Gentile readers that Jesus was not interested in political power (Matt. 4:1-11; Luke 4:1-13).

But was he? Many of his contemporaries thought so. But in a country under Roman occupation any popular preacher was seen as a potential national leader. There can be no certainty here. The possibility that the Synoptists toned down or omitted certain of

Jesus' key remarks is a very real one, and the various accounts of his trial and death are biased and (where we can check them) inaccurate.

We know more about what Jesus said than about what he did, and his teaching viewed as a whole simply does not give the impression of a political militant. Judas of Galilee had continually stressed that loyalty to God necessarily involved disloyalty to Rome. We find no hint of such a preoccupation in Jesus' sayings. On the other hand, as we have seen, he tolerated a Zealot as a disciple and gave an ambiguous reply when publicly asked whether Jews should pay taxes to Rome (Mark 12:13-17; Matt. 22:15-22; Luke 20:19-26). If only isolated sayings or facts are taken into account, seeming opposites can be paired off almost indefinitely. Thus Jesus' "Put up again thy sword" (Matt. 26:52) is matched by his "It is enough," when shown two swords (Luke 22:38). Whole books have been written around such evidence, but all they succeed in proving is that almost anything can be argued on the basis of what the Gospels do not say.

What they *do* say is that Jesus proclaimed that the Kingdom, long foretold by the Old Testament Prophets, had now arrived; it was "among you" (as "within you" should be translated in Luke 17:21). It is hard to understand exactly what Jesus meant by this. But it seems perfectly clear that the one thing he did not mean was a Jewish state independent of Rome. The Kingdom of God was a mystery that could be described only in PARABLES (Mark 4:11-12; 4:26-32; Luke 18:16-17). And yet it was close by, familiar as the everyday things mentioned in those parables. Jesus also taught more directly, using what we would call aphorisms, or pithy sayings. The list of BEATITUDES is perhaps the most famous example of these; another is the Seven Woes. This is the part of Jesus' teaching known to everyone: "Judge not, that ye be not judged" (Matt. 7:1); "Love your enemies" (Luke 6:27); "For what shall it profit a man, if he shall gain the whole world, and lose his own soul?" (Mark 8:36).

But these are not ordinary moral precepts. If they were, Jesus would have no claim to originality whatsoever, since all the purely moralistic side of his teaching can be found in the works of earlier moralists, both Jewish and Gentile. In Jesus' teaching, as in Jewish thought generally, all morality is referred back to God. To act in accordance with morality is not, as in Greek or Roman moral teaching, to follow man-made rules; rather, it is to do the will of God: "Thy will be done" (Matt. 6:10; Luke 11:2); "Nevertheless not what I will, but what thou wilt" (Mark 14:36). No theme is more prevalent in the synoptic tradition; as Rudolf Bultmann has pointed out, Jesus demands not that man choose to obey, but that he be obedient (*Jesus and the Word,* New York, 1958, pp. 72-86). Jesus taught that man exists for the sake of God, not vice versa. God is not an idol that one dusts off for special occasions or sacrifices to in order to enjoy a good meal afterward. Ritual as such is of no interest to him whatever. What he demands is perfection of thought and motive—inner, not outer, purity. Thus Jesus taught it was not enough to refrain from ADULTERY; to look at a woman with adultery in one's mind *is* adultery (Matt. 5:27-28).

To most people, Jesus appeared to be setting an impossible standard. But he was quick to point out that they thought of obeying God as difficult because they did it, if at all, out of fear. God was not only a stern judge, Jesus argued, but a loving father; only learn to love God as He loved us, and everything else would follow naturally (Luke 10:25-27). Love implied forgiveness—not a mere passive, grudging forgiveness, but an active seeking out of sinners, as in the LOST SHEEP PARABLE (Matt. 18:12-13). God would rejoice as much over the sinner who repented as the father in the parable rejoiced over the return of his playboy son (Luke 15:11-32). But forgiveness was there only for those who realized their need for it. Confronted with God, men could pride themselves on nothing; at best, they were all "unprofitable servants" (Luke 17-10). God would not listen to the professional do-gooder who boasted openly of his virtues, but to the tax collector who unobtrusively prayed, "God be merciful to me a sinner" (Luke 18:10-14).

Prayer was very important to Jesus; it both strengthened and refreshed him, and we are told how he resorted to it in times of doubt and distress (Mark 14:32-35; Matt. 14:22-23; cf. Luke 22:32). To us, after centuries of Christianity, this seems the normal behavior of a deeply religious man. To Jesus' contemporaries, however, it was decidedly unusual. Prayer had become somewhat conventionalized—a matter of recitation. Jesus prayed as if he were talking to his father (Mark 14:36; Luke 23:34). When his Disciples asked him how to pray, he taught them the LORD'S PRAYER (Matt. 6:9-13; Luke 11:1-4). In a few simple words, he expressed man's complete dependence on God. But they should not worry; God would provide for them, just as He provided for the flowers and

JESUS CHRIST 1587

Greek church in the village of Cana, where Jesus performed his first miracle (Counsel Collection).

birds (Matt. 6:26, 28-33). (On this aspect of Jesus' teaching, the painter Vincent van Gogh aptly remarked: "Christ was so infinitely great because no furniture, or any other stupid accessories, ever stood in his way."

Jesus is also recorded as having made a number of prophecies (*see especially* Mark 13; Matt. 24:1-42; Luke 21:5-36). It is very hard for a modern reader to evaluate these statements, based as they are upon a whole apocalyptic tradition of which the Book of

19th-century engraving showing Jesus preaching to his Disciples (*Counsel Collection*).

DANIEL is the only well-known example (*see also* APOCALYPTIC LITERATURE). Some scholars believe that Jesus never made any such prophecies, others that he did, but that our accounts of them are distorted because the Gospel authors misunderstood what he meant by calling himself "the Son of Man."

Still more puzzling, in the eyes of many, are the miracles: for instance, did Jesus really walk on the water? (Mark 6:47-51; John 6:16-21)—and do Christians have to believe that he did? Some non-Christians even place Jesus in the same category as the traveling conjurers whose exploits have always been a picturesque feature of life in the East. Most of the miracles can be explained in some scientific or naturalistic sense; for instance, Jesus might have been walking on the shore when the Disciples, not realizing their boat had drifted so close to land, glimpsed him through the darkness. But this is really to miss the point, which lies rather in the way these beautiful stories are told.

First, it will be noted that Jesus' miracles brought him into contact with an extraordinary variety of people—a violent lunatic (Mark 5:2-15), a leper (1:40-45), a prominent member of a synagogue (5:22-24,35-43), a Greek-speaking Syro-Phoenician woman (7:25-30), a blind beggar (10:46-52), and a Roman officer (Luke 7:1-10). Through these and many others we are given a virtual panorama of Middle

Eastern society, from outcasts to rulers. Second, all these people are in desperate need. Most pathetic of all, perhaps, are the parents of epileptic children (Mark 9:17-27; 7:25-26). We are reminded that there was almost no reliable medical knowledge in the ancient world and that certain forms of illness were considered due to possession by devils. (See DISEASES; MEDICINE.) Third, Jesus was often reluctant to perform miracles and angrily denounced all who demanded that he prove his credentials by a "sign" (Mark 8:11-12; Luke 11:29-32). Finally, and most significantly, people were cured only if they or those responsible for them had faith in Jesus (Mark 5:34; 10:51-52; Matt. 15:28; cf. 21:21). Indeed, Jesus himself often spoke as if it were their own faith that cured them, and for those who lacked faith, including the people in his home town, he could do nothing (Mark 6:4-6; Matt. 13:54-58).

In short, far from being the pointless exploits of a conjurer, Jesus' miracles were part of his teaching. They certainly helped to spread his fame. Miracles were performed as far north as SIDON (modern Saida, in Lebanon) and as far south as BETHANY (modern Al Ayzariyah, about three miles southeast of Jerusalem). But it is probably pointless to attempt to trace his exact movements during this period. The Gospels even differ on where the first miracle was performed: the St. John Gospel places it at CANA in Galilee, and the St. Mark Gospel at CAPERNAUM (near the northernmost point of the SEA OF GALILEE).

There is very little "plot" in the story of Jesus' Galilean ministry: after recruiting his Disciples (Mark 3:14-19; Luke 10:1), he traveled around with them healing people and preaching the gospel of the Kingdom of God. At one point he appears to have sent the Disciples out by themselves (Matt. 10:5-16;

Jesus and five of the Twelve Apostles on the Sea of Galilee (*Counsel Collection*).

Mark 6:7-13; Luke 10:17). It is possible that all this took place in some three-year period between A.D. 27 and 33. The Synoptic Gospels allow for only one year, but the chronology of the St. John Gospel, which allows for three, seems entirely preferable. Two important historical events can be assigned to the same period: the execution of John the Baptist by Herod Antipas, possibly in 28 B.C., and the arrival two years later of a new Roman procurator, one PONTIUS PILATE.

This man, who was to hold office for ten years, was under instructions to take a tough line with the Jews. According to the historian Flavius Josephus, he did just that. Although the story may be apocryphal, the St. Luke Gospel implies a high level of cooperation between him and Herod (23:5-12). In any case, almost as soon as Jesus' preaching began to attract public attention, he began to have trouble with what the Gospels call HERODIANS, that is, agents of Herod Antipas (Mark 3:6; Luke 13:31). Herod himself (Mark 6:14-16) is said to have responded to news of Jesus with apprehension: Could this Jesus be John the Baptist, risen from the dead? Jesus, who no doubt shared John's view of Herod's marriage, returned the compliment by calling Herod "that fox" (Luke 13:32). No wonder Jesus' life was in danger.

Jesus bringing the widow's son back to life (*Tissot, Brooklyn Museum*).

Jesus' other main enemies, according to the Gospels, were the PHARISEES, severely dealt with in the Gospel tradition as the quintessence of hypocrisy, greed, and empty ritualism (Matt. 23:13-33; Luke 11:37-44; Mark 7:1-13). Actually, Pharisaism was a relatively liberal movement, whose adherents believed that the Mosaic Law should be adapted to the changing times through learned interpretation. A whole body of such interpretations had been accumulating since about the fifth century B.C., and the Pharisees believed in taking these interpretations almost as seriously as the Law itself. Of course, this made religion a very complicated endeavor, far beyond the grasp of the ordinary person.

Perhaps this is what made Jesus so angry; he referred more than once to what he thought were the meaningless restrictions advocated by the Pharisees and told his disciples to beware of their influence (Mark 8:15; Luke 12:1-5). But Jesus himself spent much of his time reinterpreting the Scriptures, and many of his sayings resemble those of the Pharisees, or of teachers whom they admired, such as the famous Rabbi Hillel (about 50 B.C.-A.D. 10). We are told of some SCRIBES (that is, professional interpreters of the Law) who very much agreed with one of these sayings (Mark 12:28-34).

What probably annoyed both Scribes and Pharisees most about Jesus was his deliberately popular approach, which led him to associate with "publicans and sinners" (Matt. 9:10-13). In addition, they were always trying to prove that Jesus and his Disciples were not "good Jews" because they failed to observe various ritual provisions (Matt. 12:1-21; Mark 7:1-5). Nevertheless, Judaism both was and is a religion of great diversity—for instance, it has no fixed doctrine concerning life after death (*see* ESCHATOLOGY)—and the Pharisees should not be considered typical Jews. Nor were they uniformly hostile to Jesus: on one occasion, some of them tried to save his life (Luke 13:31).

We come now to the most perplexing aspect of Jesus' career: his decision to carry his ministry to Jerusalem. There is some evidence that he was not getting the kind of reception in Galilee that he wanted; most people either did not believe in him (Matt. 11:20-24; Luke 10:10-15), or believed for the wrong reasons (John 4:48; Mark 8:27-28). Jesus seems to have realized that such a step would involve his death (Mark 10:32-34). But, if our accounts are to be believed, he regarded this as inevitable.

What did he hope to accomplish? Few questions have been so hotly debated by scholars. And there has been an extraordinary variety of proposed answers: Jesus hoped to bring about the end of the world; Jesus was insane; Jesus believed that his death would redeem mankind from SIN; Jesus was taking part in an armed revolt.

The theory of insanity can be ruled out; Jesus' recorded statements exhibit a rather strong grasp of social and political reality (Mark 12:1-9; Matt. 18:23-34; Luke 16:8-9), tempered by a refreshingly forthright sense of humor (Mark 6:4; 10:25; 14:48; Matt. 15:14). The end-of-the-world, or eschatological, theory was once extremely popular; it depends on the assumption that Jesus both made and literally believed the apocalyptic prophecies attributed to him. Once again, Jesus does not seem so simple a character.

The doctrine of REDEMPTION, as far as we know, was first expounded by Paul. Still, Jesus may have chosen not to reveal it to his Disciples; their level of theological sophistication does not seem to have been high (this assumes, of course, that the author of the St. John Gospel was not one of them). As for the last theory, we are told that an armed insurrection had recently occurred (there was probably one a month), but the evidence for Jesus' participation in it is extremely tenuous. A less complicated theory is that Jesus had decided, once and for all, to preach the Kingdom of God in Jerusalem—and that he knew exactly the risk he was running. Each one of these theories has something to recommend it, and all should be kept in mind as we review the accounts of Jesus' arrest, trial, and execution.

The Synoptic Tradition, which the Church has followed in the festivals of EASTER week, implies that Jesus went up to Jerusalem six days before the Passover, on the day corresponding to Palm Sunday in the Church calendar, and that, having been arrested, tried, and convicted, he was executed on Friday of the same week. (*See also* TRIAL OF JESUS CHRIST.) This is most unlikely. Even the author of the St. Mark Gospel, with his habitual telescoping of events, supplies enough material to fill out a much longer Jerusalem ministry. In any case, Roman justice, even for noncitizens, was far more deliberate than that. If Jesus had been subject to some sort of judicial lynching, as the Gospels suggest he was, we can be quite sure that Pilate would have been recalled soon after; the Roman government could not afford to maintain a weakling in so sensitive a post.

Accordingly, many scholars have preferred to adopt a chronology based on the St. John Gospel, which shows Jesus visiting Jerusalem at the Feast of TABERNACLES, in the autumn, and staying there until HANUKKAH, the Feast of Dedication, which fell in December (John 7:2-10; 10:22-23). He then left Jerusalem for PERAEA, that is, Trans-Jordan, or rather the part of it that he had known as a disciple of John the Baptist (10:40-42). He then returned briefly to Bethany, near Jerusalem, after which he passed on to EPHRAIM (modern Et-Taiyibeh), about fourteen miles northeast of Jerusalem in the Wilderness of BETH-AVEN (11:7-18, 54). The same Gospel tells us that he decided to risk going back to Judaea because news had been brought to him that his dear friend LAZARUS was seriously ill. After Jesus had, according to the text, raised Lazarus from the dead (11:1-53), his life

"Christ on the Sea of Galilee," by the French artist Delacroix (*The Walters Art Gallery*).

JESUS CHRIST 1593

Christ performs the miracle of the feeding of the multitude (*Counsel Collection*).

was in more danger than ever. The obscure town of Ephraim, not far from BETHEL, was his last refuge. Here he would have remained until spring.

In Jesus' time the Jewish year began with the month of NISAN (March-April); the first day of the Passover, which lasted seven days, was set at Nisan 15 in order to coincide with the first full moon. No doubt Jesus had gone to Jerusalem for the Passover every year since he was twelve.

But this Passover was to be different. According to the St. John Gospel, the first day of the Passover that year fell on the SABBATH (19:31). For this and other reasons, many scholars now think that Jesus went up to Jerusalem for the last time in early April, A.D. 30. It is probably best to assume that most of the teachings and miracles assigned by the Gospels to the Jerusalem ministry had already taken place during fall or winter of the previous year. Among these, perhaps, was the event known in Christian tradition as the Cleansing of the Temple.

It is always risky to trace any kind of development in Jesus' ideas; we simply do not know enough about his life. Thus modern scholarship has completely discredited approaches such as that of Ernest Renan (1823-1892), who saw Jesus as evolving from a "delightful moralist" into an apocalyptic prophet. But the Temple episode does suggest a decisive break with teaching in favor of action. We are told that Jesus entered the outer court of the Temple—the Court of the Gentiles—carrying a whip made of "small cords," and that he proceeded to drive out all the money changers and sellers of animals for the SACRIFICES AND OFFERINGS (John 2:13-17; Mark 11:15-17; Matt. 21:12-13; Luke 19:45-46). As he did so, he quoted a phrase from the Book of the Prophet ISAIAH: "Mine house shall be called an house of prayer for all people" (56:7). He added bitterly: "Is this house, which is called by my name, become a den of robbers in your eyes?" (Jer. 7:11). Most of the violent details come from the St. John Gospel, but the St. Mark Gospel alone records that Jesus also stopped porters from taking shortcuts through the

Robert Leinweber's "Jesus Healing the Sick" (*New York Public Library*).

19th-century woodcut showing the Transfiguration of Jesus (*Counsel Collection*).

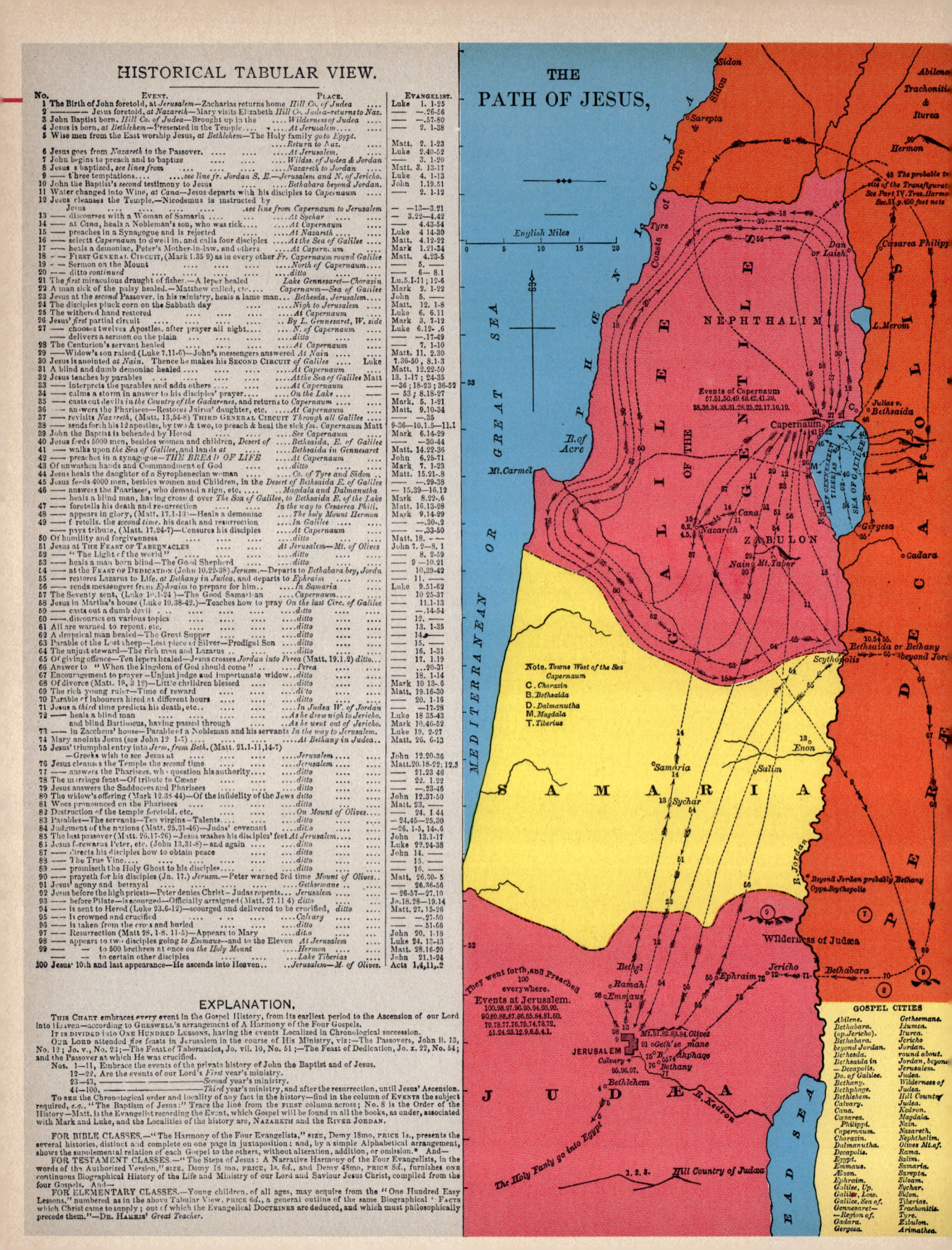

HISTORICAL TABULAR VIEW.

No.	Event.	Place.	Evangelist.
1	**The Birth of John foretold, at *Jerusalem*—Zacharias returns home**	*Hill Co. of Judea*	Luke 1. 1-25
2	——— Jesus foretold, *at Nazareth*—Mary visits Elizabeth	*Hill Co. Judea—returns to Naz.*	—— —.26-56
3	John Baptist born, *Hill Co. of Judea*—Brought up in the	*Wilderness of Judea*	—— —.57-80
4	Jesus is born, *at Bethlehem*—Presented in the Temple	*At Jerusalem*	—— 2. 1-38
5	Wise men from the East worship Jesus, *at Bethlehem*—The Holy family *go to Egypt.*	*Return to Naz.*	Matt. 2. 1-23
6	Jesus goes from *Nazareth* to the Passover.	*At Jerusalem.*	Luke 2.40-52
7	John begins to preach and to baptize	*Wildss. of Judea & Jordan*	—— 3. 1-20
8	Jesus is baptized, *see lines from*	*Nazareth to Jordan*	Matt. 3. 13-17
9	—— three temptations	*see line fr. Jordan S. E.—Jerusalem and N. of Jericho.*	Luke 4. 1-13
10	John the Baptist's *second* testimony to Jesus	*Bethabara beyond Jordan.*	John 1.19.51
11	Water changed into Wine, *at Cana*—Jesus departs with his disciples to *Capernaum*		—— 2. 1-12
12	Jesus cleanses the Temple.—Nicodemus is instructed by Jesus	*see line from Capernaum to Jerusalem*	— —13—3.21
13	—— discourses with a Woman of Samaria	*At Sychar*	— 3.22—4.42
14	—— at *Cana*, heals a Nobleman's son, who was sick	*At Capernaum*	—— 4.43-54
15	—— preaches in a Synagogue and is rejected	*At Nazareth*	Luke 4 14-30
16	—— selects *Capernaum* to dwell in, and calls four disciples	*At the Sea of Galilee*	Matt. 4.12-22
17	—— heals a demoniac, Peter's Mother-in-law, and others	*At Capernaum*	Mark 1.21-34
18	—— FIRST GENERAL CIRCUIT, (Mark 1.35 9) as in every other	*Fr. Capernaum round Galilee*	Matt. 4.23-5
19	—— Sermon on the Mount	*North of Capernaum*	—— 5. ——
20	—— ditto *continued*	*ditto*	—— 6—8.1
21	The *first* miraculous draught of fishes.—A leper healed	*Lake Gennesaret—Chorazin*	Lu.5.I-11; 12-6
22	A man sick of the palsy healed.—Matthew called, etc.	*Capernaum—Sea of Galilee*	Mark 2. 1-22
23	Jesus at the *second* Passover, in his ministry, heals a lame man	*Bethesda, Jerusalem*	John 5. ——
24	The disciples pluck corn on the Sabbath day	*Nigh to Jerusalem*	Matt. 12. 1-8
25	The withered hand restored	*At Capernaum*	Luke 6. 6.11
26	Jesus' *first* partial circuit	*By L. Gennesaret, W. side*	Mark 3. 7-12
27	—— chooses twelves Apostles, after prayer all night	*N. of Capernaum*	Luke 6.12-.6
	—— delivers a sermon on the plain	*ditto*	—— —.17-49
28	The Centurion's servant healed	*At Capernaum*	—— 7. 1-10
29	——Widow's son raised (Luke 7.11-6)—John's messengers answered	*At Nain*	Matt. 11. 2.30
30	Jesus is anointed *at Nain*. Thence he makes his SECOND CIRCUIT *of Galilee*		Luke 7.36-50, 8.1-3
31	A blind and dumb demoniac healed	*At Capernaum*	Matt. 12.22-50
32	Jesus teaches by parables	*At the Sea of Galilee*	Matt 13. 1-17; 24-35
33	—— interprets the parables and adds others	*At Capernaum*	—— —36; 18-23; 36-52
34	—— calms a storm in answer to his disciples' prayer	*On the Lake*	—— — 53; 8.18-27
35	—— casts out devils *in the Country of the Gadarenes*, and returns to *Capernaum*		Mark. 5. 1-21
36	—— answers the Pharisees—Restores Jairus' daughter, etc.	*At Capernaum*	Matt. 9.10-34
37	—— revisits *Nazareth*, (Matt. 13,54-8) THIRD GENERAL CIRCUIT	*Through all Galilee*	—— —.35
38	—— sends forth his 12 apostles, by two & two, to preach & heal the sick	*fm. Capernaum*	Matt 9-36—10.1.5—11.1
39	John the Baptist is beheaded by Herod	*See Capernaum*	Mark 6.14-29
40	Jesus feeds 5000 men, besides women and children, *Desert of*	*Bethsaida, E. of Galilee*	—— —30-44
41	—— walks upon *the Sea of Galilee*, and lands at	*Bethsaida in Gennesaret*	Matt. 14.22-36
42	—— preaches in a synagogue—*THE BREAD OF LIFE*	*At Capernaum*	John 6.25-71
43	Of unwashen hands and Commandment of God	*ditto*	Mark 7. 1-23
44	Jesus heals the daughter of a Syrophenecian woman	*Co. of Tyre and Sidon*	Matt. 15.21-.8
45	Jesus feeds 4000 men, besides women and Children, in the	*Desert of Bethsaida E. of Galilee*	—— —.29-38
46	—— answers the Pharisees, who demand a sign, etc.	*Magdala and Dalmanutha*	— 15.39—16.12
	—— heals a blind man, having crossed over *The Sea of Galilee, to*	*Bethsaida E. of the Lake*	Mark 8.22-.6
47	—— foretells his death and resurrection	*In the way to Cesaerea Phili.*	Matt. 16.13-28
48	—— appears in glory, (Matt. 17.1-13)—Heals a demoniac	*The holy Mount Hermon*	Mark 9.14-29
49	—— foretells, the *second time*, his death and resurrection	*In Galilee*	—— —.30-.2
	—— pays tribute, (Matt. 17.24-7)—Censures his disciples	*At Capernaum*	—— —.33-50
50	Of humility and forgivenness	*ditto*	Matt. 18. ——
51	Jesus at THE FEAST OF TABERNACLES	*At Jerusalem—Mt. of Olives*	John 7. 2—8. 1
52	—— "The Light of the world"	*ditto*	—— 8. 2-59
53	—— heals a man born blind—The Good Shepherd	*ditto*	—— 9 —10.21
54	—— at the FEAST OF DEDICATION (John 10.22-38) *Jerusm.*—Departs to	*Bethabara bey, Jordn*	—— 10,39-42
55	—— restores Lazarus to Life, *at Bethany in Judea*, and departs to	*Ephraim*	—— 11. ——
56	—— sends messengers from *Ephraim* to prepare for him	*In Samaria*	Luke 9.51-62
57	The Seventy sent, (Luke 10.1-24)—The Good Samaritan	*Capernaum*	—— 10 25-37
58	Jesus in Martha's house (Luke 10.38-42.)—Teaches how to pray	*On the last Circ. of Galilee*	—— 11.1-13
59	—— casts out a dumb devil	*ditto*	—— —.14-54
60	—— discourses on various topics	*ditto*	—— 12. ——
61	All are warned to repent, etc.	*ditto*	—— 13. 1-35
62	A dropsical man healed—The Great Supper	*ditto*	—— 14. ——
63	Parable of the Lost sheep—Lost piece of Silver—Prodigal Son	*ditto*	—— 15. ——
64	The unjust steward—The rich man and Lazarus	*ditto*	—— 16. 1-31
65	Of giving offence—Ten lepers healed—Jesus crosses *Jordan into Perea* (Matt. 19.1.2)	*ditto*	—— 17. 1.19
66	Answer to "When the kingdom of God should come"	*Perea*	—— ...20-37
67	Encouragement to prayer—Unjust judge and importunate widow	*ditto*	—— 18. 1-14
68	Of divorce (Matt. 19, 3 12)—Little chrildren blessed	*ditto*	Mark 10 13-.6
69	The rich young ruler—Time of reward	*ditto*	Matt. 19.16-30
70	Parable of labourers hired at different hours	*ditto*	—— 20. 1-16
71	Jesus a *third* time predicts his death, etc.	*In Judea W. of Jordan*	—— —17-28
72	—— heals a blind man	*As he drew nigh to Jericho.*	Luke 18 35-43
	and blind Bartimeus, having passed through	*As he went out of Jericho.*	Mark 10.46-52
73	—— in Zaccheus' house—Parable of a Nobleman and his servants	*In the way to Jerusalem.*	Luke 19. 2-27
74	Mary anoints Jesus (see John 12 1-7)	*At Bethany in Judea*	Matt. 26. 6-13
75	Jesus' triumphal entry into *Jerm. from Beth.* (Matt. 21.1-11,14-7) —Greeks wish to see Jesus at	*Jerusalem*	John 12.20-36
76	Jesus cleanses the Temple the *second* time	*Jerusalem*	Matt.20.18-22; 12.3
77	—— answers the Pharisees, who question his authority	*ditto*	—— 21.23 46
78	The marriage feast—Of tribute to Cæsar	*ditto*	—— 22. 1.22
79	Jesus answers the Sadducees and Pharisees	*ditto*	—— —.23-46
80	The widow's offering (Mark 12.38-44)—Of the infidelity of the Jews	*ditto*	John 12.37-50
81	Woes pronounced on the Pharisees	*ditto*	Matt. 23. ——
82	Destruction of the temple foretold, etc.	*On Mount of Olives*	—— 24. 1.44
83	Parables—The servants—Ten virgins—Talents	*ditto*	—24.45—25.30
84	Judgment of the nations (Matt. 25.31-46)—Judas' covenant	*ditto*	—26. 1-5, 14-.6
85	The last passover (Matt. 26.17-26)—Jesus washes his disciples' feet	*At Jerusalem*	John 13.1-17
86	Jesus forewarns Peter, etc. (John 13.31-8)—and again	*ditto*	Luke 22.24-38
87	—— directs his disciples how to obtain peace	*ditto*	John 14. ——
88	—— The True Vine	*ditto*	—— 15. ——
89	—— promiseth the Holy Ghost to his disciples	*ditto*	—— 16. ——
90	—— prayeth for his disciples (Jn. 17.) *Jerusm.*—Peter warned 3rd time	*Mount of Olives*	Matt. 26.30- 5
91	Jesus' agony and betrayal	*Gethsemane*	—— 26.36-56
92	Jesus before the high priests—Peter denies Christ—Judas repents	*Jerusalem*	—26-57—27.10
93	—— before Pilate—is scourged—Officially arraigned (Matt. 27.11 4)	*ditto*	Jo.18.28—19.14
94	—— is sent to Herod (Luke 23.6-12)—scourged and delivered to be crucified,	*ditto*	Matt. 27. 15-26
95	—— is crowned and crucified	*Calvary*	—— —.27-50
96	—— is taken from the cross and buried	*ditto*	—— — 51-66
97	—— Resurrection (Matt 28, 1-8. 11-5)—Appears to Mary	*ditto*	John 20. 1-18
98	—— appears to two disciples going *to Emmaus*—and to the Eleven	*At Jerusalem*	Luke 24. 13-43
99	—— — to 500 brethren at once *on the Holy Mount*	*Hermon*	Matt. 28.16-20
	—— — to certain other disciples	*Lake Tiberias*	John 21.1-24
100	**Jesus' 10th and last appearance—He ascends into Heaven**	*Jerusalem—M. of Olives.*	Acts 1,4,11,.2

EXPLANATION.

THIS CHART embraces every event in the Gospel History, from its earliest period to the Ascension of our Lord into Heaven—according to GRESWELL'S arrangement of A Harmony of the Four Gospels.

IT IS DIVIDED into ONE HUNDRED LESSONS, having the events Localized in Chronological succession.

OUR LORD attended *five* feasts in Jerusalem in the course of His Ministry, viz:—The Passovers, John ii. 13, No. 12; Jo. v., No. 23;—The Feast of Tabernacles, Jo. vii. 10, No. 51;—The Feast of Dedication, Jo. x. 22, No. 54; and the Passover at which He was crucified.

Nos. 1—11, Embrace the events of the private history of John the Baptist and of Jesus.
12—22, Are the events of our Lord's *First* year's ministry.
23—43, ——— ——— ——— ———*Second* year's ministry.
44—100, ——— ———————*Third* year's ministry, and after the resurrection, until Jesus' Ascension.

TO SEE the Chronological order and locality of any fact in the history—find in the column of EVENTS the subject required, *e.g.*, "The Baptism of Jesus:" Trace the line from the FIRST column across; No. 8 is the Order of the History—Matt. is the Evangelist recording the Event, which Gospel will be found in all the books, as under, associated with Mark and Luke, and the Localities of the history are, NAZARETH and the RIVER JORDAN.

FOR BIBLE CLASSES.—"The Harmony of the Four Evangelists," SIZE, Demy 18mo, PRICE 1s., presents the several histories, distinct and complete on one page in juxtaposition: and, by a simple Alphabetical arrangement, shows the supplemental relation of each Gospel to the others, without alteration, addition, or omission.* And—

FOR TESTAMENT CLASSES.—"The Steps of Jesus: A Narrative Harmony of the Four Evangelists, in the words of the Authorized Version," SIZE, Demy 18 mo, PRICE, 1s. 6*d.*, and Demy 48mo, PRICE 8*d.*, furnishes ONE continuous Biographical History of the Life and Ministry of our Lord and Saviour Jesus Christ, compiled from the four Gospels. And—

FOR ELEMENTARY CLASSES.—Young children, of all ages, may acquire from the "One Hundred Easy Lessons," numbered as in the above Tabular View, PRICE 6*d.*, a general outline of the same Biographical "FACTS which Christ came to supply; out of which the Evangelical DOCTRINES are deduced, and which must philosophically precede them."—DR. HARRIS' *Great Teacher.*

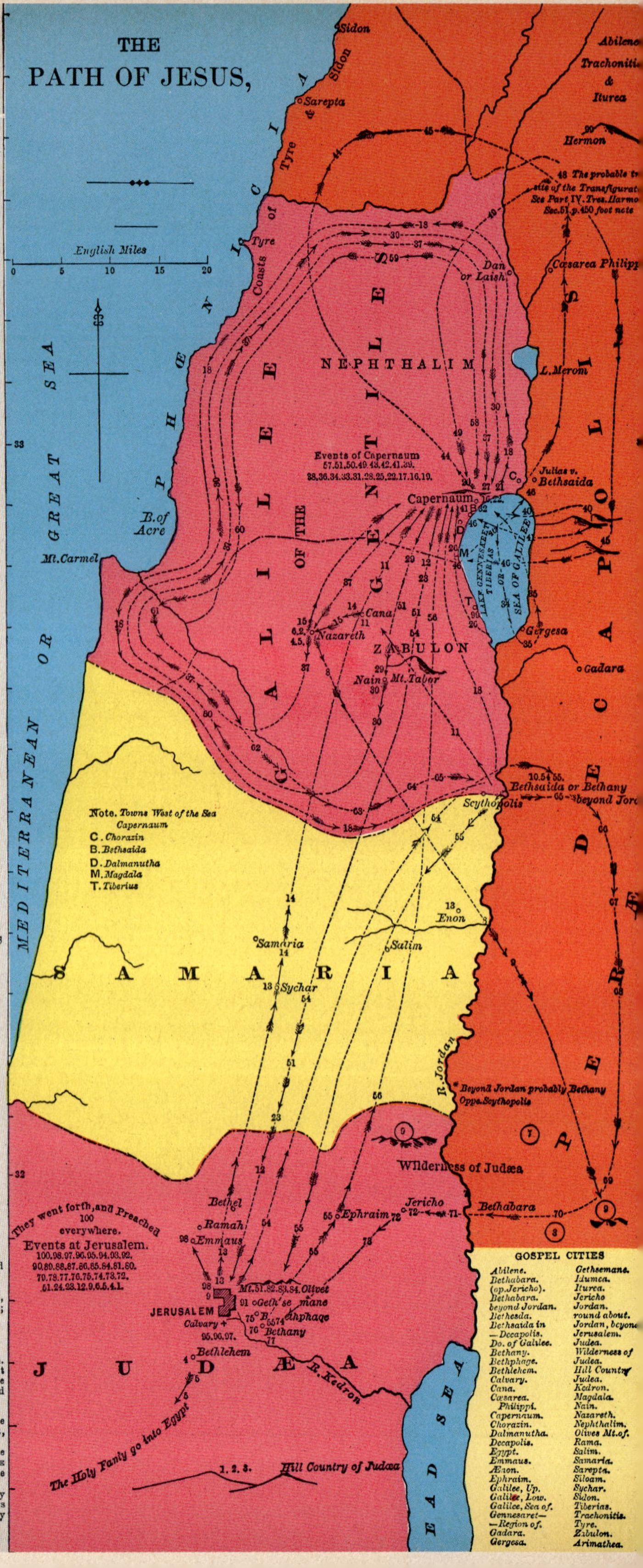
THE
PATH OF JESUS,
English Miles
0 5 10 15 20
Sidon
Sarepta
Tyre & Sidon
Coasts of Tyre
Tyre
Abilene
Trachonitis & Iturea
Hermon
48 The probable site of the Transfiguration See Part IV. Tres. Harmo Sec.51 p.450 foot note
Dan or Laish
Cæsarea Philippi
L. Merom
NEPHTHALIM
GALILEE OF THE GENTILES
PHENICIA
MEDITERRANEAN OR GREAT SEA
B. of Acre
Mt. Carmel
Events of Capernaum
57.51.50.49.48.42.41.39.
38.36.34.33.31.28.25.22.17.16.19.
Capernaum
Julias v. Bethsaida
LAKE GENNESARET OR TIBERIAS OR SEA OF GALILEE
Cana
Nazareth
ZABULON
Nain
Mt. Tabor
Gergesa
Gadara
DECAPOLIS
Bethsaida or Bethany beyond Jordan
Scythopolis
Note. Towns West of the Sea Capernaum
C. Chorazin
B. Bethsaida
D. Dalmanutha
M. Magdala
T. Tiberius
Enon
Samaria
Salim
SAMARIA
Sychar
R. Jordan
Beyond Jordan probably Bethany Oppo. Scythopolis
PEREA
Wilderness of Judæa
Bethabara
Jericho
Ephraim
Bethel
Ramah
Emmaus
They went forth, and Preached 100 everywhere.
Events at Jerusalem.
100.98.97.96.95.94.93.92.
90.89.88.87.86.85.84.81.80.
79.78.77.76.75.74.73.72.
51.24.23.12.9.6.5.4.1.
JERUSALEM
Calvary
95.96.97.
Mt. 51.82.83.84. Olivet
Geth'se mane
Bethphage
Bethany
Bethlehem
JUDÆA
R. Kedron
The Holy Famly go into Egypt
Hill Country of Judæa
DEAD SEA
GOSPEL CITIES
Abilene.
Bethabara.
(op. Jericho).
Bethabara.
beyond Jordan.
Bethesda.
Bethsaida in
—Decapolis.
Do. of Galilee.
Bethany.
Bethphage.
Bethlehem.
Calvary.
Cana.
Cæsarea.
Philippi.
Capernaum.
Chorazin.
Dalmanutha.
Decapolis.
Egypt.
Emmaus.
Ænon.
Ephraim.
Galilee, Up.
Galilee, Low.
Galilee, Sea of.
Gennesaret—
—Region of.
Gadara.
Gergesa.
Gethsemane.
Idumea.
Iturea.
Jericho
Jordan.
round about.
Jordan, beyond
Jerusalem.
Judea.
Wilderness of
Judea.
Hill Country
Judea.
Kedron.
Magdala.
Nain.
Nazareth.
Nephthalim.
Olives Mt. of.
Rama.
Salim.
Samaria.
Sarepta.
Siloam.
Sychar.
Sidon.
Tiberias.
Trachonitis.
Tyre.
Zabulon.
Arimathea.

courtyard with their bales. This would have involved control of an area more than three hundred and sixty yards long and three hundred yards wide. It is not likely, then, that Jesus did it entirely by himself.

The businesses that Jesus and (probably) his Disciples had attacked were under the control of the SADDUCEES, a conservative sect that formed the majority on the SANHEDRIN. The latter was a council of seventy members plus the High Priest that had jurisdiction over all religious matters; whether, under Roman rule, it had any real judicial power is an issue that has been much disputed (*see below*). The Temple businesses provided necessary services to the throngs of pilgrims; for instance, the money changers converted Roman money into a sacred currency that was acceptable as a Temple offering. These businesses were also extremely profitable. Thus, with a single demonstration, Jesus had not only scored the commercialism of current Temple worship but struck at its economic and political foundations. Despite the presence of an efficient Temple guard, he was not arrested. The Synoptic Gospels suggest why: the act was a popular one (Mark 11:18; Matt. 21:14-16).

The Sanhedrin was not popular; indeed, if there is one political fact that emerges from the Gospels (which are here confirmed by Josephus' account of the revolt in A.D. 66), it is that the Jewish leaders had lost touch with their people. Jesus was a son of the people who spoke their language and understood their needs. If the Sanhedrin had moved publicly

Jesus and the Apostles on his last journey to Jerusalem (*Tissot, Brooklyn Museum*).

against him, especially when hundreds of his countrymen were in town for the Passover festival, a serious riot might have ensued. As a result, the Romans would have assumed far greater control of the Jewish state, with the Sanhedrin reduced to a mere advisory committee. Moreover, there would certainly have been a new High Priest; the Romans did not hesitate to make the appointment themselves. CAIAPHAS, the incumbent High Priest, was well aware of all these possibilities (John 11:47-53). It seems very likely that these facts provide the key to the events of what is termed Holy Week in the Christian tradition.

We do not know if the Temple episode took place in Holy Week or during the last four months of the preceding year (the St. John Gospel complicates matters by making it Jesus' first recorded public act, no doubt because it symbolized everything that was to follow). In any case, the reaction of the authorities is highly significant: they asked Jesus by what authority he did these things (John 2:18; Luke 20:1-2; Matt. 21:23). This was the same question they had always asked him about his practice of telling those he healed that their sins were forgiven (Mark 2:6-9; Luke 5:20-21). Clearly, if Jesus had contented himself with being just a teacher, however unconventional, they would have left him alone; it was his emphasis on action that terrified them. After the Temple episode, Jesus was a marked man; it was only a matter of time before some excuse would be found to get rid of him (John 11:53; Mark 11:18). Jesus knew this. Perhaps that is why he decided to abandon all caution.

Previously, as soon as personal danger threatened, he had found some way to evade it (Mark 3:6-7; 9:30-32; John 7:1; Luke 4:28-30). On at least one occasion, he had entered Jerusalem secretly (John 7:8-11). But now he arranged to enter it in public, riding on a colt. When the pilgrims along the way heard that he was coming, they all began cheering (John 12:12-13; Mark 11:8-10). We are not told why the arrangements both for the triumphal procession and for the Passover meal were kept secret even from the Disciples (Mark 11:1-6; 14:12-16). Secret, too, until the last minute was Jesus' suspicion that JUDAS ISCARIOT, one of the Twelve Apostles, was planning to betray him. As far as the other Disciples were concerned, they were going up to Jerusalem in order to celebrate the Passover with their Master. Whether they ever did so is one of the great unsolved problems of New Testament interpretation.

If the first day of the Passover was Saturday (or, rather, Friday night, since the Jewish day begins at sunset), the meal known as the LAST SUPPER must have taken place on the previous Wednesday. But more important than the chronology is the meaning of the occasion for Jesus and his Disciples. They had been through a lot together. Once a crowd of five thousand men had wanted to make Jesus king (John 6:5-15). Now he had only twelve followers—and one of them was a traitor. Except for Peter, whose rugged personality is evident from nearly every mention of him, they do not seem to have been very impressive people. At this meal, with the danger of arrest and execution staring their leader in the face, they began a silly quarrel over which of them would have the best jobs in the Kingdom of Heaven (Luke 22:24-28). But Jesus, with his infinite faith in those he loved, said nothing harsh to them; instead, he washed their feet—something only a servant would normally do— in order to teach them what power was for (John 13:1-17). After this, he told them gently that he would soon be arrested, and that all of them would run away. When Simon Peter said he would never run away, Jesus replied that, on the contrary, Peter would deny ever having known him (John 13:36-38; Luke 22:31-34). Just before this, Judas Iscariot seems to have slipped away (John 13:21-30).

After supper was over, they all went out to GETHSEMANE, a place just outside the walls of Jerusalem on the west slope of the MOUNT OF OLIVES. Jesus, as he had so often done, went off by himself to pray. At no point in the Gospels does Jesus appear more deeply human. In an agony of fear and doubt, he prayed that the fate he saw before him might not be his. And yet he accepted the will of his heavenly Father (Luke 22:41-44; Matt. 26:37-42). He returned to his Disciples, only to find them asleep. It seems to have been a cold night for the time of year (John 18:18); presumably, there was a full moon shining on the olive grove. All of a sudden, the Gospels tell us, Judas appeared at the head of an armed posse. Jesus looked at them all without the slightest trace of surprise. "Why all those swords and clubs?" he said. "Am I a brigand?" The Disciples offered some resistance, and one of them—was it Peter?—drew a sword and cut off the ear of MALCHUS, the High

Christ foretelling the destruction of Jerusalem (*Counsel Collection*).

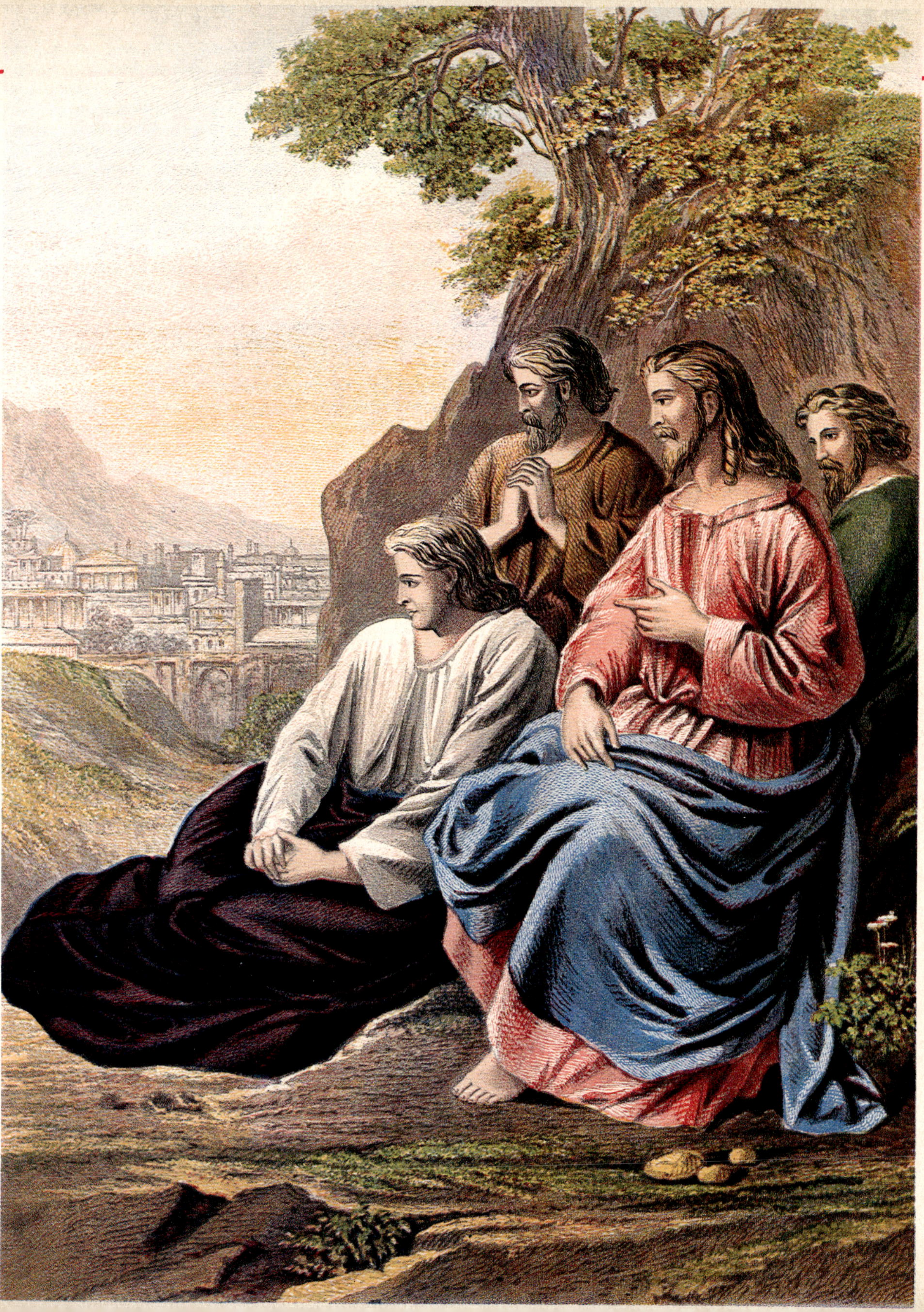

1600 THE FAMILY BIBLE ENCYCLOPEDIA

Christ washing the feet of the Disciples (*New York Public Library*).

Renaissance altar decoration showing the Last Supper (Mella, Milan).

Priest's servant. Then they all turned and ran. Jesus was led away, back to Jerusalem.

All the Synoptic Gospels agree that, when he got there, he was taken straight to the official residence of the High Priest CAIAPHAS (Mark 14:53; Matt. 26:57; Luke 22:54). The St. John Gospel (18:13) has him sent first to the former High Priest ANNAS, who was Caiaphas' father-in-law, then to Caiaphas. It is quite conceivable that Annas masterminded the whole thing; he had originally been appointed by the Romans. In any case, scholars would dearly like to know whether there were any Roman soldiers in the posse led by Judas. If there were, this would indicate that the Jewish authorities had already plotted with Pilate to bring about Jesus' downfall. Of course, they may have done so even without using Roman soldiers. Scholars would also like to know the exact nature of the judicial proceedings to which Jesus was subjected, as well as of the charges brought against him. The Gospel accounts of the proceedings in the High Priest's house sound like attempts to describe a meeting of the Sanhedrin, or of the subcommittee of it that some scholars believe was responsible for purely judicial matters. But scholars disagree over whether this could have been a formal trial.

The charge seems to have been blasphemy, for which the penalty was death by stoning. (*See also* CRIMES AND PUNISHMENTS.) According to the St. John Gospel, the Jewish authorities had attempted before to have Jesus stoned (John 11:8). But we do

1602 THE FAMILY BIBLE ENCYCLOPEDIA

not know if the Romans allowed the Sanhedrin to enforce the death penalty at this time. James the brother of Jesus was undoubtedly stoned to death for blasphemy in A.D. 62 (see JAMES, THE GENERAL EPISTLE OF). But this does not tell us what was allowed in this particular year—and Roman policy toward the Jews continued to vary right up until the revolt of 66.

According to the author of the St. Mark Gospel, as soon as it was light Jesus was taken from the High Priest's house to Pilate (who usually stayed in Herod's palace, but who probably soon moved the proceedings to the ANTONIA TOWER, a fortress at the northern end of the Temple area). Things had gone badly for Jesus before the Sanhedrin, even though the witnesses could not agree, and the most substantial charge they could bring against him was the absurd one that he had threatened to destroy the Temple. Jesus declined to answer any of these charges. But when asked if he was the Messiah, Jesus said yes—and added a prophecy that the High Priest interpreted as blasphemous (Mark 14:61-62). The Sanhedrin then condemned Jesus to death. Peter, who was sitting by the fire in the servants' quarters, was so depressed when he heard this that he denied ever having known Jesus. Brought before Pilate, Jesus maintained the same silence in the face of his accusers. Unfortunately, we do not know of what they accused him. Pilate, of course, was interested in the political aspects of the case. Was Jesus the "King of the Jews," that is, the Messiah? Jesus appears to have despaired of making this Gentile understand the first thing about his mission. At any rate, he gave a noncommittal answer.

According to many scholars, the Marcan account of the TRIAL OF JESUS CHRIST becomes progressively more incredible from this point onward. Pilate is shown as having no alternative but to accept the Sanhedrin's verdict. But since it was his custom at the Passover to grant one prisoner amnesty—"Whomsoever they desired"—he offered to release Jesus. But the "multitude" (whose presence has not previously been noted) called upon him to crucify Jesus and grant amnesty to one BARABBAS, "who had committed murder in the insurrection" (Mark 15:5-15). Quite apart from the fact that there is no evidence for the existence of any such custom, this is extraordinary behavior on the part of a Roman governor. Why did he not simply dismiss the charges against Jesus, whatever they were? Or, if his principal motive was to avoid trouble, why did he release a well-known member of the Jewish resistance movement? The St. Matthew Gospel, which is basically an expanded version of the Marcan account, offers no answers.

The account in the St. Luke Gospel (Luke 22:66-

Jesus is betrayed by Judas Iscariot—with the so-called "Judas' Kiss"— from a painting by Gonne (*Counsel Collection*).

Agony in the Garden, by Di Giovanni (*National Gallery of Art, Samuel H. Kress Collection*).

23:25) reads like a sincere attempt to plug the gaps in the Marcan narrative: Jesus is accused before Pilate of "forbidding to give tribute to Caesar, saying that he himself is Christ a King." In the Lucan narrative, Pilate, after discovering that Jesus was a Galilean, shipped him off to Herod Antipas for further questioning. When even this failed to produce confirmation of the charges, he proposed to "the chief priests and the rulers and the people" that Jesus be released after being beaten—a standard Roman punishment. But the Barabbas story is left virtually unchanged.

Finally, the St. John Gospel offers some quite extensive dialogue between Jesus and Pilate (18:33-38;

19:9-11). The Barabbas story is given second place (18:39-40). Instead, we are asked to believe that the Jewish leaders exploited Pilate's anxiety over his own career: the emperor might get to hear that he had released this subversive character, Jesus (19:12). The author does not explain why, at the same time, the Jews demanded the release of a still more subversive character: Barabbas, who was probably a Zealot (S. G. F. Brandon, *Jesus and the Zealots,* New York, 1967). Nor do any of the Synoptic Gospels enable us to determine the composition of the alleged Jewish mob that called for Jesus to be crucified (Mark 15:8; Matt. 27:20-23; Luke 23:23). According to the St. John Gospel (19:13), Pilate's final judgment took place in the paved court of the Antonia fortress. But, according to the same account, the Jews did not enter this Gentile preserve, because in so doing they would have incurred ritual defilement on the day before the Passover (John 18:28). The people doing the shouting appear to be the "chief priests...and officers" (19:6); since the author of this Gospel habitually refers to the Jewish authorities as "the Jews," there is really no evidence here that a major crowd was ever allowed to collect (this part of the Temple area could easily have been cordoned off). Moreover, if, upon every appearance of Pilate, the crowd called loudly for Jesus' crucifixion, one can only wonder why the Jewish authorities had found it necessary to take such precautions over Jesus' arrest.

During his triumphal entry into Jerusalem, Jesus was a popular figure; by Friday of the same week, he was unpopular. If this is the truth, the Gospels do not offer an explanation of it. Jesus had been condemned by a Roman governor to a Roman punishment: the Gospels agree that the official notice of his execution accused him not of blasphemy but of subversion (Mark 15:26; Matt. 27:37; Luke 23:38; John 19:19). With the two so-called "thieves" (again, probably

Christ is rejected by the people of Jerusalem (*Counsel Collection*).

JESUS CHRIST 1605

Detail from Correggio's masterpiece *Ecce Homo* (*Counsel Collection*).

1606 THE FAMILY BIBLE ENCYCLOPEDIA

17th-century painting showing the scourging of Christ by Roman soldiers (Counsel Collection).

members of the Jewish resistance movement), he was marched out of the city carrying his cross. This is the journey commemorated in Christian tradition by the third through ninth of the fourteen Stations of the Cross, each of which is associated with a particular location in the walled city of Jerusalem as it stands today.

The Crucifixion is and always has been the central

fact on which the Christian faith is based, and the accounts of it in the Gospels are as much theological as historical. Perhaps, then, it should be pointed out here that crucifixion was a slow but certain form of death, and that the theories, popular in recent years, which depict Jesus as being revived after being taken down from the cross are utterly improbable. To voluntarily undergo crucifixion in the hope of being revived later would have been like submitting to the electric chair with the same end in mind.

Jesus died—with a cry of despair, according to the Synoptists, or triumphantly, according to the St. John Gospel—but in either case with dignity and fortitude. Wealthy supporters begged his body from Pilate (a sure sign of Roman responsibility for the execution) and placed it in a tomb such as only a wealthy man would normally have had (Mark 15:43-46; John 19:41). This was on Friday, before sunset (John 19:31). On Sunday, when followers of Jesus visited the tomb, they found the body gone (Mark 16:1-6; Matt. 28:1-7; Luke 24:1-6; John 20:1-7).

The stories of Jesus' RESURRECTION appearances are not material with which the historian is competent to deal. Suffice it to say that they reflect the beliefs of the early Church. Despite some variations, the different accounts do not seriously conflict with one another (Mark 16:9-20; Matt. 28:9-20; Luke 24:13-51; John 20:11-29; 21:1-22). All of these stories are remarkable for their sober and realistic character; the Church has refused to accept the more fantastic kind of resurrection story, as found in the apocryphal *Gospel of Peter*. The post-Resurrection sayings of

Jesus being led to Pontius Pilate for sentencing (*Tissot, Brooklyn Museum*).

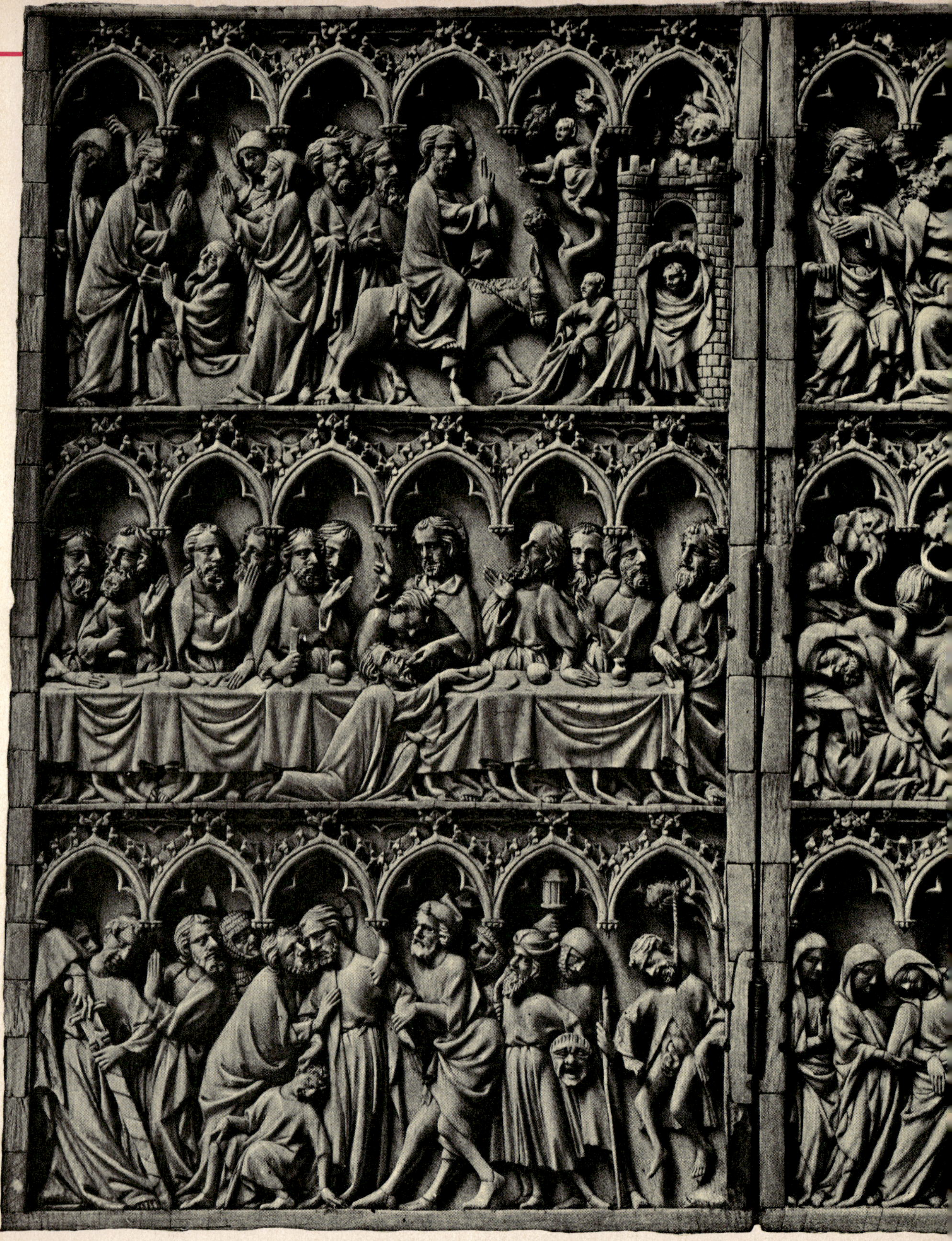

JESUS CHRIST 1609

Jesus are treasured by millions of Christians as assurance that he will always be with them.

It is perhaps ironic that one whose religion forbade making images of God should himself have become the object of so much religious portraiture. Indeed, to trace the history of Jesus in art is to follow the course of Western art as a whole. He appears first in the paintings of the Roman catacombs, usually as a beardless youth. Often he is symbolized by such pagan figures as the Greek mythological figure Orpheus, who also "descended into hell." In the Catacomb of Praetextatus he is shown crowned with thorns—the earliest known representation of his Passion, probably from the third century. No pictures of the Crucifixion have been found in the catacombs. In Byzantine art he is a bearded man in the prime of life, the *Christos Pantocrator* ("All-powerful") who mirrors the glory of the Father. The most famous example of this conception is the great series of mosaics in the church at Daphni, near Athens. Byzantium (by then Constantinople and today Istanbul) fell to the Turks in 1453, but Byzantine religious art was perpetuated by the Eastern Orthodox Church throughout Eastern Europe. Its most characteristic form is the ikon (Gr., "image") which, like the Orthodox Church itself, has preserved over many centuries an idea of Christ that can be traced back to the earliest of all Christian creeds: Christ is Lord!

In the West, the breakup of the Roman Empire very early brought about a great variety of regional styles. From the first, the tendency was in the direction of an increasing realism, first in the depiction of scenes from Jesus' life and then in the psychological portrayal of Jesus himself. Milestones along this route are *The Kiss of Judas* by Giotto (about 1266-1377) and the *Baptism of Christ* by Piero della Francesca (about 1420-1492). By the time the Italian Renaissance came to full flower, it had become acceptable to paint Jesus as a man—handsome, dignified, but with the full range of human characteristics, as shown, for instance, in the *Agony in the Garden* of Giovanni Bellini (about 1430-1516) and the *Dead Christ* by Mantegna (1431-1506). But the Christ of Italian art, and of southern European art

Hand-carved ivory sculpture, dating from 14th-century France, showing scenes from the life of Christ (*New York Public Library*).

in general, remained a somewhat idealized figure, perhaps reflecting the aristocratic Greco-Roman ideal of the perfect man.

In northern Europe, artists of the fourteenth and fifteenth centuries evolved a more disquieting form of realism that saw Christ as more of a victim. Thus the *Descent From the Cross* by Roger van der Weyden (about 1400-1464) shows a Christ who is a pathetic corpse, and the *Christ Blessing* of Hans Memling (about 1430-1494) is an intense but frail ascetic. Still more original was Hieronymus Bosch (about 1450-1516), who often painted Christ at the mercy of grotesque persecutors, as in *Christ Mocked*.

But northern realism was not to reach its highest point of development until the emergence of Dutch art in the seventeenth century. Meanwhile, the great figures of the Italian High Renaissance each made his contribution to the portrayal of Christ. Michelangelo Buonarroti (1475-1564), in his *Last Judgment*, showed Christ as a young man of almost athletic grace and power. In the only Renaissance work that can be compared with it, the *Last Supper*, Leonardo da Vinci (1452-1519) painted the meditative and sorrowing Christ of the St. John Gospel. Raphael Santi (1483-1520) is best known for his delightful portrayals of the Christ child; of his portrayals of Christ as an adult perhaps the most memorable is *The Transfiguration*. But these were all idealized conceptions.

In psychological realism, the high point was reached by the Venetian painter Tiziano Vecellio, or Titian (about 1490-1576), and Jacopo Robusti, known as Tintoretto (1518-1594). Titian's *The Tribute Money* (based on Mark 12:13-17) may be the most vital portrait of Christ anywhere. In a different vein, his *Noli Me Tangere* (Lat., "Touch me not," from John 20:17) evoked the risen Christ. Tintoretto's *Jesus in the House of Martha* showed careful study of the Gospels, as did his *Last Supper* in the Venetian church of San Trovaso. With the fading of the Renaissance, painters of religious scenes became progressively more absorbed in purely technical and aesthetic problems. But the Spanish-based painter Domenicos Theotocopoulos, known as El Greco (about 1541-1614) painted with an intense devotional spirit that made use of all the new techniques. Many highly original versions of the traditional scenes resulted, including a memorable *Jesus Stripped of His Garments*—the tenth Station of the Cross. The greatest painter of the High Baroque period, Peter Paul Rubens (1577-1640), produced, among much run-of-the-mill religious painting, an outstanding *Descent From the Cross*. But it was Rembrandt van Rijn (1606-1669) who raised the Western portrayal of Christ to a height without equal before or since. Especially in his etchings and drawings of gospel scenes, but also in such paintings as *The Supper at Emmaus* (based on Luke 24:13-31), he showed a Christ who went among men to heal and comfort them.

The beginning of the Age of Reason sounded the knell of religious painting's greatest period: henceforth (as already so in the case of Rembrandt), the truly memorable images of Christ were to be private creations, not publicly commissioned aids to faith. But despite an estimable *Crucifixion* by Giovanni Battista Tiepolo (1696-1770), the eighteenth century is a wasteland in terms of religious art. The Romantic period, which witnessed a religious revival, inspired a few major painters to treat religious subjects in a religious spirit. Among these was Eugène Delacroix (1798-1863), whose *Ascent to Calvary* is reminiscent of Tintoretto. The modern era has failed entirely to produce images of Christ that rank with the masterpieces of the past. The outstanding Christian painter of the twentieth century is perhaps Georges Rouault (1871-1958), whose many pictures of Christ show the influence of early medieval art, especially stained glass. Also worth mentioning is Stanley Spencer (1892-1959), whose *Christ in the Wilderness* series powerfully expresses Christ's oneness with nature.

In music the only types of composition in which Christian tradition permits Christ to appear in his own person are sacred cantatas and oratorios. The outstanding composers of such works are Heinrich Schütz (1585-1672), Johann Sebastian Bach (1685-1750), George Frederick Handel (1685-1759) and Joseph Haydn (1732-1809). Only in the longer works, such as Bach's *St. Matthew Passion,* does the part of Jesus offer any dramatic scope. Twentieth-century music has not enlarged on this tradition, although the *Passion According to St. Luke* of Krzysztof Penderecki (born 1933) may herald a renewal of interest.

Literary treatments of Jesus are rare; in prose there are none of the first rank, and the major West-

Medieval illumination showing the Crucifixion, with view of Jerusalem in the background (*Morgan Library*).

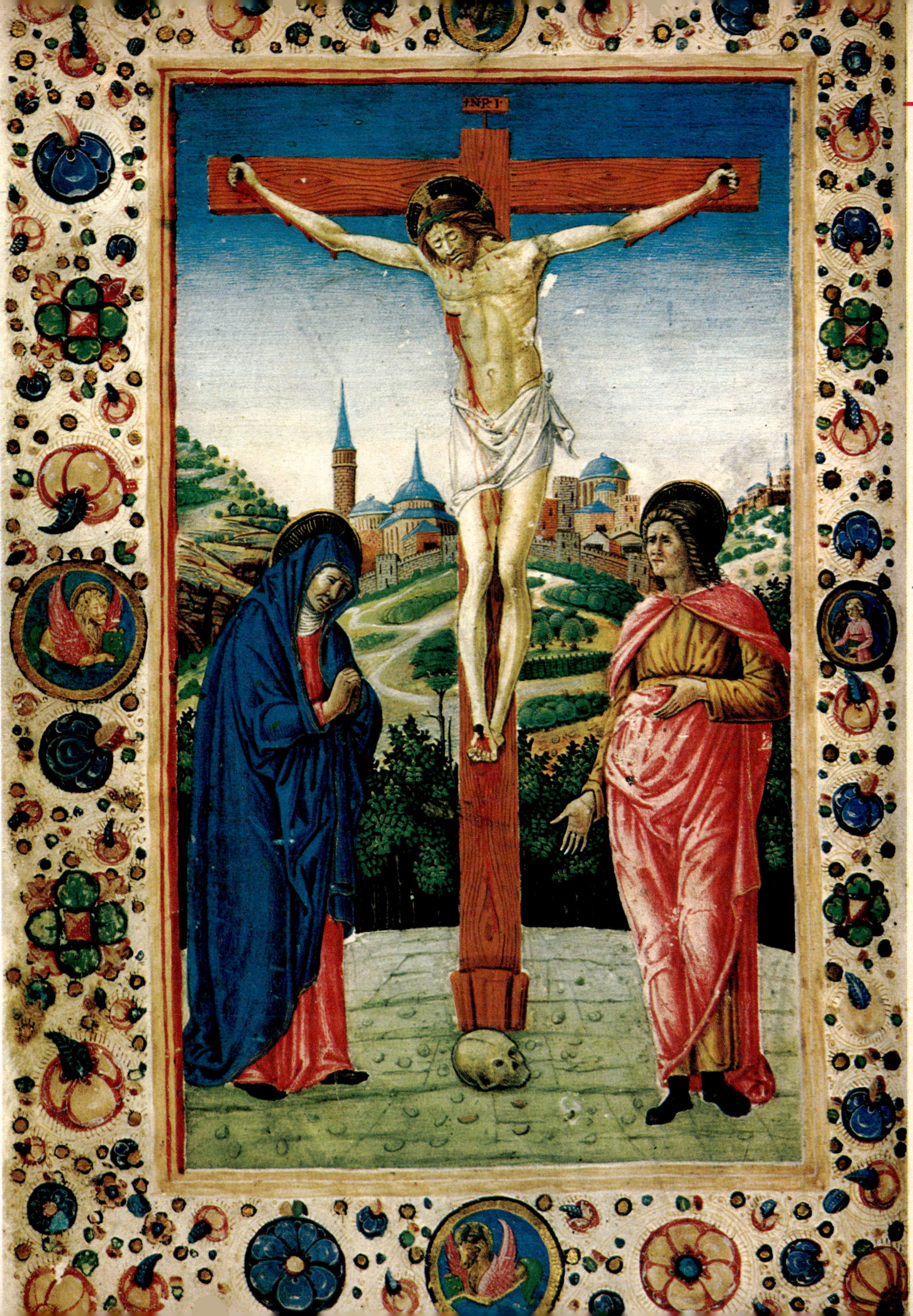
INRI

19th-century etching showing the removal of Christ's body from the Cross, witnessed by the Three Marys (*Counsel Collection*).

ern poets have shied away from treating the Gospels directly. But outstanding scholarly works exist in abundance. The first systematic historical study of Jesus was by Hermann Samuel Reimarus (1694-1768). Reimarus, who was a professor of Oriental languages at a time when this was a very unusual thing to be, argued that Jesus had never aimed to found a religion, but rather to establish Jewish independence once and for all. Johann Gottfried von Herder (1744-1803) produced the first major contribution to the study of the Synoptic Problem (like most scholars today, he thought the St. Mark Gospel was written first). Further study of the Gospel texts convinced many liberal Protestant scholars that a historically accurate life of Jesus could indeed be written. It is estimated that, since the early nineteenth century, some sixty thousand such lives have been published. Among those still read today is that of Ernest Renan (1823-1892).

The whole life-of-Jesus movement was brought to an abrupt halt by Albert Schweitzer (1875-1965), when in 1906 he published a book later translated into English as *The Quest of the Historical Jesus*. Schweitzer then abandoned scholarship as a career and went to Africa to become a medical missionary. Brilliant though Schweitzer's work is—his conclusion that the historical materials for a full-scale life of Jesus do not exist is now widely accepted—it really derived from the work of Johannes Weiss (1863-1914), perhaps the greatest New Testament scholar of modern times. Both Weiss and Schweitzer took what is known as the eschatological view of Jesus, that is, that Jesus believed the end of the world was coming, and that his death would hasten it.

One outstanding attempt to counter this approach was *The Jesus of History,* by T. R. Glover (1869-1943)—an extremely readable book by a leading classical scholar. Another was *Jesus and the Origins of Christianity* (1933) by Maurice Goguel. The classic treatment of Jesus from the modern Jewish viewpoint is that of Joseph Klausner (1922). Much material new to Christians was uncovered by the liberal

The Garden Tomb in Jerusalem, believed by some scholars and Christians to be the burial place of Jesus Christ, instead of the traditional site within the Basilica of the Holy Sepulchre (*Counsel Collection*).

Jewish scholar C. G. Montefiore in his book on the Synoptic Gospels (1910). Excellent and readable introductory treatments by two liberal Protestant experts on the New Testament are the *Prophet From Nazareth* (1961), by Morton Scott Enslin, and *A Life of Jesus* (1950), by Edgar J. Goodspeed. The thought of Rudolf Bultmann (born 1884), with which everyone seriously interested in Jesus must come to terms, is perhaps best approached through his *Jesus and the Word* (1926) and *Primitive Christianity in its Contemporary Setting* (1956).

An important recent study is *Jesus of Nazareth,* by Günther Bornkamm; while Hugh Anderson, in *Jesus and Christian Origins,* has traced the "quest" through the early 1960's. Paul Winter, in *On The Trial of Jesus* (1961), was the first to argue that the Gospel accounts of the Trial are pro-Roman distortions. This point of view was further developed by S. G. F. Brandon in his *The Trial of Jesus of Nazareth* (1968)—a work that, with the same author's *Jesus and the Zealots* (1967), opens up a new perspective on Jesus and his times. —J.M.B.E.

Caravaggio's rendition of Christ at Emmaus following his Resurrection (*below*), and (*right*) the Resurrection as interpreted by Tissot (*Mella, Milan; Brooklyn Museum*).

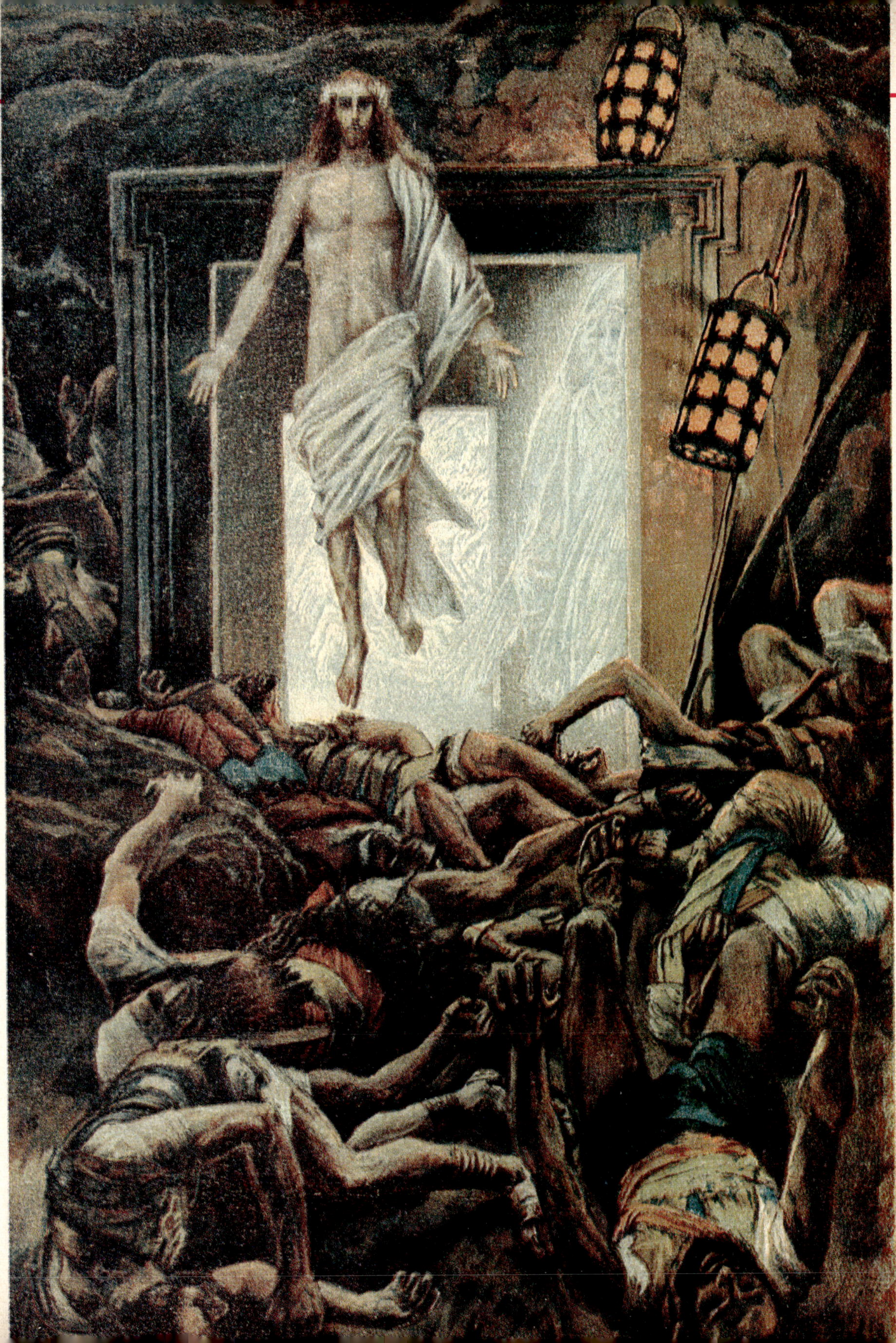

THE STORY OF JESUS CHRIST

For Younger Readers

Jesus Christ was the son of Mary and Joseph, who both belonged to the house of Judah and the family of David.

A short time before his birth, the Roman emperor, Augustus Caesar, ordered a census to be taken in his empire. Every man had to be registered in the place where he originally belonged.

Obedient to the law, Mary and Joseph set out for Bethlehem, the little town of their ancestors. Their journey was a long one, about ninety miles over rough roads. Mary rode a donkey, while Joseph trudged beside her.

When they reached Bethlehem, there was no room in the inn, so Joseph led Mary away. The most ancient tradition says that he found a cave close by. There were many caves in the hillsides around Bethlehem, which were used as stables for sheep and cattle.

Scarcely had they settled in the bleak cave when Jesus was born. Mary wrapped him in soft woolen clothes that she had brought with her, and laid him in the manger, a hole scooped out of the ground to hold grain.

Before long the child was visited by shepherds, who had been told of his birth by an angel. Three Magi, wise men from Arabia, also sought him. They were stargazers and had seen a bright new star in the sky. They believed that this was a sign that a new leader had been born.

Jesus grew up in Nazareth, a very small town in the little country of Galilee. From babyhood, many hours of his day were taken up with lessons, for Jewish children were taught by their mothers long before they went to school. Jesus learned about the ceremonies connected with the Sabbath day, and about the great festivals of his religion.

In school, he was instructed in "the Law and the Prophets." The Law contained all the rules laid down by God for His Chosen People. "The Prophets" included all the messages that the Prophets of Israel received from God and passed on to His people.

When Jesus was old enough, he helped Joseph, who was a carpenter. He no doubt learned the trade of carpentry thoroughly, because the Bible speaks of him not only as "the carpenter's son" but as "the carpenter."

Jesus grew and became strong and full of wisdom. When he was twelve, he accompanied his parents to Jerusalem, to celebrate the feast of the Passover. This great festival commemorates the deliverance of the Jews from their long captivity in Egypt.

When they had gone some way on their journey home, Mary and Joseph found that Jesus was not with the caravan. Greatly disturbed, they returned to Jerusalem, where they searched for him for three days.

To their amazement, they found the boy in the Temple, listening to the teachers and asking them questions. All who heard him were astonished at his knowledge and understanding.

Mary went to him, saying, "Son, why did you do this to us? Your father and I have been looking for you, worried." Jesus answered, "Did you not know that I must be about my Father's business?" He did not explain his words, but went home obediently with them to Nazareth.

The Bible tells us little about the youth and early manhood of Jesus. We next hear of him when he went to the Jordan River and asked John the Baptist to baptize him. When John did so, a wonderful thing happened. As Jesus came out of the water, the heavens opened and the Holy Spirit came down in the form of a dove, alighting on his head. A voice from heaven was heard, saying, "This is my beloved Son, in whom I am well pleased."

Returning from the Jordan, Jesus went into the desert to pray. While he was there, Satan tempted him three times. He offered Jesus all the kingdoms of the world if he would fall down and adore him. But Jesus cried, "Begone, Satan. For it is written, 'You shall worship the Lord your God, and Him only shall you serve.'"

When Jesus was walking one day by the Sea of Galilee, he spoke to two fishermen, Simon and his brother Andrew. "Go out into the deep," he said, "and let down your nets for a catch." Simon told him that they had caught nothing all day. "But at your word, I will let down the net."

He did so, and they caught so many fish that their nets broke. Simon, afraid, fell on his knees. But Jesus said, "Do not be afraid. From now on, you will be fishers of men." Simon and Andrew, and two brothers named James and John, became Apostles of Jesus. Later, eight more Apostles joined him.

Jesus went throughout the land, preaching and teaching. In the Sermon on the Mount, he put forth many teachings that are familiar to us, including the Beatitudes, the "golden rule," and the Lord's Prayer. He made it clear that he had not come to set aside the old Law, but to perfect it. The old Law, for instance, forbade men to kill. The new Law forbade them even to give way to anger, because anger might lead them to kill.

Jesus taught the people with stories and parables. The word "parable" means "comparison." In the parable of the Good Shepherd, for example, the Good Shepherd is really Jesus, and the sheep are his children.

Jesus performed many miracles, to prove to the people that his power came from God. He brought the dead back to life, and cured the sick, the crippled, and the blind.

Sometimes he worked a miracle out of sympathy. At a wedding feast, when the wine ran short, Jesus changed water into wine to spare his host embarrassment. On another occasion, he multiplied five loaves and two fishes so that his Disciples could feed about five thousand hungry people who had followed him to hear his words.

Jesus always taught that the one thing necessary for salvation was to love and serve God. One day he visited Martha, Mary, and Lazarus, whom he dearly loved. Martha bustled about, preparing food, but Mary sat at the feet of Jesus, listening to him. Martha complained to Jesus, saying, "Lord, do you not mind that Mary has left me alone to do the work?" But Jesus rebuked her gently. "Martha, Martha, you worry about many things," he said. "Mary has chosen the better part and it shall not be taken away from her."

When Lazarus died, Jesus came and raised him from the dead. This great miracle won him many followers, but it angered his enemies. From then on, they

"And when he was come into Jerusalem, all the city was moved,

JESUS CHRIST 1619

saying, Who is this?" (Matt. 21:10).

were determined to put him to death. So Jesus no longer walked about freely. Instead, he went into a city called Ephraim, where he continued to teach his Disciples.

Six days before the feast of the Passover, Jesus came to Bethany, where he had supper with Martha, Mary, and Lazarus. Many people came to Bethany, not only to see Jesus but to see Lazarus, the man who had been so miraculously raised from the dead.

When Jesus left Bethany, he asked two Disciples to bring him a colt. They did so, and Jesus rode it into Jerusalem. As he rode, the people threw their cloaks on the ground and strewed branches in his path. Many followed Jesus, crying out, "Blessed be he who comes in the name of the Lord."

When he reached Jerusalem, Jesus went into the Temple, where he was scandalized to see people selling doves and changing money. He drove them out of the Temple, saying, "Is it not written 'My house shall be called a house of prayer for all nations?' But you have made it a den of thieves."

The great crowd of people who followed Jesus were amazed by his teaching. This angered the Roman authorities so much that they sought a way to destroy him.

They were helped by one of his own Apostles, Judas Iscariot, who went secretly to the Roman authorities and asked them, "What will you give me if I deliver him to you?" They offered him thirty pieces of silver, which Judas accepted. From then on, he waited for his opportunity to betray Jesus.

When the Feast of Unleavened Bread approached, Jesus sent two of his Disciples into the city to prepare for it. That evening, he and his Apostles sat down in a large room in the house of a man who believed in Jesus. During the supper, Jesus took bread and blessed it. Breaking it into pieces, he gave it to the Apostles, saying, "This is my body which is given for you. Do this in remembrance of me."

Then he took a cup of wine, offered thanks, and gave it to them to drink, saying, "This is the new testament in my blood, which shall be shed for you and for many, for the forgiveness of sins."

A little later, Jesus became deeply troubled and said to the Apostles, "One of you will betray me." John, whom Jesus loved, was sitting next to him. Leaning forward, he asked, "Lord, is it I?"

Judas also asked, "Is it I, Lord?" And Jesus, in a low voice, replied "You have said it." Then Judas left the others immediately and went out into the night.

After the supper, Jesus went with his Apostles to a garden called Gethsemane. He said to them, "Wait here while I go yonder to pray." Taking Peter and the two sons of Zebedee with him, he went farther into the garden. Then, his heart heavy, he told them, "My soul is sorrowful even unto death. Stay here and watch with me." But the Apostles were so weary that they soon fell asleep.

Jesus, in agony, prayed to his heavenly Father. "O Father, if it is possible, let this cup of salvation pass from me. Nevertheless, not my will but thine be done."

After he had prayed, he returned to the sleeping Apostles and asked them, "Could you not watch one hour with me? Rise, for he who betrays me is near by."

While Jesus was still speaking, Judas came with the Roman authorities and a great crowd, armed with clubs. Judas gave the Roman authorities a signal, saying, "Whomever I kiss, that is he. Seize him and hold him fast." Then he went up to Jesus and kissed him. And the Romans took Jesus and led him away.

Jesus was bound and led for trial before the Roman governor, Pontius Pilate. Because it was a custom to release one prisoner during the festival of Passover, Pontius Pilate asked which he should set free, Jesus, or the notorious criminal Barabbas. The people cried out, "Barabbas!"

Pilate then asked what he should do with Jesus, and the crowd roared, "Crucify him!"

The Roman soldiers dragged Jesus off to their barracks. Stripping him, they began to mock him. They clothed him in a kingly red robe, and put a crown of thorns on his head and a reed in his hand. Then they spat upon him and cried out, "Hail, king of the Jews!"

They led Jesus away through the streets of Jerusalem to the place of execution outside the city. It was called Golgotha, which means "the place of skulls." There they crucified Jesus, together with two criminals.

The people who were watching mocked Jesus, shouting, "He saved others, but he cannot save himself."

At three o'clock in the afternoon, darkness fell over the land, and Jesus cried in a loud voice, "My God, My God, why have you forsaken me?" Parched with thirst, he asked for water, and a bystander handed him a sponge soaked with vinegar.

Over his head they put a sign reading, "This is the king of the Jews." One of the criminals who was crucified with him began to mock him, but the other said to Jesus, "Lord, remember me when you come into your kingdom." Jesus answered, "Truly I say to you, this day you shall be with me in paradise."

A shadow covered the sun, the earth quaked, and rocks tumbled from the hillsides. The graves opened in the graveyard. In a loud voice, Jesus called, "Father, into your hands I commend my spirit." Then he murmured, "It is finished," and bowed his head, and died.

Because the people did not want bodies to remain hanging on the crosses during the Sabbath day, they asked Pilate to have them removed. To make sure that Jesus was not still alive, a Roman soldier pierced the side of Jesus with a lance. Blood, mingled with water, flowed out.

As night fell, a rich man named Joseph of Arimathea went secretly to Pilate and asked permission to bury Jesus. Bearing away his body, Joseph wrapped it in a linen cloth. He laid it in a tomb hewn out of a rock, which he had had prepared for his own burial.

The soldiers, remembering that Jesus had said that he would rise again, set a stone at the entrance of the tomb to seal it. Then, because they were afraid that his Disciples might steal his body and say that he had arisen, they set a guard of soldiers to watch over the tomb.

JETHER (Heb., *yether*, "he who excels" or "excellence" or "abundance"), a name borne by five OLD TESTAMENT personages, two of whom were direct descendants of JUDAH (I Chron. 2:32; 4:17); a third was a descendant of ASHER (I Chron. 7:38). The fourth Jether was the father of AMASA, commander-in-chief of the armies of ABSALOM during the latter's attempt to usurp the throne of King DAVID (I Kings 2:5 [cf. I Chron. 2:17, where he is identified as a descendant of ISHMAEL]). The fifth Jether was the eldest son of GIDEON; it was he who refused to slay the captives ZEBAH AND ZALMUNNA (Judg. 8:20-21).

JETHETH (Heb., *yetheth*, "nail"), one of the TWELVE DUKES OF EDOM (Gen. 36:40; I Chron. 1:51).

JETHLAH (Heb., *yithlah*, "lofty place"), one of the towns allotted to the TRIBE OF DAN (Josh. 19:42), the precise location of which is unknown.

JETHRO (Heb., *yithro*, "excellence"), the father-in-law of MOSES; "Jethro" is an honorary title: elsewhere he is called REUEL (Exod. 2:18) and RAGUEL (Num. 10:29). The story of this priest of MIDIAN and his relationship to Moses is told in chapters two, three, four, and eighteen of the Book of EXODUS.

When Moses fled to Midian after slaying the Egyptian overseer who had been "smiting an Hebrew, one of his brethren" (2:11), he gave aid to seven girls who were being abused by shepherds at the well where they had "filled the troughs to water their father's [Jethro's] flock." When Jethro learned of this kindness shown by a stranger, he invited Moses into his home: "Moses was content to dwell with the man" who gave him his daughter, ZIPPORAH, in marriage (2:16-21). It was while tending his father-in-law's flocks (3:1 ff.) that Moses was advised of his selection by the LORD to lead the Hebrew people out of Egyptian slavery (*see also* BURNING BUSH). When Moses

Moses and his family encounter his father-in-law Jethro in the desert.

JEWELS AND PRECIOUS STONES 1623

led the EXODUS, he left his wife and two sons with Jethro, who subsequently brought them to him in the WILDERNESS (18:2 ff.). It was also Jethro who suggested to Moses that he appoint ELDERS to assist him in administering the "ordinances and laws" and otherwise supervising the Israelites during the PERIOD OF THE WILDERNESS (18:20-27).

JETUR (Heb., *yetur,* meaning uncertain), an Arabic people descended from ISHMAEL (Gen. 25:15; I Chron. 1:31); when they made war with the Israelites who dwelled in GILEAD, they were badly beaten and had to surrender part of their flocks and herds (I Chron. 5:19).

JEUEL (Heb., *yeuel,* "treasured"), a minor member of the TRIBE OF JUDAH (I Chron. 9:6).

JEUSH (Heb., *yeush,* "he will come to help"), a name borne by four OLD TESTAMENT personages: a son of ESAU (Gen. 36:5; I Chron. 1:35); a man of valor from the TRIBE OF BENJAMIN (I Chron. 7:10); a member of the LEVITES (I Chron. 23:10); and a son of REHOBOAM of the Southern KINGDOM OF JUDAH (II Chron. 11:19).

JEUZ (Heb., *yeuts,* "assembler" or "counselor"), a minor member of the TRIBE OF BENJAMIN (I Chron. 8:10).

JEWELS AND PRECIOUS STONES are frequently mentioned in the BIBLE: "And she [the QUEEN OF SHEBA] came to Jerusalem with a very great train, with camels that bare spices, and very much gold, and precious stones" (I Kings 10:2); "And the servants also of Huram, and the servants of Solomon, which brought gold from Ophir, brought algum trees and precious stones" (II Chron. 9:10). The terms "jewels," "precious jewel," and "precious stones" are sometimes used collectively in a figurative sense to signify value, beauty, or durability: "And they shall be mine, saith the Lord of hosts, in that day when I

Jewelry and other personal objects, dating from the first century B.C., excavated at the ancient seaport of Caesarea (*Counsel Collection*).

1624   THE FAMILY BIBLE ENCYCLOPEDIA

Yemenite goldsmith embedding a Torah scroll cover with jewels (*Counsel Collection*).

make up my jewels" (Mal. 3:17); "There is gold, and a multitude of rubies: but the lips of knowledge are a precious jewel" (Prov. 20:15). "Jewels" in the sense of "jewelry," that is, costly ornaments of gold, silver, and other precious metals, are discussed in the article ORNAMENTS OF THE BIBLE.

Precious jewels (in the sense of "gems") and stones and, in addition, IVORY were known and used in biblical times for objects other than jewelry (see ARCHITECTURE; MINERALS OF THE BIBLE). Inscribed seals have been found made of materials such as agate, onyx, jade, opal, and amethyst (see ARCHAEOLOGY). Modern methods of faceting were not used; instead, the items were rounded and polished, and often engraved and/or sculptured.

The most comprehensive list of precious jewels and stones in the OLD TESTAMENT is given in the description of the BREASTPLATE of the HIGH PRIEST: "And thou shalt set in it settings of stones, even four rows of stones: the first row shall be a sardius, a topaz, and a carbuncle: . . . And the second row shall be an emerald, a sapphire, and a diamond. And the third row a ligure, an agate, and an amethyst. And the fourth row a beryl, and an onyx, and a jasper" (Exod. 28:17-20; cf. 39:10-13). These jewels and stones were inscribed with the names of the TWELVE TRIBES OF ISRAEL (28:21). A related, though abbreviated, listing occurs in the description of the "covering" of the king of TYRE when he was "in Eden, the garden of God" (Ezek. 28:13). Nine of the stones are listed—the ligure, agate, and amethyst are omitted. The SEPTUAGINT version of this verse repeats the full list of twelve stones from the Book of EXODUS (28:17-20). It has been suggested that possibly the Hebrew text of chapter twenty-eight, verse thirteen, of the Book of EZEKIEL is corrupt.

Jewels set in the breastplate worn by the High Priests of ancient Israel included, in numerical order, the carnelian, peridot, emerald, ruby, lapis lazuli, onyx, sapphire, banded agate, amethyst, topaz, beryl, jasper, asteria, moonstone, sunstone, alexandrite (nos. 16 & 17), cat's eye, precious garnet, chrysoprase, quartz, bloodstone, tourmaline, almandite garnet, pearl turquoise, green garnet, cinnamon garnet, Spanish topaz, blue diamond, yellow diamond, and fire opal (*New York Public Library*).

The NEW TESTAMENT contains still another, similar listing of twelve stones in the description of the foundation of the NEW JERUSALEM (Rev. 21:19-20). Some commentators find a common thread among these lists of twelve stones (*see* NUMEROLOGY), a few regarding them as symbolic of the months of the year (*see* CALENDAR), others seeing them as symbols for the signs of the zodiac (*see* ASTROLOGY; ASTRONOMY).

Generally, the biblical peoples were more familiar with semiprecious than with precious stones. Identification of the various stones and gems given in the Bible is not always easy; the Hebrews had no scientific sense or terminology and probably only attached a very vague meaning to the names of most of these items. They were probably influenced as much by color and hardness as by any other qualities. The following are covered in separate entries in this encyclopedia: ADAMANT; BERYLS, CHRYSOLYTES; CHRYSOPRASES; JACINTH; JASPER; LIGURE; ONYX; PEARL; RUBY; SAPPHIRE; SARDIUS; TOPAZ. G.B.K.

JEWISH REVOLT, more properly, two uprisings of the Jewish people against their ROMAN EMPIRE overlords; the first began as a spontaneous reaction to Roman intractability in regard to JUDAISM which had always been the central governing factor in Jewish life. While JUDAEA was governed by Jewish kings (the HERODS) under Roman supervision, relations with

ROME were at least tolerable. Both HEROD THE GREAT and his grandson HEROD AGRIPPA I kept on good terms with the Roman emperors and were allowed to exercise a limited form of independence at least in the internal governing of the country. Upon Agrippa's death in 44 A.D., however, PALESTINE was formally annexed as a Roman province and was ruled for the next twenty-two years by a succession of PROCURATORS who were nothing but glorified tax collectors. They displayed not the slightest sympathy for or understanding of Jewish customs or religious sensibilities; were rapacious in their attempts to wring tax revenues out of the populace and dealt with the slightest hint of insurgency with brutal, bloody hands.

The general population during this period lived close to the edge or in the depths of poverty, side by side with those prosperous members of the upper classes, which included the PRIESTHOOD of the TEMPLE, who had everything to gain from the status quo and everything to lose by revolting. This foundation for insurrection and civil war was further enhanced by the ZEALOTS, a breakaway sect of the PHARISEES who believed themselves instruments of God's wrath against IDOLATRY, apostasy, and transgressions of the MOSAIC LAW. Their fanaticism was kept near the boiling point by the Romans who could not or would not understand the Jewish insistence on adhering to MONOTHEISM in the face of imperial demands for the practice of EMPEROR WORSHIP in the Temple. Carrying small daggers under their cloaks, some Zealots made a practice of assassinating anyone who collaborated with Rome. Among their victims were the wealthier citizens of JERUSALEM and many members of the Priesthood, including JONATHAN the HIGH PRIEST. The Romans called these killers, who operated in broad daylight in the midst of the crowds in

The Arch of Titus in Rome, which celebrates the destruction of Jerusalem in A.D. 70. Note representation of the Temple Candelabra, taken by Titus (*Mella, Milan*).

JEWISH REVOLT   1627

Three pieces of glass dinner service dating from the period of the Jewish Revolt (Counsel Collection).

the streets and the Temple courtyards, SICARII, signifying the type of weapon they used.

The situation came to a head during the procuratorship of Florus (A.D. 64-66) who outdid his predecessors for venality and rapaciousness. When he expropriated seventeen talents from the Temple treasury, then equivalent to about $17,000 in modern currency, the citizens of Jerusalem mocked him by taking up a collection on his behalf. Infuriated, he let loose his soldiers to sack portions of the city, condemned to crucifixion some of the leading citizens, and gave the Zealots an excuse to revolt openly. The "peace" party attempted to oppose the Zealots, even accepting military support from Agrippa, but the Zealots drove them from the city, massacred the Roman garrison, and defeated a legion sent to put them down. Preparing for the Roman retaliation that was sure to follow, the Jews mistakenly placed the defense of strategic GALILEE in the hands of young Joseph ben Matathias, who was Roman educated and a great admirer of Roman civilization.

Convinced from the outset that the revolt was doomed to failure, Joseph all but handed over Galilee to the Roman army that marched into PALESTINE under VESPASIAN, saving his own neck by prophesying that Vespasian would become emperor, which actually did occur while the Romans were waiting for the Jews in Jerusalem to kill themselves off through internecine warfare. Joseph spent the rest of the war trying to persuade his coreligionists to lay down their arms. In Rome, he enjoyed the favors of the emperors, changed his name to Flavius JOSEPHUS, and wrote histories of the Jewish people and their revolt which have become a principal source of information regarding the events of that period. The emperor Vespasian left his son TITUS FLAVIUS VESPASIANUS, the future emperor, to capture Jerusalem after a heroic siege in the Jewish month of AB, in the year A.D. 70. The Temple was reduced to ashes, most of the city was destroyed, and seven hundred choice specimens of Jewish manhood became prisoners destined for the arena, led in chains behind Titus's chariot during the triumphal procession in Rome. The fortress MASADA held out for another three years until it fell in A.D. 73.

The second Jewish revolt occurred during the reign of the emperor TRAJAN as he was trying to subdue the PARTHIANS. Seeing what they thought was a good opportunity to strike a blow for freedom, the Jews of EGYPT, CYRENE, and CYPRUS rose in revolt against both their Roman and Greek rulers. The Romans and the Greeks put down the revolt, during which both sides committed atrocities against each other with

Aerial view of the ruins of Masada and Herod's Palace (at the "prow" of the fortress) destroyed in the Jewish Revolt (*Counsel Collection*).

monotonous regularity. Trajan was so affected by what was going on in his rear that he allowed himself to be defeated by an Arab army in the desert. Hadrian, who succeeded Trajan, brought on the third revolt by threatening to rebuild Jerusalem as a pagan city and by passing a law against self-mutilation which the Jews took as an attack on CIRCUMCISION. Between revolts the Jews had managed to rebuild some semblance of national life for themselves in Palestine. Led by the scholar JOHANAN and by his successor GAMALIEL, they had established synagogues, replaced the ritual sacrifices of the Temple with organized prayer services, and taken the first steps towards the writing of the TALMUD.

This was all placed in jeopardy by Akiba ben Josef, the most renowned SANHEDRIN scholar of his day, who at the age of eighty, aroused the Jews into a state of revolt against Hadrian's threats to their religion and statehood. He found a military leader in Simon of Cozeba, a small Palestinian town, changed the man's name to Simon Bar Kochba ("son of the star"), and proclaimed him to be the MESSIAH. This second Jewish revolt erupted in A.D. 132. Hadrian responded by sending an army under Julius Severus, a veteran of the conquest of Britain. Before Severus could get into the field, Bar Kochba defeated local Roman forces, captured Jerusalem, and organized his compatriots into guerrilla bands based in caves and underground hideouts. An altar was erected on the site of the Temple, and new coins were struck and issued inscribed "First Year of the Rebellion," "Second Year of the Rebellion," and so forth for the three years the rebellion lasted.

Realizing that he was outnumbered, Severus refused to draw the rebels out into open battle, but instead concentrated on cutting their lines of supply and communication, thus isolating the individual groups before overcoming them one by one. Not being able to fortify Jerusalem effectively, the Jews lost the city within the first two years of fighting. Bar Kochba and his army were forced to retreat to the city of Bittar, where they held out for several weeks until the Romans got into the town through treachery and slaughtered them, Bar Kochba along with his soldiers. Upon the ruins of Jerusalem arose the city of Aelia Capitolina, with a temple dedicated to Jupiter Capitolinus on the site of the Temple. Judaism was proscribed in Palestine and all Jews were exiled from the new pagan city (*see* DIASPORA). Once a year, on the anniversary of the fall of the Temple, they thronged to the city gates to bribe the Roman guards to allow them to stay for a while and weep for their departed glory.

The effect of the two Palestinian revolts was almost beyond reckoning. Principal cities were laid waste, farmlands made barren, cisterns destroyed, large segments of the populations massacred or dispersed far beyond the national boundaries. Over half a million Jews are believed to have perished in the revolt of A.D. 132-135 alone, and so many Jewish slaves went on the block that their average price was reduced to that of a horse. The Romans also suffered heavily, for the Jews had fought with such savage fanaticism, making up with their ferocity for what they lacked in arms and strategists, that the Roman emperor, reporting his victory to the Senate, left out the customary ending, "I and my army are well." S.S.

JEZANIAH (Heb., *yezanyahu*, "the Lord hears"), a contemporary of GEDALIAH, governor of the Southern KINGDOM OF JUDAH at the inception of the PERIOD OF THE BABYLONIAN CAPTIVITY (Jer. 40:7-12 [cf. II Kings 25:23, where he is called "Jaazaniah"]).

JEZEBEL (Heb., *izevel,* perhaps "chaste") (died c. 842 B.C.), the wife of AHAB, seventh monarch of the Northern KINGDOM OF ISRAEL; her name has become a byword for a wicked woman. Ahab's marriage to this daughter of a Phoenician ruler, ETHBAAL, king of SIDON, reinforced an alliance that had political and economic benefits for Israel, but exposed it to the idolatrous rites and sophisticated mores of PHOENICIA. Jezebel was zealous for the cult of BAAL, adamantly opposed by the Prophet ELIJAH and the religious party, while her concept of absolute royal power was incompatible with Israel's traditions of more limited monarchy.

The imperious queen strongly influenced the king, and resistance to the policies she proposed led to bloody strife. She is accused of a mass slaughter of the PROPHETS of the LORD, and the extent to which she fostered the rival sect is indicated by Elijah's challenge to 850 pagan prophets "which eat at Jezebel's table" (I Kings 18:19). Enraged at Elijah's slaying of the Baal prophets, she drove him to flight with the message, "So let the gods do to me, and more also, if I make not thy life as the life of one of them by tomorrow about this time" (I Kings 19:2).

Her scorn for the rights of the people is seen in the story of NABOTH. When Ahab sulked over his subject's refusal to sell his vineyard to the king, she demanded "Dost thou now govern the kingdom of

Woodcut by the 16th-century Dutch artist Lucas Van Leyden showing Ahab and Jezebel.

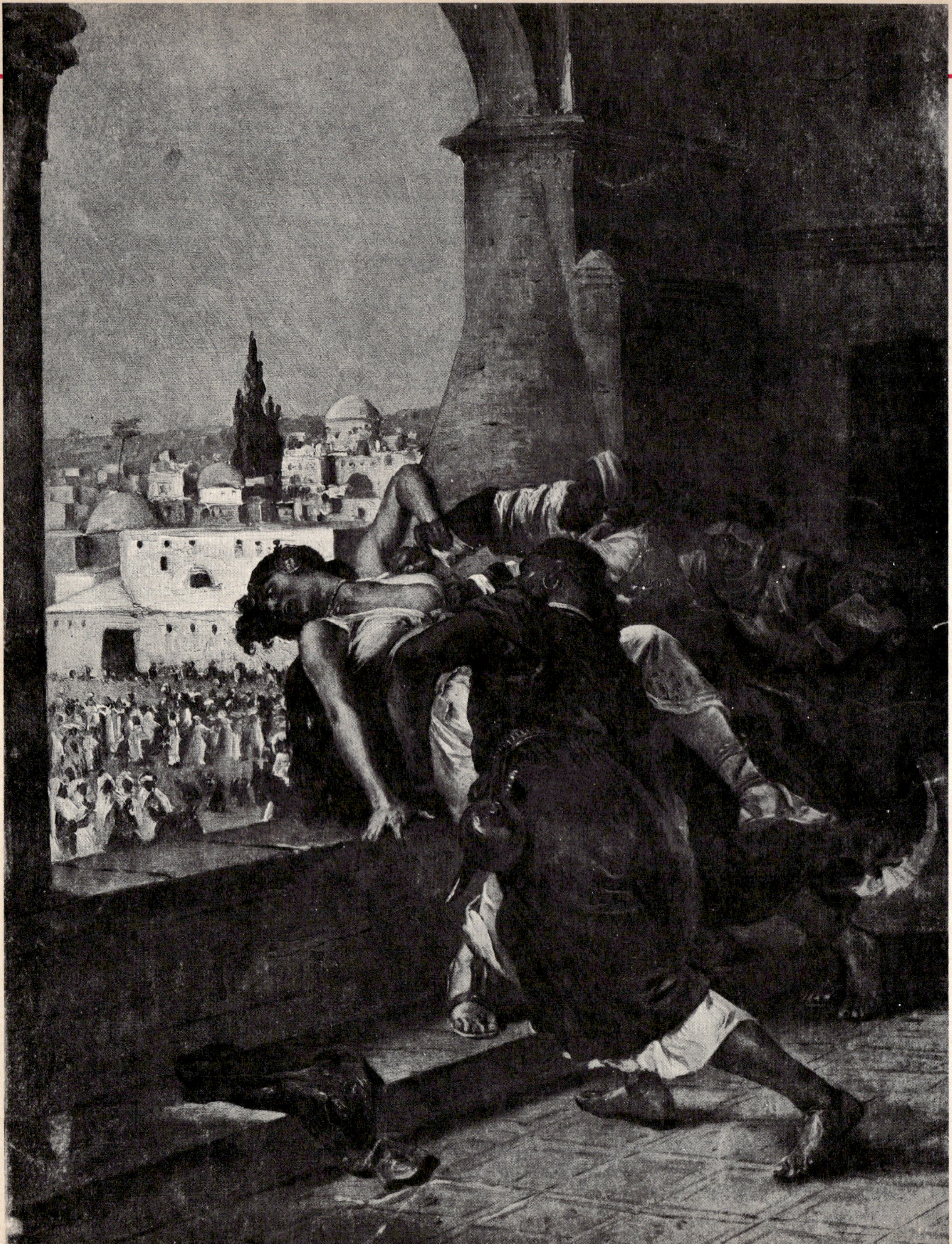

GENEALOGY OF JEZEBEL

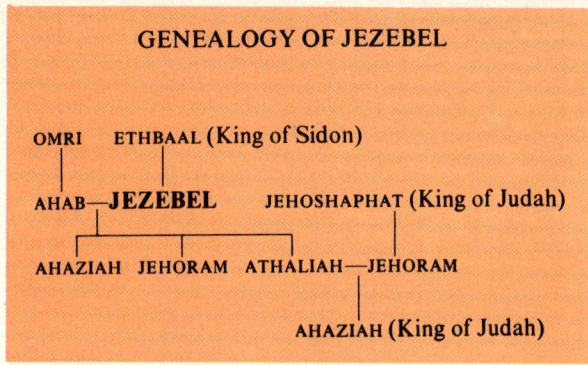

```
OMRI    ETHBAAL (King of Sidon)
  |        |
AHAB—JEZEBEL    JEHOSHAPHAT (King of Judah)
  |                    |
AHAZIAH  JEHORAM  ATHALIAH—JEHORAM
                          |
                        AHAZIAH (King of Judah)
```

Israel?" (I Kings 21:7), and devised Naboth's death by having him falsely accused of a capital offense. It was after this judicial murder that Elijah pronounced the doom, "The dogs shall eat Jezebel by the wall of Jezreel" (I Kings 21:23).

Jezebel survived Ahab to see their sons AHAZIAH and JEHORAM (JORAM) succeed to the throne in turn, to see her daughter ATHALIAH usurp the throne of the Southern KINGDOM OF JUDAH, and to see her own royal house overthrown by JEHU. The latter detested her, and before killing Jehoram taunted him, "What peace, so long as the whoredoms of thy mother Jezebel and her witchcrafts are so many?" (II Kings 9:22). The queen-mother prepared to confront the victorious rebel in full array: "And when Jehu was come to Jezreel . . . she painted her face, and tired her head, and looked out at a window" (II Kings 9:30). She addressed him in mocking words, and was flung from the window at his command. Little was left of her remains when Jehu finally ordered, "Go, see now this cursed woman, and bury her; for she is a king's daughter" (II Kings 9:34).

The biblical chroniclers, writing from their religous and moral viewpoint, abhorred Jezebel and her baleful influence on Ahab, "which did sell himself to work wickedness in the sight of the Lord, whom Jezebel his wife stirred up" (I Kings 21:25). In the REVELATION OF ST. JOHN THE DIVINE (2:20) her name is a symbol for sinfulness, and thus it has remained in popular usage.

P.J.B.

Death of Jezebel, fulfilling the prophecy of Elijah (*New York Public Library*).

THE STORY OF JEZEBEL

For Younger Readers

Jezebel, the daughter of Ethbaal, king of Sidon, was once a high priestess of Baal. The worshippers of this false god took part in all kinds of wickedness.

When Jezebel became the wife of King Ahab of Israel, she persuaded the king and his people to worship Baal. She also brought hundreds of priests and prophets of Baal from her homeland to the royal court.

Jezebel persecuted the prophets of God and caused hundreds to be slain. But some were saved by Abdias, Ahab's chief steward, who hid them in caves.

One day, the Prophet Elijah told Ahab to bring all the people of Israel and all the prophets of Baal to Mount Carmel. There he spoke to the people. "If the Lord is God, follow Him. But if Baal be God, then follow him."

As the people were silent, Elijah told them that he would prove to them which was the true God, his God, or Baal. He told the 450 prophets of Baal to choose one of two bullocks, cut it into pieces for a sacrifice, and lay it on wood. But they were not to set fire to the wood.

They did as he said, and Elijah took the other bullock and did the same thing.

Then Elijah told the prophets to cry out the name of their god. From morning to evening they did so, but there was no reply. Elijah mocked them, saying, "Cry louder. Perhaps he is on a journey, or asleep." They cried louder and louder, but there was still no answer.

Elijah then bade the people move nearer. He called out to God. "Hear me, oh

Lord, hear me, so that these people may learn that thou art the Lord God." At once fire swept down from heaven and burned up the sacrifice.

The people fell on their faces in awe. "The Lord, He is God," they said. "The Lord, He is God."

Elijah told them to seize the prophets of Baal and take them down to the waterfall of Cison. There Elijah slew them.

When Jezebel heard what had happened, she sent a messenger to tell Elijah that she would kill him on the following day. But Elijah fled into the desert and escaped her.

Jezebel came to Ahab's aid in an evil way when he wanted to buy the vineyard belonging to a man named Naboth, who did not want to sell it. She caused two witnesses to lie about Naboth, saying that he had blasphemed God and the king. This offense was punishable by death, so Naboth was stoned.

When he heard of Naboth's fate, Elijah went to meet Ahab. He told the king that God was angry with Jezebel. "On this place, where the dogs have licked the blood of Naboth, they will likewise lick your blood," Elijah prophesied. "And the dogs will eat Jezebel in the field of Jezreel."

Not long afterward, Ahab was killed by his enemies, the Syrians. His blood ran out of his chariot, and the dogs licked it up. But Jezebel lived after him until Jehu overthrew Ahab's descendants and became king of Israel.

One day, as Jehu came into the town of Jezreel, a woman mocked him from her high window. Jehu asked who she was and learned that she was the wicked queen Jezebel. He ordered his servants to cast her down from the window. They did so, and Jezebel was killed.

Later, Jehu told them to go back and give Jezebel's body decent burial because, though she was evil, she was a king's daughter. But when they came to where the body had lain, they found nothing but her skull, her feet, and her fingertips. The dogs of Jezreel had devoured Jezebel, as Elijah had foretold.

Jezebel was the mother of the wicked Athaliah, who usurped the throne of the Kingdom of Judah after killing all her sons.

JEZELUS, the APOCRYPHA rendering (I Esd. 8:32,35) of JAHAZIEL (Ezra 7:5), the ancestor of a group who returned to JERUSALEM following the PERIOD OF THE BABYLONIAN CAPTIVITY.

JEZER (Heb., *yetser*, "help" or "purpose"), the fourth son of NAPHTALI (Gen. 46:24; I Chron. 7:13), and ancestor of the Jezerites, one of the clans within the TRIBE OF NAPHTALI included in the CENSUS ordered by MOSES during the PERIOD OF THE WILDERNESS (Num. 26:49).

JEZIAH (Heb., *yetsyah*, "the Lord sprinkles" or "the Lord unites"), one of the many who agreed to divorce the foreign women they had married during the PERIOD OF THE BABYLONIAN CAPTIVITY (Ezra 10:25).

JEZIEL (Heb., *yeziel*, perhaps "God sprinkles"), a soldier who joined DAVID at ZIKLAG; he opposed King SAUL even though both were of the TRIBE OF BENJAMIN (I Chron. 12:3).

JEZLIAH (Heb., *yitslyah*, "the Lord preserves" or "the Lord sprinkles"), one of the early members of the TRIBE OF BENJAMIN (I Chron. 8:18).

JEZOAR (Heb., *yetshar*, "white" or perhaps "the shining one"), a member of the clan of HEZRON of the TRIBE OF JUDAH (I Chron. 4:7).

JEZRAHIAH (Heb., *yezrachiya*, "Yahweh shines"), one of the LEVITES who returned to JERUSALEM following the PERIOD OF THE BABYLONIAN CAPTIVITY; when they finished rebuilding the wall surrounding

"In the portion of Jezreel shall dogs eat the flesh of Jezebel . . ." (II Kings 9:36).

Jerusalem, it was he who led the people in singing the praises of the LORD (Neh. 12:42).

JEZREEL, the name of two biblical persons. The first was a descendant of JUDAH, through ETAM: "And these were of the father of Etam; Jezreel, and Ishma, and Idbash: and the name of their sister was Hazelelponi" (I Chron. 4:3). The other person bearing this name was a son of the Prophet HOSEA: "And he went and took Gomer the daughter of Diblaim; which conceived and bare him a son. And the Lord said unto him, Call his name Jezreel; for yet a little while, and I will avenge the blood of Jezreel [the city] upon the house of Jehu, and will cause to cease the kingdom of the house of Israel" (Hos. 1:3-4).

JEZREEL (Heb., *zraal,* "God sows" or "may God make fruitful"), a geographical place name in the OLD TESTAMENT which designates: the entire valley and plain, lying both north and east of MOUNT CARMEL, which separates GALILEE from SAMARIA, the western portion of which is now often called ESDRAELON; a border city of ISSACHAR situated at the foot of the northwestern spur of the MOUNT GILBOA ridge; and a town in the territory of JUDAH believed to have been situated in the general vicinity of ZIPH, Carmel, and JUTTAH.

The BIBLE records several designations for the valley which separates Galilee from Samaria, though it is not possible to determine whether these other names apply only to the great plain in its entirety, or merely to a part of it. The name "Esdraelon" (the Greek transliteration of the Hebrew word "Jezreel") appears neither in the Old nor NEW TESTAMENT; it is used only in the APOCRYPHA, in the Book of JUDITH, where it is variously rendered "Esdrelom" (1:8), "Esdraelon" (3:9; 4:6), and "Esdraelom" (7:3). Nevertheless, "Esdraelon" has become the most popular designation for this important area; some authors now reserve the name Esdraelon for the western portion of the valley, while referring to the eastern portion as Jezreel.

It seems more than likely that the name of Jezreel (the city) was applied first to its adjacent valley (Josh. 17:16) and eventually to the plain in its entirety. The references to "the valley of Megiddo" in the Second Book of the CHRONICLES (35:22), and "the valley of Megiddon" in the Book of ZECHARIAH (12:11), no doubt represent a similar extension of the name MEGIDDO to the plain, though, as indicated above, it is not possible to infer precisely what territory was meant to be delineated.

The Valley of Jezreel is among the most fertile areas of PALESTINE, a fact to which the following passage in the Book of HOSEA is usually interpreted as an allusion: "And the earth shall hear the corn, and the wine, and the oil; and they shall hear Jezreel" (2:22). It is the major corridor into Palestine's mountainous interior, and great cities, such as Megiddo and TAANACH, once lined its borders. Major transportation routes crisscross the valley, from north (i.e., Galilee, SYRIA, and PHOENICIA) to south (i.e., EGYPT and the hill country), and from east (i.e., the Jordan Valley, the Transjordan Plateau, and BETH-SHAN) to west (i.e., the Mediterranean seacoast). It is drained by the waters of the KISHON virtually throughout its area.

From very early times, the Valley of Jezreel was inhabited by CANAANITES who were so powerful militarily—their armament (*see* ARMS AND ARMOR) included chariots of iron—that the tribes of EPHRAIM and MANASSEH were unable to dislodge them (Josh. 17:16). The valley was frequently a battleground: it was here that GIDEON attacked and defeated the coalition of "Midianites . . . Amalekites and . . . children of the east [who had] pitched [camp] in the valley of Jezreel" (Judg. 6:33; *see also* 6:34-7:23), and it was from here that the "tidings came of [the deaths of] Saul and Jonathan" in battle with the PHILISTINES on Mount Gilboa (II Sam. 4:4). ISHBOSHETH briefly ruled the valley during his struggle with DAVID for the kingship (II Sam. 2:9). A passage in the Book of HOSEA states that the Lord "will break the bow of Israel in the valley of Jezreel" (1:5), undoubtedly as retribution for the bloody murders committed in the city of Jezreel during the revolution of JEHU (*see below*).

Under its various names—the Valley of Jezreel or the Plain of Esdraelon—it is often referred to as a place of battle. It was here that DEBORAH and BARAK so devastated the armies of JABIN and SISERA that "all the host of Sisera fell upon the edge of the sword; and there was not a man left" (Judg. 4:16), and it was here that King JOSIAH was murdered by the Egyptian Pharaoh NECHO. The army of the apocryphal HOLOFERNES also made camp on the plain (Judg. 7:3). Many scholars associate the area with the apocalyptic prophecy of ARMAGEDDON (Rev. 16:16).

Jezreel, the city, from which the valley takes its name, is identified with the present-day village of

JEZREEL 1635

The village of Zer'in, all that remains of the city of Jezreel (Counsel Collection).

Zer'in; the site, first mentioned in the Old Testament narratives as a town in the fifth administrative district of King SOLOMON (I Kings 4:12), besides commanding an excellent view of the entire Jezreel plain, occupied a position of great strategic importance both on the roads extending from the coast of the Mediterranean Sea to the Jordan Valley, and on those extending from northern to southern Palestine. Nearby was the scene of Gideon's exploit against the MIDIANITES and the place where the Israelites under SAUL "pitched [camp] by a fountain which is in Jezreel" (I Sam. 29:1). During the reign of AHAB, Jezreel served apparently as a base of operations against ARAM about RAMOTH-GILEAD, and also as a royal residence, or winter resort, for the king (I Kings 18:45-46); the incident involving the confiscation of the vineyard of NABOTH the Jezreelite, which drew a sharp denunciation from ELIJAH, took place here (I Kings 21:1 ff.).

According to the Second Book of the KINGS, "King Joram went back to be healed in Jezreel of the wounds which the Syrians had given him at Ramah, when he fought against Hazael king of Syria" (8:29; see also II Chron. 22:6). It was here that JORAM, JEZEBEL, and the entire house of Ahab were murdered (II Kings, chapters nine and ten); with the exception of Samaria, no community in ISRAEL experienced more horror and bloodshed as a result of Jehu's revolution. AHAZIAH of Judah was wounded there, and the heads of Ahab's slain sons were sent there from Samaria (II Kings 9:1-10:11). After bearing witness to these events, the town seems to have sunk into relative obscurity.

Another town named Jezreel was the home of AHINOAM, one of the wives of David (I Sam. 25:43); the present-day Khirbet Tarrama, situated approximately six miles southwest of HEBRON, has been proposed as the site. Though the identification is by no means certain, the suggested location seems to concur with the biblical narrative. — M.L.F.

JIBSAM (Heb., *yivsam*, "pleasant" or "fragrant"), a member of the TRIBE OF ISSACHAR in descent from the tribe's eponym (I Chron. 7:2).

JIDLAPH (Heb., *yidlaph*, "he will weep"), the seventh son of NAHOR and a nephew of ABRAHAM, who received word of his birth shortly after the attempted sacrifice of ISAAC (Gen. 22:22).

JIMNA, JIMNAH (Heb., *yimnah*, "prosperity"), the firstborn son of ASHER (Gen. 46:17; "Imnah" in I Chron. 7:30) and eponym of the Jimnites, a clan within the TRIBE OF ASHER that was included in the CENSUS ordered by MOSES at the close of the PERIOD OF THE WILDERNESS (Num. 26:44).

JIPHTAH (Heb., *yiphtah*, "opens"), a town allotted to the TRIBE OF JUDAH, located in the SHEPHELAH but otherwise unidentifiable geographically (Josh. 15:43).

JIPHTAH-EL (Heb., *yiphtahel*, "God opens"), a valley, approximately ten miles northwest of NAZARETH, which marked the boundary line between the tribes of ASHER and ZEBULUN (Josh. 19:14,27).

JOAB (Heb., *Yoav*, "the Lord is father"), the son of ZERUIAH, a half-sister of King DAVID, and the brother of ABISHAI and ASAHEL. A superb military strategist, he was his uncle's chief captain and a potent force in the establishment of his dynasty. (See PERIOD OF THE MONARCHY.) The hard outlaw years first forged a lifelong bond between them. In numerous crises, military, political, and even personal, Joab's genius for finding the effective course probably made the difference between glory and collapse for the new regime. Yet two men can hardly be imagined more different in temperament than the outgoing, greathearted reformer-king and his suspicious, unforgiving, conservative general, whose life story runs through most of the Second Book of SAMUEL. Commanding David's forces at GIBEON after Saul's death, when Saul's fleeing captain, ABNER, killed Asahel to save himself, Joab realized that immediate revenge was inexpedient. But he bided his time, and when Abner came to HEBRON to offer David Israel's army and crown, Joab waylaid and stabbed him in cold blood.

David bitterly regretted the wanton murder; but though he repudiated the deed by public mourning, he did not reject the doer. For his valor in taking the city of JEBUS (JERUSALEM), Joab was named chief captain. Through the many campaigns that firmly established David's power, "Joab the son of Zeruiah was over the host" (8:16), and always his deeds were mighty and terrible, and his loyalty to his master absolute. He slaughtered every male citizen during his occupation of EDOM. With his brother Abishai he scattered the combined forces of the AMMONITES and the SYRIANS. During the siege of RABBAH, he did not scruple to arrange for his infatuated lord the death in battle of URIAH, the husband of BATHSHEBA. And when the city finally fell, Joab renounced the glory and sent for David to lead the takeover and accept the crown and the spoils.

Though he engineered David's reconciliation with the monarch's fratricidal son ABSALOM, he later had cause to regret his peacemaking when Absalom made himself lord of Hebron and fomented open rebellion against his father. In the moment of victory against the rebel, Joab came upon Absalom hanging helpless from an oak, caught by his luxuriant hair. Despite David's direct command to "deal gently for my sake with . . . Absalom" (18:5), Joab speared him through. This news turned the triumph to mourning for the bereft father: "Would God I had died for thee, O

JOAB 1637

King David orders Joab to take a census of Israel.

Absalom, my son, my son!" (18:33). He grieved until Joab rebuked him: "Thou lovest thine enemies and hatest thy friends . . . for this day I perceive, that if Absalom had lived, and all we had died this day, then it had pleased thee well" (19:6). Though it was done for his own security, this ruthless execution was apparently more than David could forgive. He appointed his cousin AMASA captain of the host—yet again Joab regained his place. During the pursuit of the rebel SHEBA, Joab craftily killed Amasa, then took command and besieged Sheba in ABEL. Convinced they could save the city by delivering Sheba, the frightened citizens beheaded the rebel and threw his head over the wall. Thus Joab returned victorious to Jerusalem, once again "over all the host of Israel" (20:23).

But the old rapport was gone. When the aging king's son ADONIJAH prematurely seized power, Joab transferred his allegiance to the usurper. This sealed his doom, for the succession went to SOLOMON. Dying, David reminded Solomon of all Joab's bloody deeds, a clear exhortation to vengeance. "And Joab fled unto the tabernacle of the Lord, and caught hold on the horns of the altar" (I Kings 2:28), seeking sanctuary; but he could not escape the king's executioner.

Joab was truly a man of his harsh era; his brutal murders were entirely justified in his own eyes—a brother's revenge, security for his king, a commander's wrath at being supplanted. His religion was to be indispensable to his lord, and he would brook no rival. His tragedy was that he served a man who was far ahead of his age and who valued pity and forgiveness above vengeance and ruthlessness.

The name Joab was also borne by two minor OLD TESTAMENT personages: an early member of the TRIBE OF JUDAH (I Chron. 4:14); and one who returned with ZERUBBABEL following the PERIOD OF THE BABYLONIAN CAPTIVITY (Ezra 2:6).   N.P.

JOACHAZ, the APOCRYPHA rendering (I Esd. 1:34) of King JEHOAHAZ, son and immediate successor of JOSIAH on the throne of the Southern KINGDOM OF JUDAH.

JOACHIM, the APOCRYPHA rendering (Bar. 1:3) of King JEHOIAKIM, one of the last monarchs of the Southern KINGDOM OF JUDAH.

JOACIM, a name which appears only in the APOCRYPHA in the KING JAMES VERSION. Two personages bearing this name are presumably fictional characters, the husband of SUSANNA (Sus. 1:1 ff.), and the HIGH PRIEST at JERUSALEM during the period covered in the fictional Book of JUDITH (Jud. 4:6). "Joacim" is also the variant identifying kings JEHOIAKIM (I Esd. 1:37-42) and his successor JEHOIACHIN (I Esd. 1:43), two of the last monarchs of the Southern KINGDOM OF JUDAH.

JOADANUS, according to the APOCRYPHA (I Esd. 9:19), one of the LEVITES who agreed to divorce the foreign women they had married during the PERIOD OF THE BABYLONIAN CAPTIVITY.

JOAH (Heb., *yoach*, "Yahweh is a brother"), the recorder at the court of King HEZEKIAH of the Southern KINGDOM OF JUDAH; when the Assyrian army encamped directly outside the walls of the city of JERUSALEM, Joah was one of three envoys sent by the Judahite monarch to dissuade the foreigners from commencing war. Seeking to find a peaceful solution that would not mean the enslavement of Jerusalem, the ambassadors were met instead by an Assyrian captain, RAB-SHAKEH, who taunted the Hebrews, intimating that they were cowards who could not fight. Joah begged the Assyrian to speak in the Syrian tongue (which the ambassadors understood) so that the common people in the city would not hear the taunts and become disheartened; this entreaty, however, only provoked Rab-Shakeh into raising his voice and loudly yelling his taunts in Hebrew. Saddened by the conduct of the Assyrian who disdained peace and only wished for military conquest, the three ambassadors tore their clothes and returned to Hezekiah in mourning (II Kings 18:17-37; Isa. 36:1-22).

Another Joah was the recorder during the reign of King JOSIAH (II Chron. 34:8) and was also one of three people chosen to supervise the repairing of the TEMPLE; a third Joah was one of the LEVITES selected to cleanse the Temple during the reign of Hezekiah (II Chron. 29:12). Two other biblical Joahs were also Levites; their genealogies can be found in the First Book of the CHRONICLES (6:21 and 26:4, respectively).

JOAHAZ (Heb., *yoahaz*, "the Lord has held"), the father of JOAH, who was the recorder at the court of King JOSIAH (II Chron. 34:8).

JOANAN, according to the APOCRYPHA, a wealthy man who lived in JERUSALEM during the period of EZRA (ESDRAS in the text [I Esd. 9:1]).

JOANNA (Gr., *Iona* or *Ionna*, "God-given"), the wife of CHUZA; originally a morally infirm person, she was "healed" of her spiritual laxity by JESUS CHRIST (Luke 8:2-3) and subsequently gave him supplies when he was ministering in the GALILEE. Impressed by his ministry, she followed him to JERUSALEM and was with him at the time of the CRUCIFIXION; after his death she prepared spices and ointments to adorn his body in the grave (23:27,55-56). When she and two other women brought the spices to the grave, however, they found the body of Jesus absent. Afraid, they kneeled in the dust and two angels appeared before them, proclaiming the miracle of the RESURRECTION (*see also* ANGELOLOGY). Quickly, the women ran to the APOSTLES and related the miracle, but the men thought that the women were engaged in idle chatter and refused to believe them (24:1-11). A second Joanna was an ancestress of Jesus (3:27). (*See* GENEALOGY OF JESUS CHRIST.)

JOARIB (Heb., *yehoriv*, "the Lord fights"), an ancestor of the MACCABEES (I Macc. 2:1; 14:29, where the name is rendered JARIB).

JOASH 1639

JOASH (reigned c. 835-800 B.C.) (Heb., *Yoash,* "the Lord has given"), ninth king of the Davidic Monarchy, successor to his grandmother, the usurper queen ATHALIAH, in the Southern KINGDOM OF JUDAH; his story is told in chapters 11-12 of the Second Book of the KINGS and chapters 23-24 of the Second Book of the CHRONICLES. When Joash's father AHAZIAH died after a reign of barely a year, the throne was usurped by Ahaziah's mother, Athaliah, who had fostered the pagan BAAL-worship in the kingdom and who gained the throne by murdering or causing to have murdered all of Ahaziah's surviving heirs—or so she thought. For the infant Joash was hidden in the TEMPLE by his aunt JEHOSHEBA and her husband, the High Priest JEHOIADA. Seven years later Joash was crowned as the rightful king through the efforts of Jehoiada who, having deposed Athaliah, abolished IDOLATRY throughout the kingdom and returned the people to the worship of YAHWEH "as it was ordained by David" (II Chron. 23:18) (*see also* MONOTHEISM).

During the king's minority he was under the healthy influence of Jehoiada and thus "did that which was right in the sight of the Lord all the days of . . . the priest" (24:2). Unfortunately, the monarch had inherited the ways of his antecedents, for no sooner had Jehoiada died than Joash asserted his independence and led the people in a reversion to pagan worship. When Jehoiada's son and heir as HIGH PRIEST remonstrated against the people and the PRIESTHOOD for this recidivism, he was stoned to death at the

Athaliah is condemned to death at the coronation of her grandson Joash (*Counsel Collection*).

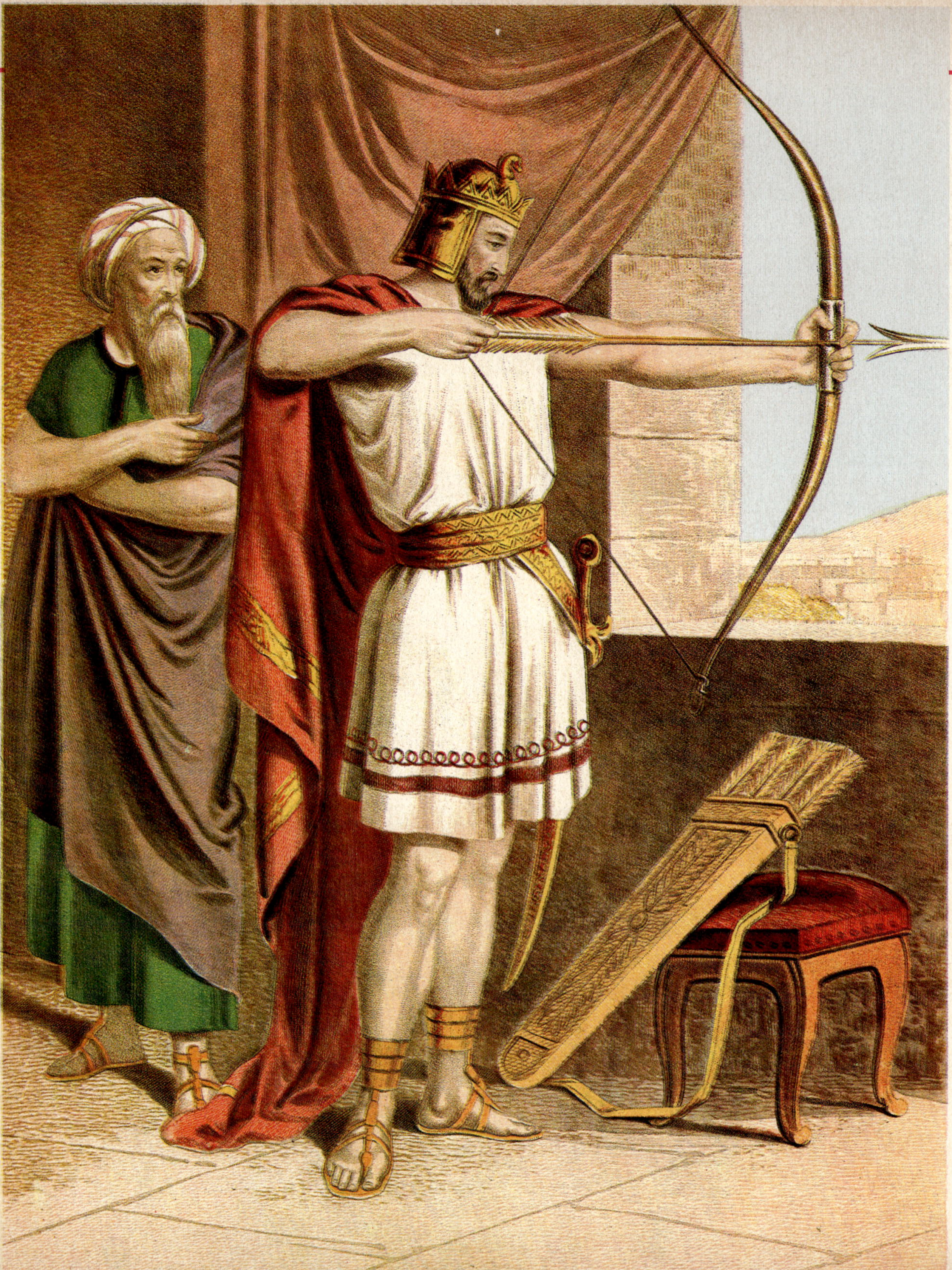

king's command. Within a year, the Syrians invaded the Southern Kingdom and sacked the religious and political capital of JERUSALEM. In the version given in II Kings, Joash sent the Temple treasures to HAZAEL when the Syrian king "set his face to go up to Jerusalem" (12:17), and the inference is that Judah was spared by this act of tribute ("and he went away from Jerusalem"); however, if Hazael spared the Southern Kingdom, it was only temporarily—or perhaps a feint on his part. For in II Chronicles we learn how the Syrians "came to Judah and Jerusalem, and destroyed all the princes of the people from among the people, and sent all the spoil of them unto" Hazael (24:23). According to this version, the Syrians "came with a small company of men" and were victorious because the inhabitants of Judah "had forsaken the Lord God of their fathers," thus delivering punishment upon the people for their reversion to the paganistic Baal-worship.

Following the Syrian sacking of Jerusalem, because he had condoned the murder of the High Priest, and also presumably because of an "arrangement" he had with the Priests regarding the moneys collected in the Temple, Joash was assassinated by a group of his own servants. (According to II Chronicles, he was denied burial in the royal sepulcher; this contradicts the version in II Kings, wherein Joash is described as having been buried "with his fathers"). He was succeeded by his son AMAZIAH, who may have been co-regent for a brief period. It should be noted that "Joash" is the shorter form of the name "Jehoash," and the two are used interchangeably; in order to preclude any confusion, the history of Joash of the Northern Kingdom of Israel will be treated under the entry JEHOASH.

A number of other biblical personages bore the name Joash, of whom the most prominent was the father of GIDEON. When Gideon destroyed the altar of Baal which his father had erected, Joash refused to surrender his son for punishment for this sacrilege, arguing that if Baal really were a god he should "plead for himself, because one hath cast down his altar" (*see* chapter six, verse seven of the Book of JUDGES). Others named Joash were: one of the sons of BECHER given in the genealogical listings of the TRIBE OF BENJAMIN (I Chron. 7:8); one of the "mighty men, helpers of the war" who joined DAVID at ZIKLAG during the future king's period of outlawry (I Chron. 12:1-3), and a servant of King David "over the cellars of oil" (I Chron. 27:28). (The last two may have been one and the same person.)   M.A.B.

King Joash shooting arrows at the command of the Prophet Elisha (*Counsel Collection*).

GENEALOGY OF KING JOASH OF JUDAH

```
      AHAB—JEZEBEL      JEHOSHAPHAT
              |              |
           *ATHALIAH—JEHORAM
                       |
   ZIBEAH—AHAZIAH    JEHOSHABEATH—JEHOIADA
              |                    (High Priest)
       JOASH—JEHOADDAN
              |
         AMAZIAH—JECHOLIAH (Jecoliah)
```

*Athaliah usurped the throne of Judah following the death of her son Ahaziah, and was in turn dethroned by her son-in-law Jehoiada who put Joash on the throne at the age of 7.

JOATHAM, the NEW TESTAMENT rendering (Matt. 1:9) for JOTHAM, tenth hereditary monarch of the Southern KINGDOM OF JUDAH and thus a direct descendant of King DAVID; the reference here is to his position in the MATTHEW genealogy of JESUS CHRIST, which was intended to establish his descent from David (*see also* GENEALOGY OF JESUS CHRIST).

JOAZABDUS, the APOCRYPHA rendering (I Esd. 9:48) of the LEVITE known as JOZABAD, in the OLD TESTAMENT account of the Return following the PERIOD OF THE BABYLONIAN CAPTIVITY (Neh. 8:7); he assisted EZRA (called ESDRAS in the apocryphal account) in expounding the MOSAIC LAW.

JOB (Heb., *iyyov,* etymology uncertain, but possibly "persecuted"), titular hero of the eighteenth book of the OLD TESTAMENT in the KING JAMES VERSION (*see following entry*). A wealthy man of high rank, Job was noted for his piety and righteousness, "perfect [blameless] and upright"; his household included a wife, seven sons and three daughters, and many servants, and he possessed thousands of sheep, camels, and oxen—the property of a seminomadic chieftain—

The afflicted Job offering a sacrifice to the Lord (*Counsel Collection*).

"so that this man was the greatest of all the men of the east." He was so devout that, after feast days, he would offer special sacrifices and offerings for each of his sons in case they had unwittingly sinned (1:1-5). Job is cited by the Prophet EZEKIEL, together with NOAH and the Prophet DANIEL, as one of the three most righteous men (Ezek. 14:14,20), suggesting a hero figure of great antiquity. The TALMUD enlarges upon his piety and his character: like the Patriarch ABRAHAM, he is supposed to have had an intuitive understanding of GOD; since he owned nothing that had been taken unjustly, his prayers were pure. He is cited in rabbinical literature as a man whose doors were always open to travelers and to the poor.

The biblical account—one of the great masterpieces of world literature—begins on "a day when the sons of God came to present themselves before the Lord, and Satan came also among them" (1:6). Asked whence he had come, SATAN replied, "From going to and fro in the earth . . . from walking up and down in it" (1:7). When God spoke in praise of his "servant Job . . . a perfect and an upright man; one that feareth God, and escheweth evil" (1:8), Satan replied that if Job's possessions were to be taken away, "he will curse thee to thy face" (1:11). God gave Satan permission to test Job: "Behold, all that he hath is in thy power; only upon himself put not forth thine hand" (1:12).

News soon came to Job that the Sabeans had seized his oxen and asses and had killed the servants who had been taking care of them; another messenger brought word that a fire had destroyed Job's sheep and the servants with them; immediately after came a report that the CHALDEANS had carried off his camels and slain the servants. The crowning blow was the death of all his children, killed when a house collapsed. Job mourned and prostrated himself and worshipped, "Naked came I out of my mother's womb, and naked shall I return thither: the Lord gave, and the Lord hath taken away; blessed be the name of the Lord" (1:21). The next time the "sons of God" (2:1) assembled, Satan told God that Job had remained steadfast because his own person had not been harmed, but "touch his bone and his flesh, and he will curse thee to thy face" (2:5). Now given permission to afflict Job's body, so long as his life was spared, Satan smote Job "with sore boils from the sole of his foot unto his crown" (2:7; the disease has been interpreted as leprosy and as elephantiasis, but may have been a terrible skin infection of ulcerous boils common in the Middle East and known as "Baghdad button" or "Jericho rose"). At this point Job's wife said to him, "Dost thou still retain thine integrity? curse God, and die," to which Job answered, "What? shall we receive [accept] good at the hand of God, and shall we not receive evil?" (2:9-10). (Her role as temptress was not overlooked by St. Augustine and John Calvin, both of whom considered her a tool of the devil, and postbiblical rabbinical traditionalists made the point that Job, unlike ADAM, was not influenced by his wife.)

When his friends—ELIPHAZ, BILDAD, and ZOPHAR —heard what had befallen Job they came "to mourn with him and to comfort him" (2:11). Such was their sympathy and devotion that they sat silently beside him on the ground for seven days and nights, the traditional period of mourning for the dead but did not speak because comforters were not to do so until the bereaved chose to break the silence.

Job is often referred to as a man of patience—the phrase "the patience of Job" is proverbial—but the term does not fit him; furthermore, the term frequently causes the essential lesson of Job's travails to be overlooked. Actually he stormed and railed at his fate, complaining bitterly and sometimes almost blasphemously. His first words to his friends were: "Let the day perish wherein I was born . . . Why died I not from the womb?" (3:3,11). Job's outstanding characteristics were not patience and submissiveness, but a questioning spirit, moral courage, and uncompromising honesty—traits that are demonstrated in his subsequent conversations with the three comforters. His friends, drawing upon the only dogma they knew, offered him the stock religious answer of their day: that Job was being punished for his sins and that if he would repent and beg God for forgiveness, his suffering might be eased. They are the voices of orthodoxy. Eliphaz, the eldest of the three and the first speaker, may be said to represent the proof of authority; Bildad speaks on the basis of experience; and Zophar voices the fervor of religious conviction. Job, at first, dared not challenge the ancient and sacred tradition by protesting his innocence. Nevertheless, in his heart he knew that he was not guilty of evildoing, and he soon found himself unable to accept the bankrupt ideas of his age; eventually, he challenged them bluntly.

The ensuing intellectual confrontation develops in a series of three dialogues with each of his three friends. At the outset, the discussion is gracious and

Medieval illumination depicting Job appealing to the Lord (*New York Public Library*).

understanding: Eliphaz's first discourse is a marvel of tact. It is not long, however, before the three who had come in such devotion speak harsh and accusing words. Zophar angrily declares: "Know therefore that God exacteth of thee less than thine iniquity deserveth" (11:6), and Eliphaz asks Job: "Is not thy wickedness great? and thine iniquities infinite?" (22:5), ending with a series of wild accusations. The three friends are committed to the ancient doctrine of divine retribution: anything else is unthinkable to them, for it would mean that God is unjust. Job responds to their heartlessness and lack of understanding with increasing bitterness. He points out that God does not necessarily reward people according to their merit and that the wicked, in many cases, live long and happy lives. He, therefore, seeks to know the real reason why evil has come upon him, rejecting the easy answers he knows to be false.

At length he realizes that he must turn for answers to God Himself: "Oh that one would hear me! behold, my desire is, that the Almighty would answer me, and that mine adversary [God] had written a book" (31:35). When his friends charge that he is defaming God, Job replies that they are doing Him no service by speaking lies: "Will ye speak wickedly for God? and talk deceitfully for him? . . . Will ye contend for God? . . . He will surely reprove you, if ye do secretly [show partiality]" (13:7-10). This speech reveals Job's deep conviction that one must be honest with God. He is confident that God will have the faith in him that his friends do not: "Also now, behold, my witness is in heaven, and my record is on high" (16:19). Despite what has befallen him, he still trusts in God and counts on Him for vindication: "For I know that my redeemer liveth, and that he shall stand at the latter day upon the earth: And though after my skin worms destroy this body, yet in my flesh shall I see God" (19:25-26). At the last, a very self-confident young man, ELIHU, enters the conversation, impatient with Job for the position he has taken and with the three friends because they cannot cope with him. It turns out that Elihu has little that is new to say, his main contribution being the idea that the purpose of affliction may be disciplinary, a means of keeping man from pride and sin (36:8-11).

As Elihu speaks, a storm comes up, and Job is granted a THEOPHANY (one of the few such manifestations recorded in the Old Testament to take place in the daytime) and out of the storm God addresses Job. His first discourse—one of four—is considered one of the most sublime passages in the Scriptures (38:1 ff.). Its general statement is that man in his finity understands but little of God, whose power and works are beyond mortal ken. Job, reduced to silence by an awareness of his own ignorance of God, asks only to learn of Him: "Hear, I beseech thee, and I will speak: I will demand of thee, and declare thou unto me" (42:4). Then God vindicates Job, reprimanding the others for misrepresenting Him. He says to Eliphaz: "My wrath is kindled against thee, and against thy two friends: for ye have not spoken of me the thing that is right, as my servant Job hath" (42:7).

Job is restored to his former estate, not because he has been faithful or patient, but because he has spoken only the truth, even to the Almighty. (The Talmud says that his sufferings lasted twelve months; according to other noncanonical writings they lasted seven years.) Afterward God gave him twice as much as he had had before, including seven sons and three daughters (42:13), apparently considered the ideal number of children in ancient times. (Too many daughters were not looked on as a blessing, for they were additional mouths to feed and had to be provided with dowries before they could be married off; pagan Arabs often buried girl babies at birth.) Job's daughters were considered the most beautiful in the land and therefore it would be easy to find husbands for them. Also, he seems to have been advanced in his attitude toward girls; he "gave them inheritance among their brethren" (42:15), an act which was particularly notable when the sons were still living. Job lived another 140 years; thus he was able to see "his sons, and his sons' sons, even four generations" (42:16)—one generation more than the Patriarch JOSEPH (Gen. 50:23). Extrabiblical tradition claims that the entire world mourned when he died. In summation, Job is a symbol of the questing spirit, of man's lonely and often agonizing search for truth—which alone is acceptable to God in those who would worship Him. He was a man who maintained that he had a right to question and a right to doubt.

There is a wide difference of opinion as to the time in which Job was supposed to have lived, ranging from the PERIOD OF THE PATRIARCHY (about 2100-1550 B.C.) to the PERSIAN EMPIRE Period (about 539-333 B.C.), with the weight of opinion favoring the earlier dating. In the apocryphal appendix to the SEPTUAGINT, Job is identified with JOBAB, a king of MOAB who was a grandson of ESAU, the brother of JACOB, and therefore a great-great-grandson of ABRAHAM: according to this version Jacob's daughter DINAH became Job's second wife. Other traditions connect Job with JETHRO, the father-in-law of MOSES, and with the Mesopotamian prophet BALAAM, which would place him several hundred years later in the late thirteenth or early twelfth century B.C. According to this tradition, the Egyptian PHARAOH consulted the two on how to reduce the numbers of the Israelite population in EGYPT (prior to the EXODUS) and Job's suffering was in punishment for his silence regarding the intended genocide.

The early datings of these interpretations were undoubtedly influenced by the patriarchal setting of the story, which is presented in the Book of Job with a wealth of authentic detail and without lapses into anachronism. In this context, the ideas expressed by Job and his friends are of special interest, in that they reveal the religious concepts in the Patriarchal Period outside the family of Abraham and before the religious legislation of Moses during the PERIOD OF THE WILDERNESS. The religion mirrored in the book is a patriarchal form of worship, entirely domestic, with no PRIESTHOOD and little ritual besides sacrifices. God is represented as omnipotent, the master of all the forces of nature, revealing a practical MONOTHEISM. The book in no way indicates whether or not Job was a Jew, and there is considerable disagreement on this point. Some of the talmudists believed that he was a pious GENTILE, and certain of them specified that he was one of the prophets of the Gentiles. Others among the postbiblical rabbis placed Job among those who returned following the PERIOD OF THE BABYLONIAN CAPTIVITY (about 537 B.C.), obviously considering him an Israelite. Some modern scholars feel it is incredible that a Gentile would have been presented in that age as articulating such exalted concepts of God. Others maintain that a Gentile would have been especially selected for the story so as not to introduce the problem of departure from orthodoxy by a Jew.

There are three theories regarding the historicity of Job: that he was a real person, that his story is religious fiction, and that a character like Job, in all probability, lived but that details about him may be fictional. Early Christian scholars did not challenge the authenticity of the character. The traditional Christian view was later expressed by Martin Luther, who stated that while he believed Job's story to be true, he did not believe "that all took place just as it is written, but that an ingenious, pious, and learned man brought it into its present form." Many of the traditional rabbis took the same position, although most of them took it for granted that Job had really lived. The third-century A.D. scholar Rabbi Hananeel declared, "Job never existed: the book is a parable."

Literature of the ancient Near East contains a number of accounts of a righteous man of high estate who suffered greatly, showing that the character is rooted deep in antiquity: there may have been a historical personage behind the stories. A Sumerian poetic essay dating to about 2000 B.C. tells about a "righteous sufferer" and gives much the same answers to the theological questions as does the Book of Job. A similar character appears in an Accadian composition (about 1700 B.C.) but may be derived from a still more ancient source. A long epic poem from Ugarit recounts the tale of a king named Keret who suffered a series of catastrophes similar to Job's, was eventually restored to his position, and acquired a new wife and family. Another Mesopotamian literary work, widely known as the "Babylonian Job," reveals many parallels to the biblical story.

Another theory that has emerged claims that Job is based on characters in Greek drama. As far back as the fourth century A.D., Theodore of Mopsuestia, a leading teacher of the ancient Church, saw a relationship between Job and certain figures in the Homeric epics. Some scholars find a similarity between Job and the Prometheus of Greek mythology. On the other hand, there is a school of thought that looks on Job as a symbolic figure representing ISRAEL, like the "suffering servant" in chapters 52-53 of the Book of the Prophet ISAIAH. These scholars regard Job as the earlier of the two symbolic characters. Opponents of the theory maintain that it is not likely that an EDOMITE (a member of a brother race but one which was deeply hated), as Job is held by some to have been, would have been selected as an Israelite symbol. BIBLICAL CRITICISM regards the hero of the Book of Job as a legendary figure. It does not consider it possible to ascribe any historic basis to his story, since no facts about him can be ascertained. It may be assumed, critics say, that the story originated in Edom, since that land remains as the background of the Old Testament version. Nevertheless, a number of traditions connect different locales and relics with the presence of Job. Not far south of JERUSALEM, near the junction of the VALLEY OF HINNOM and the VALLEY OF JEHOSHAPHAT, there is a deep well of sweet water that is known as the Well of Job (the modern-day Bir Ayub and the biblical EN-ROGEL [Josh. 15:7; 18:16; II Sam. 17:17; I Kings 1:9]). A stela of RAMESES II found at the Tel Sheikh Sa'ad about twenty-three miles east of the SEA OF GALILEE (identified as the site of the biblical CARNAIM) is known as the Job Stone because of the Arab tradition that connects the site with Job. St. John Chrysostom, the great fourth-century A.D. Church Father, noted a place in Arabia known as Job's dunghill to which he said pilgrims came from all ends of the earth.

A vast literature has grown up around the figure of Job and his spiritual struggle. He was prominent in early rabbinic literature and numerous legends cluster about his name, particularly with regard to his piety and hospitality. In modern times, the Swiss psychiatrist Carl Jung (1875-1961) felt impelled to write his own "reply" to Job in *Antwort auf Job*. The Prologue to *Faust*, the masterwork of Johann Wolfgang von Goethe (1749-1832), was taken from the Book of Job. A play, *The Masque of Reason,* by Robert Frost (1875-1963), is a witty, ironic version of Job, and Archibald MacLeish (1892-   ) gave a modern treatment of the Job story in his drama *J.B.,* which was produced on Broadway in 1958.

Numerous artists also have found inspiration in Job. He is the subject of a stone relief on the Cathedral of Chartres, a series of six frescoes by Francesco da Voltero (c. A.D. 1370), and a sculpture by the Florentine artist Donato di Donatello (1386-1466). Jean Fouquet (c. 1415-1480) depicted Job's life in a group of glowing miniatures, and *Job and His Wife* are seen in a painting by Albrecht Dürer (1471-1528).

The three friends of Job attempt to reason with him in his affliction (*Counsel Collection*).

JOB 1647

A drawing by Rembrandt van Rijn (1606-1669) shows *Job Conversing with His Friends,* and in his *Vision of the Book of Job,* William Blake (1757-1827) executed a complete set of engravings illustrating the life of Job.

Among contemporary artists, Léon Bonnat (1833-1922), Yehuda Epstein (1870-   ), and Max Liebermann (1847-1935) have painted Job. In Frankfurt, Germany, there stands a statue of *Job* by the German sculptor Gerhard Marcks (1889-   ), erected in 1957 as a memorial to victims of Nazi concentration camps. Among musical works inspired by Job are oratorios by the late nineteenth-century English composer Sir Charles Hubert Hastings Perry and by the American Frederick Shepherd Converse (1871-1940).

H.G.G.

JOB, THE BOOK OF, eighteenth book of the OLD TESTAMENT in the KING JAMES VERSION; it tells the story of a wealthy man of exemplary piety and righteous conduct who suffered a series of catastrophes in which he lost his family, his property, and his health (*see preceding entry*). The book consists of forty-two chapters (1,065 verses) including a prologue and an epilogue. In the Hebrew Scriptures it is placed in the HAGIOGRAPHA, between the books of PSALMS and PROVERBS (*see* CANON OF THE OLD TESTAMENT). Job falls into five parts of unequal length: the Prologue (chapters one and two), the Dialogues (chapters 3-31), the ELIHU speeches (chapters 32-37), the THEOPHANY (chapters 38-42:6), and the Epilogue (42:7-17). The Prologue describes Job's prosperity and how he came to be visited by calamity. The Epilogue recounts his restoration to health and his former high estate. The Dialogue in between, which takes place among Job and the three friends who have come to comfort him in his distress (ELIPHAZ, BILDAD, and ZOPHAR) is the heart of the book; the Elihu speeches add little to the insights, and the theophany (wherein GOD confronts Job) brings about the denouement of the story.

The discussion, which unfolds in a series of three dialogues with each of the three friends, formulates the issue clearly. The text addresses itself to the eternal mystery of undeserved human suffering in a universe that is supposed to be ruled by a just God. Why is there human suffering, it asks. The traditional answer to the question in ancient times was provided by the doctrine of divine retribution. Misfortune was held to be God's punishment of evil, and good fortune His reward of virtue. The hero of the Book of Job, however, was pictured as pious and righteous beyond question, a man who was careful not to sin, even inadvertently. When calamity befell such a person, the stock answer no longer applied; another answer had to be found. Job's three friends, accepting without question the religious dogma of their day, took it for granted that he had sinned; it remained for Job, who alone knew otherwise, to seek another explanation.

The dialogues with the three comforters brilliantly depict Job's intellectual and spiritual progress as he rejects the false answers and searches for the truth (although this progress is not to be taken as a rejection of all orthodoxy). The discussion proceeds logically through various stages of reasoning, with rich elaborations and skillful transitions as Job's moods and understanding change. His friends find themselves unable to refute his arguments, and an observer named Elihu accomplishes little more. There remains only one source for an answer, God Himself ——and it is to the Almighty that Job now makes his appeal. God appears in an awesome storm (the theophany) and speaks to Job in a group of four discourses, the first of which is universally acknowledged to be one of the literary masterpieces of all time. It points out the vastness of God's power and the finitude of man's understanding thereof. In the Epilogue, God vindicates Job and reprimands the three would-be comforters for their thoughtless parroting of outworn and untrue concepts of Him.

No other answers are given to the basic theological problem posed in the book, because the author did not know them and was too honest to contrive comfortable and convenient solutions. He left the problem where he found it, having accomplished his goal of dispelling the false dogma that had closed people's minds to further searching. His faith nonetheless undiminished, the writer retained his belief (as does Job) in an omniscient and just Deity, recognizing the human inability to fathom the divine purpose. The door has been opened to freedom of thought, and to future growth and understanding. And while the Book of Job may not answer all questions about the existence of suffering, it tells man how to receive it and how to triumph over it.

It presents a number of ideas that were new to people of ancient times and is a milestone in religious thought. The first new idea is that God does not apportion good and bad fortune in accordance with

JOB, THE BOOK OF 1649

Job reproved by his friends, who attempt to shake his faith (Counsel Collection).

human behavior: the events in a man's life are not a reflection of God's will. This important reversal in thinking makes it incumbent upon man to do good for its own sake, rather than for personal gain. It keeps the fortunate individual from becoming self-satisfied and complacent about his own virtue and the unlucky one from being automatically branded a wrongdoer who is deserving of his fate. It takes away the sense of guilt that must otherwise oppress anyone whose life does not go well.

Job is so advanced in its thinking that many people have not yet been able to accept its conclusions, but cling to a belief in a system of divine punishment and reward. Yet, it has continued to engage men's minds and hearts, perhaps the main argument for its acceptance into the Old Testament Canon. (Only the Syrian theologian Theodore of Mopsuestia challenged its inclusion.) The Book of Job also teaches that man has a right to question even God, so long as his purpose is truth. Absolute honesty is necessary to all relationships, it says, and especially that between God and man. And no one should admit to sins he has not committed in order to placate the Lord. Job was right in insisting, "Till I die I will not remove mine integrity from me. My righteousness I hold fast, and will not let it go: my heart shall not reproach me so long as I live" (27:5-6). Furthermore, people should be patient and understanding of words uttered in pain, even as God was with Job's.

Some commentators have seen in the text the doctrine of vicarious ATONEMENT, whereby an innocent person suffers for the sake of others as the "suffering servant" of the Book of the Prophet ISAIAH, who "bare the sin of many, and made intercession for the transgressors" (53:12).

The modern-day scholar J. H. Rowley sees in the testing of Job not an idle wager but the testing of the mutual faith of God and man. Many scholars regard the main object of the book as the showing of the effect of the most terrible adversity on a truly religious spirit. An even bigger overall purpose is sensed by others: not just illumination of the problem of undeserved suffering, but of suffering in general. Suffering is in the natural order of things: pain, loss, injustice, and death are part of the cycle of living. The lot of mortal man is sorrowful at best, they realize: the Book of Job is a tragedy because life is tragic.

The language of the text shows great antiquity. It is closer to the Arabic than is any other Hebrew work. It also reveals a strong Aramaic influence in its vocabulary and grammatical forms, which are characteristic of the antique style. (*See also* POETRY OF THE BIBLE.) It contains more rare words and words that are used only once than does any other biblical book. It has been suggested that the book may have been drawn from other SEMITIC languages. The many idiosyncrasies of the Hebrew text have led some scholars to speculate that the language may be Edomite (a closely related Semitic language) and the author an EDOMITE rather than an Israelite. (*See also* LANGUAGES OF THE BIBLE.) The Edomite setting of the book (indicated in Job's residence, "the land of Uz" [1:1] and in the home of Eliphaz, TEMAN) encourage this view. Edomite and Hebrew were both variations of the CANAANITE language and hence very similar. Some scholars, including the medieval Jewish commentator Abraham Ibn Ezra, have theorized that the book may originally have been written in another language, perhaps Arabic, although this idea is considered highly improbable. The contemporary Israeli scholar N. H. Tur-Sinai holds the view that the original was a sixth-century B.C. Babylonian dialect of Aramaic and that only the more difficult phrases were translated some generations later for the benefit of the Israelite reader. Despite the ingenious details of the theory, it has not been widely accepted.

The entire Book of Job has an archaic grandeur, and many portions of it are correspondingly obscure and difficult. The Greek version, in the SEPTUAGINT, occasionally sheds light on the text but more often complicates a problem. It is four hundred lines shorter than the original Hebrew version and the gaps in the text increase the difficulties. The *Peshitta* (*see* BIBLE, SYRIAC VERSION), which was taken directly from the Hebrew, clarifies some Hebrew terms but little of the text. The Targum (the Aramaic paraphrase of the Old Testament) does not solve textual problems. (*See also* BIBLE, ARAMAIC VERSIONS.) Theological bias on the part of the translators (whether Greek, Massorete, or English) has compounded the problem. The Latin version, or VULGATE, while sometimes literal, is occasionally very free in translation, and hence cannot serve as a basis for correcting the Hebrew. The MASSORETIC TEXT (the traditional Hebrew version), although frequently corrupt or obscure, remains the chief source. The text obviously has been tampered with, has suffered in transmission, and leaves whole passages incomplete.

The form of the Book of Job has defied classification beyond its inclusion in the WISDOM LITERATURE. It draws on various elements of biblical literature—narrative, proverb, hymn, lament, and oracle—and on the dialogue of Babylonian theodicy and of western Semitic fables or Contest Literature. It has been called, among other things, an allegory, an epic, a tragedy, a religious tractate, and a dramatic poem. It is considered one of the two earliest Hebrew dramas, the other being the SONG OF SOLOMON. The American educator Horace M. Kallen in *The Book of Job as a Greek Tragedy* (1918) presents the biblical work in what he believes was its original form—as a drama in the style of the Greek dramatist Euripides, complete with Greek choruses and *deus ex machina* (the theophany). The choruses accommodate four disputed passages that have otherwise been considered extraneous by some biblical critics (*see* BIBLICAL CRITICISM). The poetry has a free rhythm without a rigid metrical pattern and without rhyme, and is marked by the parallelism characteristic of Hebrew poetry, in this case usually synonymous parallelism. The brevity and terseness of the original have not been matched in the English translation.

The work represents a mature stage of literary culture, and is more finished and powerful than even DEUTERO-ISAIAH (Isa. 40-66). Regarded merely as literature, it is a foremost expression of the Hebraic genius. The highly individual form of the book probably evolved out of a combination of sources. The first, critics say, is an ancient folktale that came down to the Israelites from MESOPOTAMIAN and western Semitic literature and that is retained in the Prologue and Epilogue of the biblical work. This portion, which contains many antique concepts, is written in an epic prose style that has its own poetic quality. It refers to God by the Hebrew designation YHWH (sometimes vocalized as YAHWEH), which it naively puts into the mouths of the Edomite characters.

The Dialogue, by contrast, is poetry. In it the Deity is spoken of as *El, Eloah,* or ELOHIM (forms of the Hebrew word for God) and as SHADDAI (Al-

Job after he has been restored to prosperity by the Lord.

mighty), a usage that goes back to the PERIOD OF THE PATRIARCHY. Whereas the Prologue is detached and impersonal, the Dialogue is emotional and highly personal. A different authorship is therefore ascribed to these two portions, although even this point of view is contested: some scholars maintain that the author devised the Prologue and Epilogue as an antique setting for his poetic work. The ancient part, whether transmitted orally or in writings, was probably fixed in form and content. The Dialogue, which may be the Israelite conribution to the work, was written at a much later date.

The TALMUD ascribed authorship of the Book of Job to MOSES (late thirteenth century B.C.). Most modern scholars assume that it is not the writing of one man but a composite work that has gone through many hands. The Dialogue, however, has a uniform style and a literary quality that bear the stamp of a single author. The writer, despite his stature, is entirely unknown to us, and his identity will probably never be ascertained. There is no proof that he was an Israelite: the forms he used were typical not only of the Old Testament but of other literature of the ancient Near East, and the theme was one which had for centuries occupied the attention of the peoples in that part of the world.

Although the setting seems to reflect PALESTINE, it may have been consistent also with other lands.

Job surrounded by the children born to him after the end of his adversity (*Tissot, Brooklyn Museum*).

Many scholars consider it impossible for work of such religious breadth, loftiness of the doctrine of God, and highly developed concepts of morality to have emerged from any ancient people but Israel; moreover, they assume that it must have been the product of a later period when Israel had attained the spiritual heights for which it was to be remembered. Yechezkel Kauffman, insisting that the work is entirely Israelite, maintains that it is classical Hebrew at its best, that it was composed before the PERIOD OF THE BABYLONIAN CAPTIVITY (tenth century B.C.), and that its author deliberately used an antique literary style.

Whatever the case, the writer reveals a familiarity with world literature of that time and with mythologies of the countries outside Israel. He came under strong Aramaicizing influences and may have lived near Aramaic- or Arabic-speaking peoples, perhaps in the far southeast of Palestine (Cheyne). He was cultured, well-traveled, and cosmopolitan—a member of the intellectual elite. He is seen clearly as a teacher, a *hacham* (scholar or wise man) in the Hebraic tradition. Such knowledge of EGYPT is demonstrated in the book that some commentators have thought he must be Egyptian; however, the information in the Egyptian references was known in the land of Israel.

The period in which the author lived is as much a mystery as his birthplace. The consistent patriarchal setting suggests great antiquity. Parallels to the story and the character of Job are found in the literature of almost every ancient Mesopotamian and western Semitic people: the literary roots of the story go back to 2000 B.C. The early rabbis placed the Book anywhere from the Period of the Patriarchy (eighteenth century B.C.) to the fourth century B.C. Early Christian scholars also considered it very ancient, the ancient Greek historian Eusebius placing it before the time of Moses, and the fourth-century A.D. Cappadocian theologian Saint Gregory of Nazianzus setting it in the time of King SOLOMON (late tenth century B.C.). Those who argue for an early date cite the book's failure to reflect any awareness or influence whatsoever of the MOSAIC LAW or of the EXODUS from Egypt—the major influences in Jewish life and thought after the twelfth century B.C.

The style of the writing is as antique in its stark grandeur as that of the PENTATEUCH itself. The gathering of "the sons of God" (1:6), a holdover from the pagan pantheon of gods, the naive view of God, a theophany in the full light of day, and the extremely old age to which Job is supposed to have lived (42:16) all give the book the stamp of the remote past. In every detail of life and customs, of setting and atmosphere, in all of its allusions, the book accurately mirrors the period between the Patriarch ABRAHAM and Moses. Nonetheless, most informed opinion today inclines toward a later dating, the authenticity of the Patriarchal background being attributed to the skill and scholarship of the author. Some scholars think that the poem reflects not only personal adversity but a national disaster; certain passages (3:20, 7:1, 9:24, 12:6, 24:12) suggest to them widespread misery and havoc. The calamities wrought upon Israel by the ASSYRIAN EMPIRE in the late eighth century B.C. or by the NEO-BABYLONIAN EMPIRE in the sixth century B.C. could explain such references. W. F. Albright considers it likely that the author lived in the sixth or fifth century B.C., that he wrote the book in Hebrew, and that he was familiar with ancient pagan literature.

Because of certain similarities in theme between this book and the later chapters of the Book of the Prophet ISAIAH, some scholars have seen an affinity between the author of Job and Deutero-Isaiah (Isa. 40-66), both of them anonymous poets of the highest rank. Still, the figure of Job is generally conceded to have preceded the "suffering servant" of the Isaiah text. Some commentators note a remarkable similarity between Job's curse of the day of his birth (3:3-10) and a lament of the Prophet JEREMIAH (Jer. 20:14-18), who lived in the seventh and sixth centuries B.C. Nonetheless, the author of Job had more literary power than Jeremiah. Some critics say that the SATAN concept shows Persian influence (about mid-sixth to mid-fourth centuries B.C.).

If the author was an Israelite living in the sixth or fifth century B.C., it is hard to understand how his work would not have in some way reflected the great national revival that took place with the restoration of the Jewish nation (JUDAEA) and the end of the Babylonian Captivity (about 537 B.C.). The selection of an Edomite as the hero of the book is also inconceivable after the fall of JERUSALEM to NEBUCHADNEZZAR in 586 B.C.: the gloating of the Edomites over the destruction of the TEMPLE and the fall of the Southern KINGDOM OF JUDAH, as well as the advantage they took of those tragic circumstances, earned them Israel's undying hatred. Some critics assume the date to be a considerable time after the Captivity —possibly the fifth or even the fourth century B.C. On the other hand, many scholars contend that the various relics of archaism bespeak a preexilic date.

Portions of the book were found among the DEAD SEA SCROLLS discovered at QUMRAN, showing that the work was in circulation before the first century B.C. The wide range of views testifies to the inconclusiveness of all the arguments. With all this, the unity of the Dialogue is not seriously questioned: the consistency of style, language, and viewpoint all point to one author. A few portions are viewed as doubtful by some critics. The poem on Wisdom (chapter twenty-eight, one of the finest in the Old Testament), is regarded as extraneous to the context of the argument, but its style and language are so similar to that of the rest of the book that it is sometimes judged to be a separate work by the same author.

Many critics look on the Elihu speeches (chapters 32-37) as interpolations, for they seem to add little either as literature or as religious thought. They also contain more Aramaicisms than the rest of the book. It is considered significant by many that Elihu is completely disregarded in the Epilogue, which winds up the action, although the three friends are mentioned. Yet such is the diversity of opinion regarding the Book of Job that others consider the Elihu speeches the climax of the Dialogue and the best statement of the problem of evil. In any event, the passages have been added with such skill as to give every appearance of unity. There are those who doubt the authenticity of God's second discourse, claiming that it does not meet the lofty standards set by the first. The majority of scholars accept both, excluding only one passage (40:15-41:34) whose florid language suggests that it is a later addition.

The Book of Job has given us memorable lines and passages of piercing beauty. Many troubled and bereaved souls have echoed the words, "Naked came I out of my mother's womb, and naked shall I return . . . : the Lord gave, and the Lord hath taken away; blessed be the name of the Lord" (1:21). Much quoted and discussed is Job's cry of faith: "Though he slay me, yet will I trust in him" (13:15). Equally famous

1654 THE FAMILY BIBLE ENCYCLOPEDIA

Job in his deep affliction, after all that he treasured has been lost (*Counsel Collection*).

JOB, THE BOOK OF 1655

is the brooding passage that opens: "Man that is born of a woman is of few days, and full of trouble. He cometh forth like a flower, and is cut down: he fleeth also as a shadow, and continueth not" (14:1-2). The passage beginning "I know that my redeemer liveth..." (19:25), the theme of the great aria in Handel's oratorio *The Messiah,* speaks to all men of faith. And God's words to Job in his first discourse are a rallying cry to mankind: "Deck thyself now with majesty and excellency; and array thyself with glory and beauty" (40:10). Its last line is a prescription, a philosophy, a challenge, and a summons to action: "Then will I also confess unto thee that thine own right hand can save thee" (40:14). The Talmud records that before YOM KIPPUR (the DAY OF ATONEMENT) the Book of Job was read by the HIGH PRIEST as a diversion. To dream about Job was considered an omen of bad luck.

Following is a chapter by chapter capsule analysis of the Book of Job:

Chapter 1 (22 verses): the piety of Job; Satan obtains leave to tempt him.

Chapter 2 (13 verses): the affliction of Job; the visit of his three friends.

Chapter 3 (26 verses): Job curses the day he was born.

Chapter 4 (21 verses): Eliphaz declares that the end of the wicked is misery.

Chapter 5 (27 verses): Job is told to confess his sins and ask God for forgiveness.

Chapter 6 (30 verses): Job asks wherein he has erred.

Medieval painting showing the massacre of Job's children (*New York Public Library*).

Job's wife, who is unable to accept her husband's compliance with the Lord's will (*Counsel Collection*).

Chapter 7 (21 verses): Job reproves his friends for their unkindness.

Chapter 8 (22 verses): Bildad explains God's justice—let Job turn to Him.

Chapter 9 (35 verses): Job asks how man can be just before almighty God.

Chapter 10 (22 verses): Job expostulates with God.

Chapter 11 (20 verses): Zophar reproves Job—let him put evil from him.

Chapter 12 (25 verses): Job declares that God raises up and God casts down.

Chapter 13 (28 verses): Job professes his confidence in God.

Chapter 14 (22 verses): Job speaks of the shortness and trouble of human existence.

Chapter 15 (35 verses): Eliphaz reproves Job severely; a picture of the evil conscience.

Chapter 16 (22 verses): Job appeals to God for answers.

Chapter 17 (16 verses): Job's misery and anguish.

Chapter 18 (21 verses): Bildad recounts the fate of the wicked.

JOB, THE BOOK OF 1657

Chapter 19 (29 verses): Job expresses his great misery and appeals for pity.

Chapter 20 (29 verses): Zophar describes the portion of the wicked.

Chapter 21 (34 verses): Job reminds him that often the wicked prosper in their lives and die in peace.

Chapter 22 (30 verses): Eliphaz accuses Job of many sins and urges him to return to God.

Chapter 23 (17 verses): Job longs for vindication from God.

Chapter 24 (25 verses): Job points out that the wicked, though they flaunt their wickedness, often go unpunished.

Chapter 25 (6 verses): Bildad declares that man is impure.

Chapter 26 (14 verses): Job reproves Bildad and speaks of God's greatness.

Chapter 27 (23 verses): Job will not renounce his integrity.

Chapter 28 (28 verses): Job speaks of wisdom, an excellent gift of God.

Chapter 29 (25 verses): Job remembers God's former kindness to him when he had the respect of others.

Chapter 30 (31 verses): Job describes his afflictions; the prospect of death.

Chapter 31 (40 verses): Job solemnly protests his integrity; he reviews the deeds of his life.

Chapter 32 (22 verses): Elihu angrily attempts to refute Job.

Chapter 33 (33 verses): Elihu declares that the purpose of affliction is discipline.

Chapter 34 (37 verses): God omnipotent cannot be wrong or unjust.

Chapter 35 (16 verses): Elihu states that righteousness benefits a man.

Chapter 36 (33 verses): Calamity is a warning from God that man should repent.

Chapter 37 (24 verses): God's wisdom is unsearchable; a storm begins to rise.

Chapter 38 (41 verses): God appears in a whirlwind, shows Job that man is ignorant and finite.

Chapter 39 (30 verses): God speaks of His wonders, revealed in nature and creation.

Chapter 40 (24 verses): Job replies with humility; and marvels of God's creation.

Chapter 41 (34 verses): Man's weakness and ignorance compared with the greatness of God.

Chapter 42 (17 verses): Job, repentant, asks to know more of God; God reprimands the three comforters; Job is restored to health and fortune. *H.G.G.*

THE STORY OF JOB

For Younger Readers

Job, an Old Testament hero, was an eastern chieftain of high rank. He owned seven thousand sheep, three thousand camels, five hundred yoke of oxen, and five hundred she-asses.

He was a devoted father. He had seven sons and three daughters who respected and loved him. On Job's birthday, they always gave a feast in his honor.

One day God praised Job to Satan, saying that Job was a perfect man. Satan replied that if God took Job's possessions away, Job would curse God to His face. So God gave Satan permission to test Job.

Soon afterward, a messenger ran up to Job. "The Sabeans have carried off your oxen and slain the herdsman," he cried. "I am the only one who has escaped to tell you."

Before he finished speaking, another messenger came. "The Chaldeans have seized your camels and killed the men who were tending them," he said. "I am the only one who has escaped to tell you."

As he spoke, a third messenger came hurrying. "While your sons and daughters were eating together in the home of your eldest son, a mighty wind blew from the desert and struck the house. It fell upon your children and they are all dead."

"And Job spake and said, Let the day perish wherein I was born . . ." (Job 3:2-3).

Job was filled with sorrow. He tore his cloak and cut his hair, which in those days was a sign of mourning. But he said nothing against God.

Satan told God that if Job himself were hurt, he would curse God. So God let Satan afflict Job with painful boils all over his body. Even then, Job did not speak against God.

But Job's wife was bitter. She told Job to curse God. Then he would die and be rid of his pain. But Job scolded her for being a foolish woman. "We accept good things from God," he said. "Why should we not accept evil things?"

Three of Job's friends, Eliphas, Bildad, and Zophar, heard what had happened and came to comfort Job. For seven days and nights they sat with him on the ground. As was the custom, they waited for Job to speak first. At last he cried out that he did not understand why he was being punished. He wished he had never been born, and he wanted to die.

He and his friends began to argue at great length about the ways of God. Eliphas said that God was making Job suffer for his sins and that God wanted him to repent. Zophar said that his sufferings would not only take Job's sins away but would stop him from sinning again. At times both Eliphas and Zophar said things about God that were not correct.

Then Job spoke directly to God, begging Him to explain why he was being punished so harshly. But God did not explain. Instead, He reminded Job that He was the Almighty, the Creator, whom men must not question.

Job replied humbly, "Though I have spoken once, I will not do so again."

God rebuked Eliphas and Zophar for the wrong things they had said. But He was pleased with Job and gave Him twice as much as he had had before. He blessed Job with a second family of seven sons and three daughters. Job lived to see his grandchildren and his great-grandchildren and did not die until he was one hundred and forty years old.

JOBAB (Heb., *yovav*, "scream loudly" or "howl"), a king of MADON; during the PERIOD OF THE CONQUEST AND JUDGES, he joined forces with other monarchs in CANAAN in an effort to annihilate the Israelites; at the WATERS OF MEROM his forces were defeated, his chariots were burned, and he was slain (Josh. 11:1-9; 12:19). Another Jobab was a descendant of SHEM (Gen. 10:29; I Chron. 1:23), and a third was a king of EDOM (Gen. 36:33; I Chron. 1:44). Also named Jobab were two men of the TRIBE OF BENJAMIN (I Chron. 8:9, 8:18, respectively).

JOCHEBED (Heb., *yokhevedh*, "the Lord is glorified"), the mother of MOSES, AARON, and MIRIAM (Exod. 6:20; Num. 26:59); she married her nephew AMRAM, the son of her brother KOHATH. The appositive phrase "daughter of Levi" (Num. 26:59) does not mean that she was a daughter of LEVI but rather that she was a woman of the tribe of which Levi was the eponym; since Amram was also of the TRIBE OF LEVI, Moses' descent from Levi was a collateral one.

JOD, the tenth letter of the Hebrew alphabet; as such, it is used to introduce the tenth section of Psalm 119, every verse of which, in the original Hebrew text of the Book of PSALMS, begins with this letter.

JODA (Gr. from the Heb. *yehudah*, "Judah"), in the APOCRYPHA one of the LEVITES who returned to JERUSALEM with ZOROBABEL following the PERIOD OF THE BABYLONIAN CAPTIVITY; he supervised the rebuilding of the TEMPLE (I Esd. 5:58).

JOED (Heb., *yoedh*, "the Lord witnessed"), a member of the TRIBE OF BENJAMIN, mentioned only in the Book of NEHEMIAH (11:7).

JOEL (Heb., *Yael,* "the Lord is God"), second of the twelve Minor PROPHETS according to their order in the CANON OF THE OLD TESTAMENT and the presumed author of the Book of JOEL (*see following entry*); nothing is known about him other than that he was born in the Southern KINGDOM OF JUDAH and lived in the capital city of JERUSALEM, at least during the years that he preached. Even the dates of his ministry are not certain; it has been estimated that he preached either before 800 B.C., since he makes no mention of the Assyrian invasion of the Kingdom of Judah, or after 500 B.C., as he makes no mention of the Babylonian domination or of NEBUCHADNEZZAR. His interest in the TEMPLE and in religious ritual has led some scholars to suggest that he was a member of the PRIESTHOOD but, even in that conjecture, there are no grounds for certainty. Unlike the other Prophets, Joel was not concerned with political matters, but

The Prophet Joel, as depicted by Michelangelo on the Sistine Chapel ceiling (*New York Public Library*).

rather with foretelling natural disasters such as a devastating plague of locusts. (Some scholars, however, consider the locusts to be a symbolic reference to an attack by Assyria or SCYTHIA.) Joel is one of the Prophets portrayed in the powerful sculpture *The Well of Moses,* by the Flemish artist Claus Sluter, and *The Frieze of the Prophets,* by the American painter John Singer Sargent.

The name "Joel" is a fairly common one in the OLD TESTAMENT among the other Joels are: an ancestor of SAMUEL (I Chron. 6:36); the first son of Samuel (I Sam. 8:2); a prince of the TRIBE OF SIMEON (I Chron. 4:35); a chief of the TRIBE OF REUBEN (I Chron. 5:4); a chief of the TRIBE OF ISSACHAR (I Chron. 7:3); an overseer of the TRIBE OF BENJAMIN (Neh. 11:9); one of the LEVITES who aided King DAVID in carrying the ARK OF THE COVENANT up to JERUSALEM (I Chron. 15:7); a soldier in the army of David (I Chron. 11:38); one of David's officers (I Chron. 27:20); and a man who married a foreign wife during the PERIOD OF THE BABYLONIAN CAPTIVITY (Ezra 10:43). (*See also* JUEL and UEL.) H.G.G.

JOEL, THE BOOK OF, twenty-ninth book of the OLD TESTAMENT in the KING JAMES VERSION, and the second book of the Minor Prophets in the Hebrew Scriptures (*see* CANON OF THE OLD TESTAMENT); it consists of the surviving chapters of the writings of the Prophet Joel (*see preceding entry*). Composed of three chapters (73 verses), it can be divided into two parts: chapters 1:1-2:17 and chapters 2:18-3:21. The first part, addressed to the elders of the Southern KINGDOM OF JUDAH, predicts a terrible visitation of LOCUSTS (1:2-7) and a FAMINE which will bring misery to the land (1:10-12; 16:20); the Prophet sees this double affliction as ushering in the DAY OF THE LORD (1:15) unless the people are truly repentant of their misdeeds, and he exhorts them to fast, weep, and mourn, and to "rend your heart, and not your garments" (2:13).

The second part, which is generally considered APOCALYPTIC LITERATURE, describes how the people, by obeying the Prophet's injunctions, avoid the disaster. GOD answers their prayers (2:19 ff.); He will bring relief from famine through abundant rain and fruitfulness of the land. (The words "I will pour out my spirit upon all flesh" [2:28] sound a note of universality.) The land will be filled with the prophetic spirit: "And your sons and your daughters shall prophesy, your old men shall dream dreams, your young men shall see visions" (2:28). There will be terrifying portents of the Day of the Lord—"blood, and fire, and pillars of smoke" (2:30). All nations will be gathered into the VALLEY OF JEHOSHAPHAT, where the enemies of the Jewish people (3:2-5) will meet their retribution (3:5-8): "Multitudes, multitudes, in the valley of decision . . ." (3:14). It will do them no good to "prepare war, wake up the mighty men . . ." (3:9).

With irony, Joel says to the other nations, "Beat your plowshares into swords, and your pruning hooks into spears" (3:10)—a reversal of the famous "and they shall beat their swords into plowshares" passage found in the books of ISAIAH (2:4) and MICAH (4:3). But it will be to no avail: God will sit in JUDGMENT on them all. "The Lord will be the hope of his people, and the strength of the children of Israel" (3:12-16). Judah will become fruitful and well-watered, whereas EGYPT and EDOM will be reduced to a wilderness (3:18-19).

Joel's magnificent picture of "the day of judgment" influenced later writings and was elaborated upon in legends indigenous to both JUDAISM and CHRISTIANITY.

The dating of the book presents numerous difficulties. Some scholars place it early in the reign of King JOASH of Judah, in the latter part of the ninth century B.C., mainly because neither the ASSYRIAN EMPIRE nor the BABYLONIAN EMPIRE is mentioned. Tradition favors the early date, as is seen by Joel's placement between the Prophets HOSEA and AMOS in "The Twelve," the Old Testament compilation of the works of the Minor Prophets. Others judge Joel to have lived a century later, during the reign of King JOSIAH.

Nevertheless, most modern scholars date the book around 444 B.C., after the canonization of the TORAH by EZRA, on the following grounds: that there is no mention of the Northern KINGDOM OF ISRAEL, which had been conquered by the Assyrians in 721 B.C.; that JERUSALEM, the capital of the Southern Kingdom, had long since fallen (3:17); that royalty (the Davidic monarchy) is not mentioned, whereas there is emphasis on the PRIESTHOOD and ritual; and that the book shows the influence of the other Literary Prophets. A number of scholars, medieval as well as modern, think it belongs to the PERSIAN EMPIRE period about one hundred years later, convinced, both from the pure literary style and from the contents of the Books, that Joel came some time between DEUTERO-ISAIAH (c. 538 B.C.) and Ezra, that is, around the time of the Prophet MALACHI (c. 460 B.C.). (It is to be noted that Malachi also speaks of a plague of locusts, drought, and crop failures [Mal. 3:9,11].)

Some critics argue that the first two chapters of Joel are preexilic (i.e., before the PERIOD OF THE BABYLONIAN CAPTIVITY, which began in 597 B.C.) and the last chapter, postexilic. It is true that the evidence supporting the early date is found mainly in the first two chapters, while indications of a later period occur in the last; yet most scholars do not challenge the unity of the book (although a few go so far as to maintain that it is a revision of an older work at a later time), and some of the most authoritative Jewish commentators (including Rashi and Kimchi) feel that there is not enough internal evidence to justify any conclusion.

Opinions on whether the locusts mentioned are to be taken literally or figuratively are as many and as varied; both interpretations present problems. Critical to the discussion is the word *ha-tsephoni,* literally "the northern one" (2:20), which some read as an allusion to Assyria. (The translation, "the northern army," in the King James Version, does not conform to the original Hebrew text.) Those who accept the early date usually choose the literal interpretation: they consider the description of the insects a faithful record of a plague of locusts, corroborated in every detail by travelers' accounts, both ancient and modern. On the other hand, opponents of this interpretation point out that locusts do not attack the country from the north, but from the southeast, whereas NEBUCHADNEZZAR as well as the SCYTHIANS did descend on Judah from the north. Those who prefer the postexilic date generally see the locusts as figurative. The early Church Fathers interpreted them as symbols of human lusts or of the enemies that attacked the reconstructed Jewish state. This latter view is upheld by the tenth-century scholar Jepheth ben Ali, the leading biblical commentator of the Karaites (an anti-Talmudic Jewish sect founded in Persia in A.D. 765), who interprets the four species of locusts as symbolizing the four invasions by hostile nations. Some scholars read "the northern one" as a reference to the wars of GOG AND MAGOG, which are supposed to usher in the Messianic era (*see* MESSIAH.)

The Book of Joel rates high as literature. It is smooth and polished in diction, elegant in its turn and use of language. It has a strong oratorical feeling, marked by vigorous language and vivid illustrations. The poetry is cited for its perfection of form and its originality of expression. The book contains numerous examples of literary parallelism, word play, and Oriental hyperbole. — H.G.G.

Tissot's concept of Joel (*Brooklyn Museum*).

JOELAH (Heb., *yoelah,* "let him help"), a brave warrior who joined DAVID at ZIKLAG; he opposed King SAUL, although both men were of the TRIBE OF BENJAMIN (I Chron. 12:7).

JOEZER (Heb., *yoetser,* "aided"), a warrior who joined DAVID at ZIKLAG; he opposed King SAUL, even though both men were of the TRIBE OF BENJAMIN (I Chron. 12:6).

JOGBEHAH (Heb., *yoghbehah,* "high" or "lofty"), a city of GILEAD, east of the JORDAN RIVER, which was allotted to the TRIBE OF GAD (Num. 32:35); the town, which has been identified with the present-day village of Judeihat about five miles northwest of the Jordanian capital of Amman, is also mentioned in the Book of JUDGES (8:11) in the pursuit by GIDEON of the MIDIANITES. (*See also* JUDGES OF ISRAEL.)

JOGLI (Heb., *yogli,* "exiled"), a member of the TRIBE OF DAN during the PERIOD OF THE WILDERNESS; his son BUKKI was one of the princes who helped MOSES divide the PROMISED LAND among the TWELVE TRIBES OF ISRAEL (Num. 34:22).

JOHA (Heb., *yocha,* "given life"), a minor member of the TRIBE OF BENJAMIN (I Chron. 8:16). Another Joha was one of "thirty mighty warriors" in the army of King DAVID (I Chron. 11:45).

JOHANAN (Heb., *yohanan,* "the Lord has been gracious" or "the Lord's mercy"), a name borne by eleven OLD TESTAMENT personages, of whom perhaps the most important from a historical point of view was the Johanan who was active during the brief governorship of GEDALIAH following the conquest of the Southern KINGDOM OF JUDAH by NEBUCHADNEZZAR in 586 B.C., and the ensuing PERIOD OF THE BABYLONIAN CAPTIVITY. After razing JERUSALEM and exiling the leading citizens of Judah, Nebuchadnezzar chose Gedaliah to be governor over the "remnant of Judah" (i.e., those who had been left behind after the deportation), with headquarters at MIZPAH (II Kings 25:23 ff.). As a captain serving Gedaliah, Johanan was in a position to learn of the plot against the governor's life being engineered by ISHMAEL (not to be confused with the firstborn son of ABRAHAM) who, being a descendant of King DAVID, hoped to overthrow the hegemony of Nebuchadnezzar and re-establish Judah as an independent kingdom. Johanan warned Gedaliah of the royalist plot, but Gedaliah paid him no heed, and when the governor was assassinated, Johanan tried to avenge his death (Jer. 40:13-14; 41:11-15). After the abortive royalist uprising, Nebuchadnezzar completed the destruction of Judah, and Johanan—against the advice of the Prophet JEREMIAH—was one of the leaders who led the remnant, including the unwilling Jeremiah, in flight to EGYPT.

Other biblical Johanans include: the eldest son of King JOSIAH, who appears to have died young, as there is only one reference to him (I Chron. 3:15); a descendant of King David (I Chron. 3:24); the father of AZARIAH, who was the HIGH PRIEST at JERUSALEM during the reign of King SOLOMON (I Chron. 6:10); two men (one of the TRIBE OF BENJAMIN, the other of the TRIBE OF GAD) who joined David at ZIKLAG during his period of outlawry (I Chron. 12:4; 12:12,14); a leader of the TRIBE OF EPHRAIM at the time of the destruction of the Northern KINGDOM OF ISRAEL in 721 B.C. by the ASSYRIAN EMPIRE (II Chron. 28:12); one of the men who accompanied EZRA back to Jerusalem following the Babylonian Captivity (Ezra 8:12); one of the AMMONITES who, during the royal governorship of NEHEMIAH, married a Jewess (Neh. 6:18); a High Priest during Nehemiah's time (Neh. 12:22); and the man in whose chamber Ezra mourned for the sin committed by those Jews who had married foreign women during the Captivity (Ezra 10:6). M.A.B.

JOHANNES, a Greek variant of *Yohanan* ("the Lord has been gracious" or "the Lord's mercy") found only in the APOCRYPHA to identify two OLD TESTAMENT personages: one of the Hebrews who married a foreign woman during the PERIOD OF THE BABYLONIAN CAPTIVITY (I Esd. 9:29; cf. Ezra 10:28, JEHOHANAN), and one of those who returned to JERUSALEM with EZRA (rendered ESDRAS [I Esd. 8:38; cf. Ezra 8:12, JOHANAN]).

JOHANNINE EPISTLES, a collective name for the twenty-third, twenty-fourth, and twenty-fifth books of the NEW TESTAMENT, the writing of which has been ascribed by tradition to JOHN, nominal author of the GOSPEL ACCORDING TO ST. JOHN and the REVELATION OF ST. JOHN THE DIVINE (*see below*).

JOHN (the Gr. form [*Ioannes*] of the Heb. *yehohanan,* "the Lord has been gracious"), a name borne by a number of personages in the APOCRYPHA and the NEW TESTAMENT. The name was popular among the MACCABEES (the most frequently used Hebrew variant being "Jonathan"). The father of MATTATHIAS OF MODIN was named John (I Macc. 2:1), as were two of the brothers of JUDAS MACCABEUS—JOHN MACCABEUS and JONATHAN MACCABEUS. A descendant of Mattathias and the first monarch of the HASMONAEAN DYNASTY (regnal name of the Maccabees in JUDAEA) was JOHN HYRCANUS. Also, a number of minor personages associated with the Maccabees bore the given name John, as recorded in the First and Second Books of the MACCABEES.

In the New Testament, with the exception of an otherwise unidentified member of a priestly family named John (Acts 4:6), all of the Johns are significant. JOHN THE APOSTLE, a son of ZEBEDEE and younger brother of the Apostle JAMES (also identified as the son of Zebedee) is credited in Christian tradition with being the author of five New Testament books: the JOHANNINE EPISTLES, the GOSPEL ACCORDING TO ST. JOHN, and the REVELATION OF ST. JOHN THE DIVINE. Tradition also identifies him with JOHN THE BELOVED DISCIPLE. If this tradition is correct, then John "The Elder," identified in the opening words of the Second and Third Epistles of John as author of those Johannine Epistles, and JOHN THE DIVINE (so called in the KING JAMES VERSION), nominal author of the Revelation of St. John the Divine, are the same person—John the Apostle.

JOHN THE BAPTIST is one of the New Testament's most colorful and important individuals. He spent his childhood in the wilderness of Judaea, emerging as a young man clothed in a camel's hair garment with a leather girdle, sustained by a diet of locusts and wild honey (Mark 1:6), "preaching the baptism of repentance for the remission of sins" (Luke 3:3). Accepted by CHRISTIANITY as the forerunner of JESUS CHRIST, John the Baptist had a large following of DISCIPLES, some of whom continued in his name following his death by beheading at the hands of HEROD AGRIPPA I, and some of whom joined the disciples of Jesus.

The nominal and traditional author of the GOSPEL ACCORDING TO ST. MARK had two names, as was a custom of the times. MARK was his Roman name, and John his Jewish name (Acts 12:12,25; 15:37); he is often referred to as John Mark. His first appearance is in JERUSALEM, where he apparently lived with his mother MARY (not to be confused with the mother of Jesus), in a home proposed by some interpreters as the scene of the LAST SUPPER. John Mark would have been a boy at the time, and may have witnessed some of the final events in the life of Jesus. Another interesting conjecture is that John Mark was the young man dressed in a linen cloth who was following Jesus, was grabbed by the authorities about to seize Jesus, and fled them naked, leaving the linen cloth (Mark 14:51-52). John Mark was an assistant to PAUL THE APOSTLE and BARNABAS on the First Missionary Journey to ANTIOCH (Acts 12-15) but left them at PERGA in PAMPHYLIA (Acts 13:13) and returned to Jerusalem; presumably he had some sort of quarrel with Paul, the effects of which were apparently not permanent (cf. Col. 4:10; Philem. 24).   G.Y.

JOHN, THE FIRST EPISTLE GENERAL OF, THE SECOND EPISTLE OF, THE THIRD EPISTLE OF, twenty-third, twenty-fourth, and twenty-fifth books of the NEW TESTAMENT, where they are usually reckoned among the CATHOLIC EPISTLES, that is, those canonical letters addressed to no particular church or individual (*see also* CANON OF THE NEW TESTAMENT). However, only the first of them falls unambiguously into this category; the other two do contain formal greetings, apparently to individuals. Both tradition and modern scholarship incline to attribute all three to the author of the GOSPEL ACCORDING TO ST. JOHN. But neither in this Gospel nor in these three epistles does the author ever identify himself, except as an anonymous "elder" (II John 1:1; III John 1:1), and there is no good reason to believe, as some commentators do, that he was the same person as the author of the REVELATION OF ST. JOHN THE DIVINE. If the authorship of the three Johannine epistles is a mystery, their purpose is reasonably clear: they are warnings against false teaching. Only I John is long enough to be called a sermon; neither of the others could have covered more than one sheet of papyrus, and they do in fact read like notes.

The opening of I John, however, is not at all like that of a letter; indeed, it seems more like a footnote to chapter one of the St. John Gospel. "That which was from the beginning . . . That which we have seen and heard declare we unto you, that ye also may have fellowship with us . . ." (I John 1:1-3; cf. John 1:1,14; 20:30-31). With these words, the author introduces his two main themes: that JESUS CHRIST was a real person; and that belief in Jesus is not complete unless it shows itself in love for one's fellow believers. Adoption of the first theme was made necessary, according to many commentators, by the prevalence of a first-century A.D. heretical sect called the Docetists (Gr., *dokein,* "seem"), who maintained that the earthly Christ was not truly human, but rather some kind of supernatural being who had borrowed a human body. Proponents of this heresy were thus able to claim that Christ had only *seemed* to suffer on the cross; the real Christ, being all-powerful, had already managed to evade his enemies. Docetism was a form of GNOSTICISM, a rather loose term used to denote any religion of the ROMAN EMPIRE that advocated a form of salvation based on secret knowledge (Gr., *gnosis*). Having acquired this knowledge, Gnostics tended to feel rather pleased with themselves; after all, they reasoned, with a passport to heaven in one's pocket, there was little to fear of an earthly nature. This was another trend that the author of I John was determined to oppose.

JOHN, THE EPISTLES OF

In contrast to the gloomy wisdom of the Gnostics, who saw this world and everything about it as basically evil, the author of I John brought a message of joy (1:4; some early texts have "our joy" in place of "your joy," but this makes little difference). "God is light"—that is, He is goodness, through and through. The Gnostics believed that, after being initiated into their sect, they could do no wrong. Christians, on the other hand, began by confessing their own sinfulness. They recognized that their own nature fell so far short of God's that it was only through being forgiven by Him, and by obeying His commandments, that they could gain knowledge of Him. All this was so familiar that the author apologized to his readers for reminding them of it (1:5-2:7).

Nevertheless, he continues, they seem to have forgotten Christ's "new commandment" that they love one another; to hate each other is to be in darkness, far removed from GOD (2:8-11; cf. John 13:34). The world is passing away; Christians should overcome earthly desires and obey God (2:12-17). At this point, the author voices his conviction that the world's last age has come. That is why so many Antichrists have appeared (2:18-19; I and II John are the only NEW TESTAMENT books in which the word ANTICHRIST is actually used, though there are obvious parallels in Mark 13:22 and Rev. 13:5-6). An Antichrist is someone who teaches that Jesus was not the Christ; such teachers, the author felt, Christians could do without. Instead, they should remember their vows, lest they be put to shame at Christ's SECOND COMING (2:20-29).

The rest of the epistle recapitulates and reinforces the same themes. Christians should give proof of their love for one another, just as Christ's sacrifice proved God's love for them (3:1-24, a passage of deep spiritual beauty). Preachers who deny Christ are not preachers of God's word (4:1-3). But those who accept Christ are God's own children; through the HOLY SPIRIT, God is in them and they in Him. Unlike the Gnostics, they have no reason to fear God: "perfect love casteth out fear" (4:4-18). Loving God is incompatible with hating one's fellow man (4:19-5:2). Only through belief in God and His son Jesus Christ can they overcome the world and enter into eternal life (5:3-13). (The following words should probably be deleted from 5:7-8, since they do not occur in the best manuscripts: ". . . in heaven, the Father, the Word, and the Holy Ghost: and these three are one. And there are three that bear witness in earth. . . .")

They can be confident that God will forgive any kind of SIN except the "sin unto death" (5:14-17). Apparently, the author was not sure whether real Christians should be considered capable of sin (5:18-19). The important fact, however, is that "the Son of God is come." The epistle concludes with a warning against idols, that is, against all the false teachings criticized above (5:20-21).

The first surviving reference to I John is in the writings of the second-century A.D. Church Father Irenaeus (about 125-202); the epistle was also known to the author of the Muratorian Canon (about A.D. 200). Both references suggest a date of composition well into the second century, which would certainly be consistent with the theory that the "many Antichrists" are Gnostic heretics. Of course, this rules out any of the TWELVE APOSTLES, including JOHN the son of ZEBEDEE, as author. But it could have been one of this John's DISCIPLES. Ancient tradition itself is confused on the subject. Thus an early Christian writer called Papias, a man of "very small intelligence," according to Eusebius, refers to a "presbyter John" who seems to be different from John the son of Zebedee, and whom Eusebius identifies with the author of Revelation (*History of the Church,* book 3, chapter 39).

More significant, perhaps, is a story that Eusebius' sources attribute to St. Polycarp. One day the Apostle John was about to take a bath in a public bathhouse when he was told that Cerinthus, a leading Gnostic heretic, was in the same building. He ran into the street, shouting to his friends: "Let's get out of here! If that heretic Cerinthus is inside, the building will probably fall down!" (*History of the Church,* book 3, chapter 28). With such a tradition of hostility to Gnosticism in John's circle, it would not be surprising if one of his disciples wrote the Johannine epistles. Perhaps that explains why both II and III John are attributed to "the elder" (presbyter), since there is little else distinctively Johannine about them.

In II John, this elder warns against the "many deceivers" who deny that "Jesus Christ is come in the flesh" (verse 7). Traveling preachers who bring a message like this should be shown the door. The conclusion of the epistle (verse 13) makes clear that the "elect lady" to whom it is addressed is really a church. It is curious that III John, which copies II John in many respects, should make precisely the opposite point. The epistle is ostensibly a note of thanks to one GAIUS, who has offered hospitality to certain visiting preachers after DIOTREPHES, apparently the head of Gaius' church, has declined to receive them. This alleged action of Diotrephes, "who loveth to have the preeminence among them," has often been used as evidence that the office of BISHOP was just beginning to emerge in this period and was meeting with some resistance. (*See also* CHURCH AND CHURCH GOVERNMENT.) However, the fact that "Gaius" was the ancient equivalent of "John Doe" makes one hesitate to take the epistle at face value. Perhaps, as one contemporary scholar has suggested, it was written by some pseudo-Johannine author expressly in order to counteract the effects of II John (Morton Enslin, *Literature of the Christian Movement,* New York, 1956, p. 350). Curiously, the chief importance of the Johannine epistles in Christian tradition is the authority they give to the Roman Catholic distinction between "venial" (that is, forgivable) and "mortal" sin (cf. I John 5:16-17).

J.M.B.E.

JOHN, THE GOSPEL ACCORDING TO ST., fourth book of the NEW TESTAMENT and last of the FOUR GOSPELS. According to a tradition preserved in the Muratorian Canon (*see* CANON OF THE NEW TESTAMENT), it was written by JOHN the son of ZEBEDEE (Mark 3:17), after ANDREW (John 1:40) had received a vision that John should write a Gospel and then hand it over to his friends to be edited. The most generally received form of the tradition is that it was written by John in his old age at EPHESUS (now a ruin about forty miles south of Smyrna, in Turkey), and that he also wrote the JOHANNINE EPISTLES and the REVELATION OF ST. JOHN THE DIVINE. He is also usually identified as the Disciple "whom Jesus loved" (John 13:23).

There is no strong evidence for any of this. Only the author of Revelation identifies himself as "John," and there is no apparent connection between this John and John the son of Zebedee. The author of II and III John identifies himself simply as "the elder," while both I John and the St. John Gospel are completely anonymous. (*See preceding entry.*) Ancient scholarly opinion provides no answers. In addition to the tomb of John the Apostle there appears to have been a tomb of "John the Elder [or Presbyter]" at Ephesus (Eusebius, *History of the Church,* book 3, chapter 39). Even so, it is not clear whether he and the Apostle John were the same person. Other suggestions are that the author was JOHN MARK (Acts 12:12), NATHANAEL (John 1:45-49), and even LAZARUS (John 11:1-44). In spite of these doubts about authorship, the St. John Gospel was deeply respected in antiquity and appears to have been in circulation by the early second century.

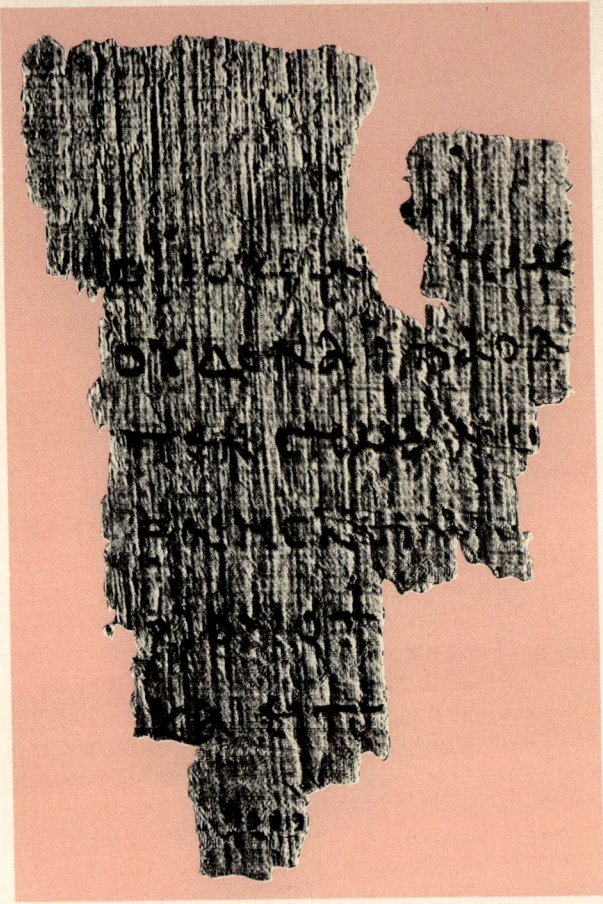

This papyrus fragment, describing the arraignment of Jesus before Pontius Pilate (John 18:31-33), and dating from the early-2nd century B.C., is the oldest Gospel text yet discovered (*New York Public Library*).

Two papyrus fragments, known as Rylands Papyrus 457 and Egerton Papyrus 2, provide the earliest evidence. The Rylands Papyrus, which is no later than A.D. 150 and may be earlier, contains John 18:31-33 and 37-38; it is the oldest surviving New Testament manuscript. The Egerton Papyrus, about the same date, seems to show knowledge of at least five chapters of the St. John Gospel. In addition, the Bodner Papyrus II (P 66), dated about A.D. 200, contains chapters 1-14 and parts of the remainder. The first surviving literary reference to this Gospel is in the work of the second-century A.D. Church Father Irenaeus. It is just possible, then, that the Apostle John may have written it when he was very old. There seems to be some allusion to his great age in the Gospel itself (21:21-24).

More puzzling than the work's authorship is its difference from the other canonical Gospels. There is nothing in it about the VIRGIN BIRTH, the childhood of JESUS CHRIST, his BAPTISM by JOHN THE BAPTIST, the temptation in the wilderness, the TRANSFIGURATION, or the ASCENSION. On the other hand, it contains material that occurs nowhere else: hints of an early ministry in JUDAEA, the marriage incident at CANA in GALILEE, the stories of NICODEMUS and the woman of SAMARIA, and the so-called farewell discourses of Jesus to his DISCIPLES.

The author's literary method is also quite different: he records only seven miracles and spends altogether less time on narrative. These differences were of some concern to the early Church Fathers, but the best explanation they were able to produce was the one by Clement of Alexandria. He thought that John, having decided that the basic facts of Jesus' life had been adequately described in the SYNOPTIC GOSPELS (the first three New Testament books), decided to write "a spiritual gospel," that is, one more concerned with teaching. Such an explanation is not satisfactory. The Synoptic Gospels all resemble each other closely in structure. Despite minor discrepancies, they read as if they are presenting the same events in the same order, and that these events (apart from the stories of Jesus' birth and childhood) took place within a period of about one year. The St. John Gospel has not only a different structure but a different time scale: its events seem to require a minimum of three years. Moreover, its historical discrepancies with the synoptic tradition are not minor.

Thus, in the St. John Gospel the cleansing of the TEMPLE (2:13-17) is Jesus' first significant public act. The Synoptists, however, place it after the triumphal entry into JERUSALEM that preceded his arrest and CRUCIFIXION. Of course, they could not have placed it anywhere else, since they record only one visit to Jerusalem by Jesus during his entire ministry. The St. John Gospel, on the other hand, records no less than four such visits, each one in connection with a specific religious festival (for the chronology, see R. H. Lightfoot, *St. John's Gospel*, London, 1960, pp. 48-49). This seems altogether more plausible than the synoptic version, and most scholars now agree that Jesus' ministry lasted for about three years.

It is not possible to regard the St. John Gospel as a purely historical narrative, or even as a loosely connected series of historical reminiscences. Careful study shows that the chief points it is designed to make are what we would call theological, not historical, though it is doubtful whether the author made any such distinction. The same is true of the other Gospels, but with one important difference: their authors, though able men, were neither theological nor literary geniuses—the author of the St. John Gospel was both. For profundity of thought, he is matched in the New Testament only by PAUL THE APOSTLE: for beauty of language, his only equals in the entire scriptures are DEUTERO-ISAIAH and a few of the many authors of the Book of PSALMS. If Shakespeare had been an evangelist, we would expect him to have produced a gospel unlike any other. We should abandon all our preconceptions about "Galilean fishermen" and admit that the author of the St. John Gospel falls into the same category. But since the structure of this Gospel is exceedingly loose, dividing it into parts becomes a major problem of interpretation.

Three distinct interpretive approaches (all others are merely combinations of these) have established themselves in recent years. First, the theological-symbolic approach regards the St. John Gospel as a work so completely devoted to conveying a particular religious and philosophical message that even the smallest details in it have deep symbolic meaning. For example, at the marriage in Cana of Galilee (2:1-11)—an incident found only in this Gospel—there were six water pots set aside for ritual purification; Jesus had them filled with water, which then became wine. Since there was nothing in Jewish custom that required six of them rather than any other number, commentators of the theological-symbolic school would have us believe that they were meant to symbolize the "failure" of JUDAISM because they fell short of the mystically perfect number seven (*see* NUMEROLOGY). In the same way, they point out that although each of the Four Gospels describes how Jesus drove the money changers and animal dealers out of the Temple, only the St. John Gospel says that he drove out the animals as well (2:15). This is supposed to symbolize Jesus' role as the one sacrifice acceptable to GOD. Interpretation of this kind may seem farfetched until one comes across such passages as "And as Moses lifted up the serpent in the wilderness, even so must the Son of man be lifted up . . ." (3:14; cf. Num. 21:8-9). The St. John Gospel is indeed full of symbols—but it is hard to tell which details were meant to be symbolic.

Second, the eyewitness approach assumes that most, if not all, of the details were drawn from the author's personal experience. Thus the author undoubtedly knew a great deal about Jewish customs (7:22-23; 19:31) and history (2:20; 4:9). His use of Hebrew and Aramaic words (1:38; 5:2; 9:7; 19:7) seems to mark him out as a native of PALESTINE. Various place descriptions with no discernible symbolic relevance have been proved entirely accurate by recent excavation (the most celebrated is that of the Pool of Bethesda, finally uncovered in 1932, which does indeed have the "five porches" mentioned in 5:2, see also ARCHAEOLOGY). But perhaps most convincing of all to the ordinary reader are such vivid narrative details as the "five barley loaves, and two small fishes" at the feeding of the five thousand (6:10), or the napkin "wrapped together in a place by itself" in the empty tomb (20:7). There are also the human touches, as when the man born blind shows irritation at being questioned (9:24-34), or Jesus weeps at the tomb of Lazarus (11:35). Such details are so numerous that it seems illogical to interpret them all symbolically.

Third, the source criticism approach maintains that the St. John Gospel, no less than the Synoptic Gospels, contains earlier materials in edited form. Thus Rudolf Bultmann, one of the greatest of contemporary New Testament scholars, suggests that there was one source for the miracles, another for the so-called discourses (the long monologues by Jesus that are such a feature of this Gospel), and a third for the passion (Crucifixion) narrative. (See BIBLICAL CRITICISM.) Some of these sources, he believes, were not even Christian, but originated with a Jewish sect called the Mandaeans, supposedly founded by John the Baptist. This theory has not found much acceptance. It is true that the author of the St. John Gospel gave far more attention to John the Baptist than did any of the Synoptists and that the Baptist played a large part in the scriptures of the Mandaeans. It is also true that the Mandaeans had their own gospel of salvation, according to which the Supreme Being, whom they called the King of Light, had sent His own son to earth in human form. But most of our information about the Mandaeans dates from the seventh century A.D. or later, and it is far more likely that the St. John Gospel influenced them than vice versa. The emphasis on the Baptist in that Gospel may stem from its author's familiarity with the Judaean ministry, which he alone mentions (3:22; cf. Eusebius, *History of the Church,* book 3, chapter 24). Indeed, study of his geographical references has convinced many scholars that he was most familiar with the southern half of Palestine.

No matter which of these three approaches they choose, most scholars agree that the St. John Gospel has four major sections: 1:1-18; 1:19-12:50, 13:1-20:31; and 21:1-25. The problem is how to label these sections and whether to subdivide them. The magnificent prologue (1:1-14) is unique in Christian literature (if we except I John 1:1-3, which is clearly an imitation of it). But it is unique, not because it is theological—all three Synoptic Gospels have theological prologues—but because of the lofty, almost rapt character of the author's thought. It is like the opening of some great symphony. Still more remarkable, the same level of intensity is maintained throughout, almost without a break; even the more homely incidents vibrate with feeling. Parts of the book read like the utterances of a man in a trance, a man who is seeing and hearing what he describes. Whether or not one believes in visions, the St. John Gospel is much easier to read if one supposes that its author's methods of composition were closer to a poet's than to a historian's. There are no half-tones in this vision: light, which is truth and the certainty of truth, is pitted against darkness, which is sin, deceit, and refusal to acknowledge the truth.

From the very first, the real "children of light" (12:36)—John the Baptist, Andrew, PETER, and the others—recognized that Jesus was the truth (1:15-51). Jesus' first miracle in Galilee was a triumph; the divine bridegroom had appeared (2:1-11). Immediately, he set out to remake the Jewish religion, dealing firmly with those who hesitated or refused to believe (2:12-22). The Baptist, his mission fulfilled, endorsed Jesus even more heartily than before (3:23-36). A conversation between Jesus and a Samaritan woman (a kind of rural Merry Widow, it seems!) showed that his message was not confined to Jews (4:1-42). Jesus then healed the son of an imperial official, as "nobleman" should be translated here (4:43-54). Many commentators believe the official was the same person as

SAINT JOHN'S GOSPEL.

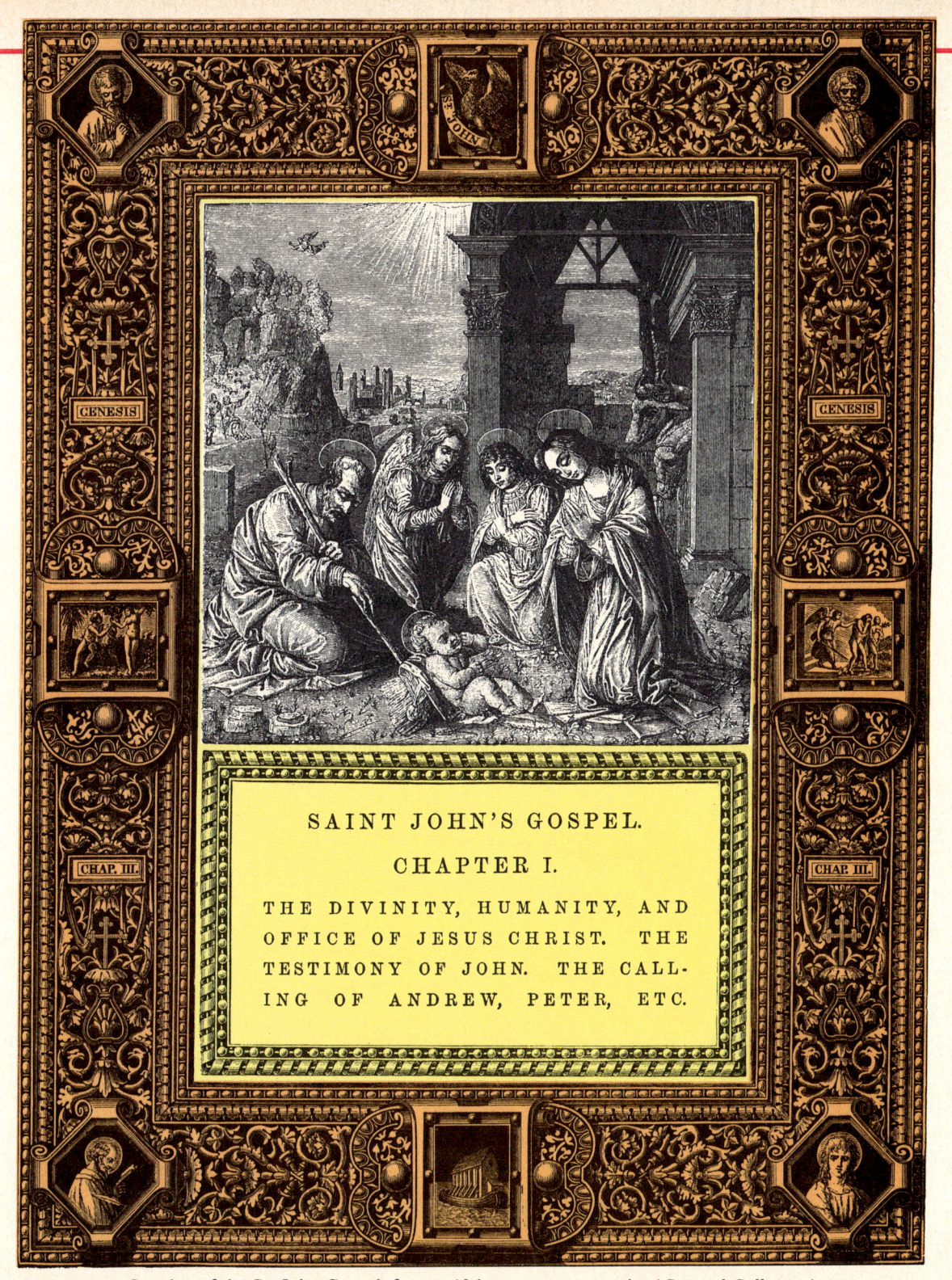

CHAPTER I.

THE DIVINITY, HUMANITY, AND OFFICE OF JESUS CHRIST. THE TESTIMONY OF JOHN. THE CALLING OF ANDREW, PETER, ETC.

Opening of the St. John Gospel, from a 19th-century manuscript (*Counsel Collection*).

the centurion in the synoptic tradition (Matt. 8:5-13; Luke 7:1-10). If so, the intended message was probably the same: GENTILES with faith would be saved, and Jews without faith would not. As Jesus gained ever greater public support through a whole series of miracles and pronouncements, the Jewish leaders' opposition to him grew in proportion (chapter 5).

Then came a mysterious turning point in his career: After he had miraculously fed a crowd of five thousand—all men, it seems (6:10,14)—he went off by himself, because he saw that "they would come and take him by force, to make him a king" (6:15). From now on, Jesus' only close relations were with the TWELVE APOSTLES: his public pronouncements grew increasingly defiant and bitter. He knew that the community leaders, the Establishment as it were, had decided to kill him, and that it was only a matter of time before they succeeded. During this period, he performed several more miracles and made several public attempts to explain the meaning of the death that was to be his. But this aspect of his teaching was met with derision (6:16-10:42). Turning from the crowd, Jesus found joy in the company of his friends (here it should be noted that the author, for all his theology, agreed with the synoptic tradition that in his private life Jesus was both friendly and sociable). But a dear friend had just died—Lazarus, the brother of MARY and MARTHA, who lived at BETHANY near JERUSALEM, and with whom (it is implied) Jesus often stayed. In language of unequaled vividness and solemnity, we are told how Jesus raised Lazarus from the dead (11:1-44). The Jewish leaders then decided that Jesus would gain so much support through this miracle that the Romans would come "and take away both our place and our nation." They therefore, according to the text, decided to have him put to death—for the good of the country (11:45-57). There is a deliberate historical irony here, since the author was writing after the destruction of Jerusalem in A.D. 70 (see JEWISH REVOLT). Neither this incident nor the miracle of Lazarus occurs in the other canonical Gospels.

The next section (12:1-17:26) is all preparatory to the Crucifixion. The author began with the anointing of Jesus by Mary, Martha's sister (12:1-8). As the chief priests laid their plans (which now included the elimination of Lazarus), Jesus entered Jerusalem in triumph (12:9-19). He delivered his last public sermons (12:20-50). In the few days remaining, he had no time to teach any but his immediate disciples. Accordingly, after various preparations, he dispatched JUDAS ISCARIOT, who he knew was planning to inform on his whereabouts to the religious authorities (13:1-30). "And it was night" (13:30). With these simple words the author signified that the forces of darkness—"the prince of this world" (12:31)—were about to triumph over the forces of light. Ringed around by darkness, the little circle of Jesus and his friends (now, we begin to realize, symbolizing the Church) seemed an oasis of light in a world wholly dominated by evil. Against this evil, man unaided could do nothing; even the faithful Simon Peter would turn traitor (13:36-38).

There follow the sublime farewell discourses (14:1-17:26). From a theological point of view, they are probably best interpreted as teachings about the Sacraments and the HOLY SPIRIT. But what shines out above all is Jesus' love for his Disciples—not only for those present at this LAST SUPPER, but for all those who would acknowledge him in the future. The discourses are pictured as taking place in one night. At their conclusion, Jesus went outside "over the brook Cedron, where there was a garden" (18:1) (GETHSEMANE). Here he was arrested, by a posse sent by the chief priests and guided by Judas Iscariot. After questioning by PONTIUS PILATE, the Roman PROCURATOR, he was sentenced to be crucified. The nature of the charges against him is left mysterious, but Pilate had a notice fixed to his cross: "JESUS OF NAZARETH THE KING OF THE JEWS." The chief priests asked Pilate to take it down, but he refused. (See also I.N.R.I.; TRIAL OF JESUS CHRIST.) Jesus on the cross suffered no agony of self-doubt; we hear nothing of the despairing cry recorded by the Synoptists. Instead, after commending his mother to the care of the Beloved Disciple, he died with a triumphant, "It is finished!" (18:1-19:30). Because the next day was the SABBATH, the bodies of Jesus and those crucified with him were taken down. Jesus was buried nearby, in a tomb hewn out of the rocky hillside; it is implied that everything was taken care of by JOSEPH OF ARIMATHAEA, a previously unnamed follower of Jesus, and that the Twelve had nothing to do with it (19:31-42).

The day after the Sabbath, MARY MAGDALEN came early to the tomb and found it empty. After fetching Peter and the Beloved Disciple, who entered the tomb and found no body—only grave clothes—she remained there alone. Looking into the tomb, she saw two angels, who asked her why she was crying.

Jesus healing the lepers at Capernaum (*Tissot, Brooklyn Museum*).

Raphael's rendition of Jesus and Mary Magdalene following Christ's Resurrection (*Counsel Collection*).

(*See also* ANGELOLOGY.) Suddenly, a man was asking her the same question. It was Jesus. "Touch me not," he said, "for I am not yet ascended to my Father" (20:17). After that he appeared twice to all the other Disciples, seemingly in Jerusalem, and a third and last time to seven of them as they were fishing in the SEA OF GALILEE. The narrative ends on a note of calm and simplicity. It was the same Jesus that they had always known, and his last recorded words were, "Follow thou me" (21:1-22). In a postscript the author is identified—but obliquely.

The St. John Gospel presents a number of unresolved problems of interpretation. For instance, it is impossible to prove that the author knew and used the Synoptic Gospels as source material, although the hypothesis that he assumed his readers knew them seems quite plausible. The hypothesis that his real purpose was to write a gospel for Christians of Greek culture has been somewhat shaken by the discovery of the DEAD SEA SCROLLS, which show that many concepts previously considered Hellenistic were already familiar to the QUMRAN community, an ascetic Jewish sect (the ESSENES) with whom both Jesus and John the Baptist may have studied (*see also* HELLENISM). The alleged influence of GNOSTICISM on this Gospel seems less obvious now that more Gnostic texts have come to light. Discussions of whether or not the text is a unity tend to begin and end with the story of the woman taken in adultery (8:1-11), which does not occur in the best manuscripts. C. H. Dodd, the greatest of contemporary Johannine scholars, believes that this Gospel depends on at least eight different kinds of traditional material (*Historical Tradition in the Fourth Gospel,* Cambridge University Press, 1963, pp. 429-430). Some of this material may preserve memories of a "revolt in the desert" of which the Five Thousand wanted to make Jesus leader (A. M. Hunter, *According to John,* Philadelphia, 1968, p. 44).

But why was the author of the Fourth Gospel so anti-Jewish and so pro-Roman? He never loses an opportunity to refer to Jesus' enemies as "the Jews," even though most of the time he means the Jewish religious authorities. And his account of Pilate's behavior is clearly designed to let the Roman authorities off the hook. Perhaps the best thing to bear in mind when reading this Gospel is that its author, by his own admission, planned it as both an aid to faith (20:30-31) and a selective historical account (21:25). Following is a chapter-by-chapter capsule analysis of the Gospel According to St. John.

Chapter 1 (51 verses): John the Baptist hails Jesus

Church dome (*right*) marks the site of Christ's miracle of the wedding feast at Cana (*Counsel Collection*).

as Son of God and Redeemer; Jesus calls Andrew, Simon, (who is renamed "Cephas" [Peter] by him), Philip, and Nathanael; Jesus proclaims his own divinity.

Chapter 2 (25 verses): the marriage in Cana; Jesus and his disciples visit Capernaum, then Jerusalem, where he cleanses the Temple.

Chapter 3 (36 verses): Jesus tells Nicodemus that God has sent His Son to save the world, then baptizes in Judaea.

Chapter 4 (54 verses): the incident of the woman of Samaria; Jesus converts many Samaritans, returns to Galilee where he cures the official's son.

Chapter 5 (47 verses): Jesus visits Jerusalem again and cures the paralytic at the Bethesda pool; "the Jews" decide to kill Jesus.

Chapter 6 (71 verses): Jesus, in Galilee again, feeds the five thousand men, rejoins his Disciples by walking on the water, and discourses on himself as the bread of life; many of his followers are offended, and leave him; Jesus predicts that one of the Twelve will betray him.

Chapter 7 (53 verses): Jesus returns to Jerusalem where he preaches openly in the Temple, proclaiming that he has been sent from God and foretelling his death and the coming of the Holy Spirit.

Chapter 8 (59 verses): Jesus proclaims himself the light of the world, discourses on his heavenly father, and severely rebukes the people for not recognizing his divine nature.

Chapter 9 (41 verses): Jesus restores the sight of a blind man and then tells the Pharisees that they are spiritually blind men who claim they can see.

Chapter 10 (42 verses): Jesus preaches at the Feast of the Dedication and leaves Jerusalem for the area "beyond Jordan... where John at first baptized."

Chapter 11 (57 verses): the death and raising of Lazarus; the chief priests and Pharisees, afraid that Jesus will attract a following large enough to provoke a Roman invasion, begin in earnest to plot his death.

Chapter 12 (50 verses): Jesus' triumphal entry into Jerusalem riding an ass, and the premonition that his hour has come.

Chapter 13 (38 verses): Jesus washes his Disciples' feet, announces that one of them will betray him, predicts that Peter will deny him.

Chapter 14 (31 verses): the first Farewell Discourse.

Chapter 15 (27 verses): the second Farewell Discourse.

Chapter 16 (33 verses): the third Farewell Discourse.

Chapter 17 (26 verses): Jesus prays to his Heavenly Father to preserve his Disciples and all who believe in him.

Chapter 18 (40 verses): the arrest of Jesus; Peter's denial; interrogation of Jesus by Pilate.

Chapter 19 (42 verses): the Crucifixion, the removal from the cross, and the entombment.

Chapter 20 (31 verses): Mary Magdalen finds the tomb empty; Jesus appears first to Mary, and then to the Disciples in the upper room; the author of the Gospel states his purpose.

Chapter 21 (25 verses): Jesus at the Sea of Galilee; his instructions to Peter, final words.   J.M.B.E.

JOHN THE APOSTLE, a son of ZEBEDEE, and brother of JAMES THE APOSTLE, both of whom worked with their father as fishermen on the SEA OF GALILEE prior to becoming two of the TWELVE APOSTLES of JESUS CHRIST (Matt. 4:21-22; Mark 1:19-20). Apparently John and James were members of a financially secure family, since the fishing ship that they abandoned to join Jesus contained "hired servants" (Mark 1:20). Since James is usually mentioned before John, the latter was probably the younger. John was one of the three apostles who were closest to Jesus (along with James and PETER). They were present when Jesus raised the daughter of JAIRUS from the dead (Mark 5:37; Luke 8:51), at the TRANSFIGURATION (Matt. 17:1; Mark 9:2; Luke 9:28), and when Jesus left them to pray alone in the Garden of GETHSEMANE prior to his arrest (Matt. 26:37; Mark 14:33). Because of their undisciplined and sometimes misdirected zeal (Mark 10:37; Luke 9:49-50; 54-55), Jesus early nicknamed John and James BOANERGES ("Sons of Thunder," Mark 3:17).

If John the Apostle was the "beloved disciple," it was he who sat closest to Jesus at the LAST SUPPER (John 13:23), who was, at the CRUCIFIXION, entrusted by Jesus with the care of his mother MARY (19:26-27), and the Disciple who outran Peter to Jesus' tomb and was the first to believe the RESURRECTION (20:1-8; *see also* JOHN THE BELOVED DISCIPLE). In the ACTS OF THE APOSTLES John is mentioned in three passages (1:13; 3-4; 8:14-15), the latter two of which find him in association with Peter, who is the spokesman and leader of the two. PAUL THE APOSTLE mentions him but once. After returning from a trip to JERUSALEM, Paul in-

JOHN THE APOSTLE 1675

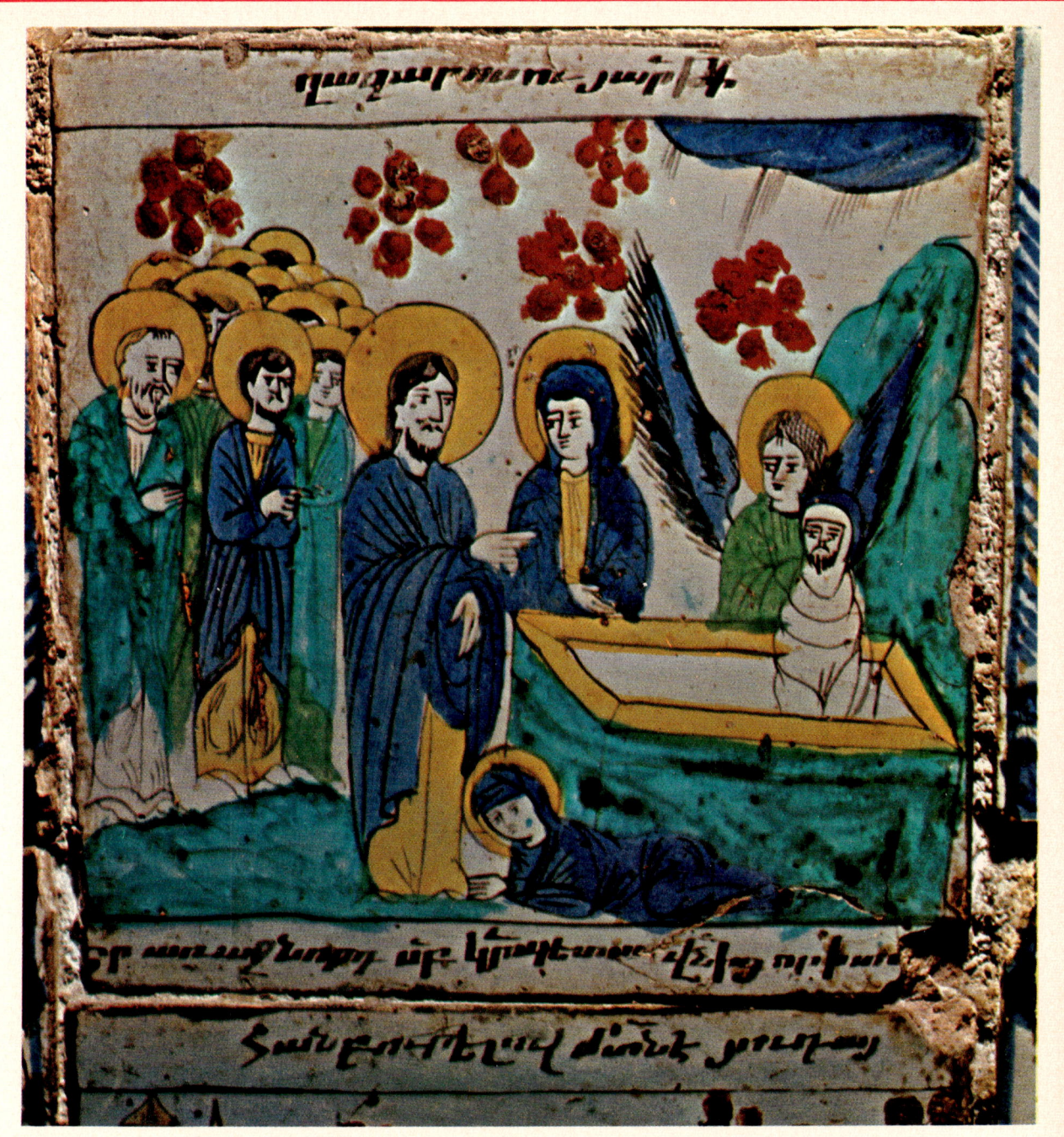

17th-century Armenian painting, now in the St. James Cathedral, Jerusalem, shows Lazarus coming forth from his tomb at the command of Jesus (*Counsel Collection*).

dicates that John was apparently one of the "pillars" of the Church there (Gal. 2:9).

According to Church tradition John the Apostle moved to EPHESUS after years of leadership at Jerusalem and there wrote the GOSPEL ACCORDING TO ST. JOHN, the JOHANNINE EPISTLES, and the REVELATION OF ST. JOHN THE DIVINE. Revelation, however, is the only one of these five books which names its author

St. John, from a 13th-century Turkish illuminated manuscript (*Counsel Collection*).

JOHN THE APOSTLE 1677

(1:1,9, and elsewhere; the titles of the books in English were added later). This author gives his name simply as John, never calling himself an apostle or otherwise providing a fuller identity. Both the Second and Third Epistles of John begin with "the elder" as their author, with no further identification either by name or title. Not only does the Gospel of John not name its author (although 21:20-24 identifies him as the disciple "whom Jesus loved"), it never mentions John the Apostle by name.

According to tradition John lived to be very old and died a natural death at Ephesus. An earlier tradition places him on the island of PATMOS under a sentence of banishment; however, the early Church historian Eusebius says that he returned to Ephesus and lived until the time of the Roman emperor TRAJAN (*History* III.18.1; 20.9; 23.4). Another tradition that John the Apostle was martyred may be the result of a confusion between him and JOHN THE BAPTIST. Most scholars think it very unlikely that the same John wrote all five NEW TESTAMENT books, known collectively as the "Johannine writings." The earliest tradition has him as the author of Revelation, however, and possibly the "elder" who wrote the Second and Third Epistles was the same person who wrote the First Epistle of John and the Gospel of John. John the Apostle could have been the source of the witness recorded in the Gospel of John.

G.Y.

Medieval painting showing Mary Magdalene washing the feet of Jesus with her hair (*New York Public Library*).

St. John, from a painting by Blondel (*Counsel Collection*).

JOHN THE BAPTIST, so called because he practiced the rite of BAPTISM during his ministry, was a PROPHET of priestly descent on both sides of his family. His mother, ELISABETH, was related to MARY the mother of JESUS CHRIST, and his father was the aged priest ZACHARIAS. John was six months older than Jesus (inferred from Luke 1:36) and began his ministry preaching "the baptism of repentance for the remission of sins" (Luke 3:3). He is viewed in the NEW TESTAMENT as the forerunner of Jesus, who came to prepare the way for the MESSIAH. The baptism of Jesus by John the Baptist in the JORDAN RIVER (Matt. 3:13 ff.; Mark 1:9 ff.; Luke 3:21) marks the beginning of Jesus' ministry (Luke 3:23). Shortly thereafter John the Baptist was imprisoned and executed by HEROD ANTIPAS.

John the Baptist had a number of devoted followers known as Baptists who continued his ministry after his death and who had their own literature when the New Testament was being written. Some scholars believe that verses 5-80 in chapter one of the GOSPEL ACCORDING TO ST. LUKE were originally a Baptist document which Luke included in his narrative as an introduction to his account of the birth of Jesus. (After identifying Luke's—or a subsequent editor's—Christian interpolations in this section, scholars view the purely Baptist material as Luke 1:5-25,47-55,57-80.) While this source probably contains some legendary material about John, they hold that the historically reliable information includes his parentage and priestly descent, his birth in JUDAEA (1:65), and his youthful sojourn in the "deserts" (1:80).

It was there in the deserts, or "wilderness," that John began his ministry (Matt. 3:1; Mark 1:4; Luke 3:2). He preached the JUDGMENT of GOD and called on ISRAEL to repent of its sins. Many people from JERUSALEM and the country of Judaea, as well as from the land around the Jordan, came to hear him (Matt. 3:5; Mark 1:5; Luke 3:3,7), and many believed him and were baptized (Matt. 3:6; Mark 1:5). John preached that divine judgment was very near at hand, making REPENTANCE an urgent matter, for the wrath of God would soon come down on the unrighteous (Matt. 3:7-12; Luke 3:7-9, 16-17). He exhorted people to share their possessions, and when PUBLICANS (tax collectors), not the most popular of citizens, asked what they should do (Luke 3:12), John advised them, "Exact no more than that which is appointed you" (3:13). Soldiers who came to him with the same question were told, "Do violence to no man, neither accuse any falsely; and be content with your wages" (3:14). It should be understood that John was not preaching pacifism toward a legitimate enemy, but telling the soldiers not to take advantage of the civilian population. The NEW ENGLISH BIBLE renders this

JOHN THE BAPTIST 1679

passage, "No bullying; no blackmail; make do with your pay!"

John the Baptist wore clothing of camel's hair, with a leather girdle around his waist, and lived on a diet of locusts and wild honey (Mark 1:6). Such food and clothing were readily available in the wilderness and entirely appropriate for a Prophet uninterested in status symbols; it is significant that John's food was ceremonially clean, in accordance with Jewish dietary laws (cf. Lev. 11:21-22; *see* CLEAN AND UNCLEAN). His was a time when messianic expectations were at their highest in JUDAISM, compelling him to emphasize that he was not the Messiah. "I indeed baptize you with water unto repentance: but he that cometh after me is mightier than I, whose shoes I am not worthy to bear: he shall baptize you with the Holy Ghost, and with fire" (Matt. 3:11; cf. Mark 1:7-8; Luke 3:16). Some interpreters suggest that John immediately recognized Jesus as the Messiah, on the basis of his professed unworthiness to baptize Jesus (Matt. 3:14) and the explicit statements attributed to him in the GOSPEL ACCORDING TO ST. JOHN (1:29-34). If John did accept Jesus as the SON OF GOD after baptizing him, he later had his doubts, for after his im-

John baptizing Jesus, from a small 15th-century Dutch altarpiece (*The Walters Art Gallery*).

prisonment John sent two of his disciples to ask of Jesus, "Art thou he that should come, or do we look for another?" (Matt. 11:3). Jesus sent John's disciples back with the message (a paraphrase of Isa. 29:18-19), "The blind receive their sight, and the lame walk, the lepers are cleansed, and the deaf hear, the dead are raised up, and the poor have the gospel preached to them. And blessed is he, whosoever shall not be offended in me" (Matt. 11:5-6).

After John's disciples left with Jesus' message, "Jesus began to say unto the multitudes concerning John, What went ye out into the wilderness to see? A reed shaken with the wind? . . . A man clothed in soft raiment? behold, they that wear soft clothing are in kings' houses . . . A prophet? yea, I say unto you, and more than a prophet. For this is he, of whom it is written, Behold, I send my messenger before thy face, which shall prepare thy way before thee. . . . Among them that are born of women there hath not risen a greater than John the Baptist: notwithstanding he that is least in the kingdom of heaven is greater than he" (Matt. 11:7-11). The questions about the reed shaken with the wind, and the soft clothing, are ironical, referring to John the Baptist's strength and courage even while in prison, and to his austere manner of dress. Jesus' statement that "he that is least in the kingdom of heaven is greater" than John the Baptist is not meant to depreciate John, for he obviously held John in high esteem. The statement rather humbles all men in general (of whom John represents the best) in contrast to those men in particular who enter the KINGDOM OF GOD.

John the Baptist's ascetic way of living and the radical character of his ethical teaching (including the sharing of worldly goods) is strongly suggestive of the life-style and ethical teaching and practices of the ESSENES. Thus, some scholars have suggested that John was an Essene. Further evidence to substantiate this theory is that John spent his early years in the wilderness of Judaea, where we now know that the Essenes had their headquarters community, and that it was a practice of the celibate Essenes to adopt boys and rear them in their religious discipline. The Essenes—who considered themselves people of the NEW COVENANT and "Sons of Light," in a constant state of military preparedness for a literal battle with the "Sons of Darkness" (whom they identified with the ROMAN EMPIRE)—were a militant people. Therefore, they were constrained by an order which was preserved in the DEAD SEA SCROLLS, reading, "Let no man put forth his hand to shed the blood of a man of the Gentiles for the sake of property and gain; also let him not carry off anything of their property" (Zadokite Document 12.6-7). This is similar in spirit to the exhortation of John the Baptist to the soldiers, "Do violence to no man, neither accuse any falsely; and be content with your wages" (Luke 3:14).

Another point made in favor of this theory is John's apparent view of baptism, which echoes the ritual baths taken by the Essenes to keep their encampments free from impurity and ensure the presence of the angelic warriors who would help them in their battle against ROME. Possibly the rite of baptism as practiced by John was a part of, if not the high moment in, a ceremony of initiation into a growing eschatological "New Covenant" community expectantly awaiting the Messiah (see also ESCHATOLOGY). Both the Essenes and John the Baptist emphasized that the efficacy of baptism was conditioned upon repentance and the confession of sins, and both preached a rigid standard of ethics on the occasion of baptism.

True to his devotion to the Jewish law, John the Baptist denounced Herod for taking his own brother's wife, HERODIAS, and true to the nature of kings in such circumstances, Herod had John arrested and imprisoned (Mark 6:17-18). Herodias was more upset than her husband and wanted John killed, but Herod declined because he "feared John, knowing that he was a just man" (6:19-20). However, at Herod's birthday party, "a convenient day," the daughter of Herodias (SALOME) danced for her stepfather and pleased him so much that he offered her anything she wanted. After conferring with her mother, Salome told Herod that she wanted the head of John the Baptist (6:21-25). "And the king was exceeding sorry; yet for his oath's sake, and for their sakes which sat with him, he would not reject her. And immediately the king sent an executioner, and commanded his head to be brought: and he went and beheaded him in the prison, and brought his head in a charger, and gave it to the damsel: and the damsel gave it to her mother" (6:27-28). John's disciples were allowed to take his body from the prison and bury it (6:29). Matthew's account of John the Baptist's execution (14:3-12) par-

John the Baptist preaching in the wilderness (Counsel Collection).

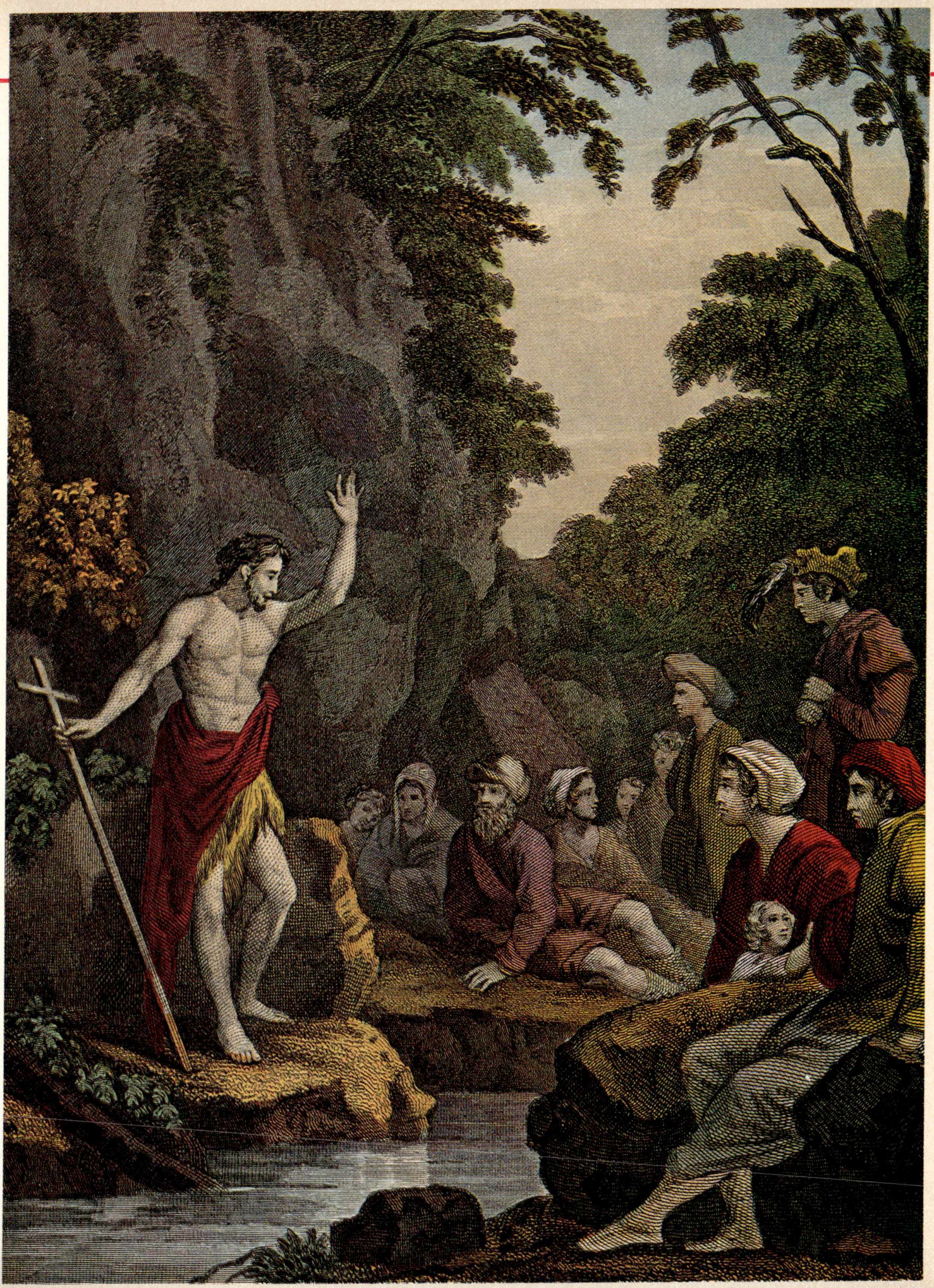

Remains of St. John the Baptist Church in the ancient city of Samaria, dating from Crusader times, erected over the traditional burial site of the Baptist. It was also here that Philip the Evangelist preached, and where the Apostle Peter denounced the sorcerer Simon Magus (*Counsel Collection*).

allels that of Mark, and some scholars suspect that these accounts contain much legendary material. They note that Luke merely records the confrontation between Herod and John and John's subsequent imprisonment, but says nothing of the execution (3:19-20), suggesting that perhaps Luke recognized some difficulties in fitting details of the story with information provided in the histories of the contemporary Jewish historian FLAVIUS JOSEPHUS.

According to Josephus, it was for political reasons that Herod had John the Baptist executed. His account goes as follows: "But some of the Jews believed that Herod's army was destroyed by God, God punishing him very justly for John called the Baptist, whom Herod had put to death. For John was a pious man, and he was bidding the Jews who practiced virtue and exercised righteousness toward each other and piety toward God, to come together for baptism. . . . And when everybody turned to John—for they were profoundly stirred by what he said—Herod feared that John's so extensive influence over the people might lead to an uprising [for the people seemed likely to do everything he might counsel] . . . So because of Herod's suspicion, John was sent as a prisoner to Macherus . . . and there put to death" (*The Antiquities of the Jews,* 18:2).

Meanwhile, word of Jesus was rapidly spreading, and soon after the death of John the Baptist some people (including Herod) were wondering if Jesus were not John the Baptist risen from the dead, or perhaps ELIJAH (Mark 6:14-16; 8:28). In the dramatic encounter between Jesus and some ecclesiastics who questioned his authority (Mark 11:27-33), Jesus answered, "The baptism of John, was it from heaven, or men? answer me" (11:30). It was a shrewd question, for if they said "from heaven" he would then ask why they had not believed him. On the other hand, "But if we shall say, Of men; they feared the people: for all men counted John, that he was a prophet indeed" (11:32). Undoubtedly "the people" feared by Jesus' interrogators were former supporters of John, now looking to Jesus for leadership.

A number of John's disciples viewed him as the Messiah, and at times there was conflict between them and the disciples of Jesus (although apparently not during Jesus' lifetime). The rebaptism by PAUL THE APOSTLE of twelve men who had received only the baptism of John (Acts 19:1-7) indicates that the Church may have been troubled then by the influence of a messianic community centered around the ministry and martyrdom of John the Baptist. A small Baptist sect known as Mandeans, claiming to perpetuate the movement begun by John the Baptist, exists today in Mesopotamia.
G.Y.

THE STORY OF JOHN THE BAPTIST

For Younger Readers

John the Baptist was so called because of the many hundreds of people whom he baptized. He was the son of the aged priest Zacharias and his wife, Elisabeth. Through his mother, John was related to Jesus Christ, because Elisabeth was a cousin of Mary, the mother of Jesus.

Tradition says that John was born at Ain Karim, a village lying five miles west of Jerusalem. Zacharias had been told by an angel that his son would be the forerunner of the Messiah and would prepare the people for his coming. Thus John was brought up to study the Hebrew Scriptures and be very devout.

When he grew to manhood, John prepared for his mission by leading a life of prayer, fasting, and self-discipline in the lonely deserts of Judaea. He wore coarse clothing, made of goat's hair, and a leather girdle. He fed upon locusts and wild honey. Locusts are insects which were then eaten as food and are still enjoyed sometimes in the Near East.

When John began his ministry, he went about through all the country around the Jordan, preaching on both sides of the river. He told the people that the Lord was soon coming and cried out, "Make ready the way of the Lord, make straight His paths."

John taught the people that they must repent and be baptized, so that their sins would be forgiven. He baptized great crowds of men and women in the waters of the Jordan River, telling them, "I indeed baptize with water, but one mightier than I is coming. He will baptize you with the Holy Spirit, and with fire."

"*I indeed baptize you with water unto repentance . . .*" (Matt. 3:11).

JOHN THE BELOVED DISCIPLE 1685

Jesus himself came from Galilee to the Jordan and asked John to baptize him. But John at first refused, saying, "It is I who should be baptized by you. Why do you come to me?"

Jesus told him that it was right for everyone to be baptized. So John did as Jesus asked. And as soon as Jesus had been baptized, the heavens opened and the Holy Spirit alighted on the head of Jesus in the form of a dove. A voice from heaven said, "This is my beloved Son, in whom I am well pleased."

Though the poor welcomed the preaching of John, the upper classes rejected his teaching. The Roman authorities feared his influence, so Herod, the prince of Galilee, had John cast into prison.

On his birthday, Herod gave a great feast and his daughter, Salome, danced for the guests. Herod was so pleased with her performance that he told her he would give her anything she wished, even up to half of his kingdom.

Salome went to her mother, Herodias, for advice. Herodias, who hated John the Baptist because he had rebuked her for her evil ways, said, "Ask for the head of John the Baptist."

Returning to her father, Salome said, "Give me the head of John the Baptist on a platter." So Herod regretfully ordered John to be beheaded, and his head was brought in and given to Salome.

Thus John the Baptist died a cruel death. But his mission had been fulfilled and many of his followers became disciples of Jesus Christ.

JOHN THE BELOVED DISCIPLE, traditionally assumed to be JOHN THE APOSTLE, a DISCIPLE of JESUS CHRIST, referred to as "the disciple whom Jesus loved" only in the GOSPEL ACCORDING TO ST. JOHN. At the LAST SUPPER he is the one "leaning on Jesus' bosom" (13:23; "reclining close beside Jesus" in the NEW ENGLISH BIBLE) who, at a signal from PETER, asked Jesus who would betray him. While on the CROSS Jesus entrusted the care of his mother to the disciple "whom he loved" (19:26-27), and when MARY MAGDALEN found Jesus' sepulcher [tomb] empty she ran and told Peter and "the other disciple, whom Jesus loved," who then outran Peter to the sepulcher (20:1-4). There he stooped and looked in, but did not enter (20:5) until Peter caught up and went directly inside (20:6); whereupon "that other disciple which came first to the sepulcher" went in, "and he saw, and believed" (20:8). Finally, in chapter twenty-one (which many scholars believe to be a subsequently added appendix or postscript) the disciple whom Jesus loved is identified as the author of the Gospel of John (21:24).

Attempts to identify the beloved disciple have followed several lines of thought. It is argued that he must have been one of the TWELVE APOSTLES, and a prominent one. Of the three closest to Jesus, Peter is ruled out because he is often mentioned along with the beloved disciple, and JAMES THE APOSTLE was martyred early (Acts 12:2), making John the Apostle the likely choice. This identification is further strengthened by Peter and John appearing together in Luke (22:8) and in the ACTS OF THE APOSTLES (3:1; 8:14), as Peter and the beloved disciple do in the Gospel of John. The ancient Church tradition supports this identification, and many early Church writings name John the Apostle as the beloved disciple.

Other investigators have examined internal evidence in the Gospel of John itself, however, leaving the above (admittedly strong) external evidence to stand on its own merits. Three views have arisen from this method. One suggests that the beloved disciple was not an actual individual, but a figure representing the ideal disciple of Jesus Christ, who should not be identified with any particular one of Jesus' followers. Another theory, based solely on the identification of the beloved disciple with the unnamed disciple who "was known unto the high priest" (18:15), holds that he must have been a JERUSALEM disciple of priestly family and connections, an unlikely status for John the Apostle, a Galilean fisherman, to have.

John the Evangelist, from a medieval illuminated manuscript (*New York Public Library*).

The strongest internal evidence points to LAZARUS of BETHANY as the beloved disciple. He is the one man in the Gospel of John whom Jesus is specifically said to love (11:3,5,36), and twice they share a meal together (12:2; 13:23). Living at Bethany, which was near Jerusalem, Lazarus could have conveniently taken Jesus' mother home with him after the CRUCIFIXION. Finally, it was Lazarus whom Jesus raised from the dead (11:43-44); it would thus have been highly significant that he was "the other disciple, whom Jesus loved," who was the first to reach the empty tomb, the first to believe that Jesus had been resurrected from the dead (20:2-8), and the first to recognize the risen Christ standing on the shore of the SEA OF TIBERIAS (21:7). If this theory is correct, Lazarus is the likely author of the Gospel of John.

The main difficulty with the identification of Lazarus as the beloved disciple is that he is never mentioned as being among Jesus' closest followers, and the presence of the beloved disciple at the Last Supper certainly suggests that he was one of the Twelve (unless more than twelve were present). Until more conclusive evidence supporting Lazarus is forthcoming, the weight of tradition will continue to favor John the Apostle as the beloved disciple. G.Y.

JOHN THE DIVINE, the author of the REVELATION OF ST. JOHN THE DIVINE, identified by himself only as John (I:1,4,9). The term "divine," included in the caption (but not in the text) of the KING JAMES VERSION, means "theologian." From the middle of the second century A.D. it was the general belief in the Church that he was JOHN THE APOSTLE. Some modern scholars, however, have identified the author of Revelation with John Mark (see also MARK), John the Elder (see also EPISTLES OF JOHN), or some otherwise unidentified John. Of the five NEW TESTAMENT books attributed to a personage named John, Revelation is the only one in which the author is identified by name (see also JOHN).

JOHN HYRCANUS (fl. c. 134-104 B.C.), the son and successor of SIMON MACCABEUS as leader of the MACCABEES in their wars of independence against the SELEUCID DYNASTY of the Syrian Empire; the story of how he foiled the attempted coup on the part of his brother-in-law Ptolemee and became ETHNARCH of JUDAEA comprises the concluding verses of the First Book of the MACCABEES; the comparatively scant information about Hyrcanus, during whose reign the Jewish people reached their period of greatest prosperity during the entire Second Commonwealth era of the INTERTESTAMENTAL PERIOD, is to be found in volume 13, chapters 8-10 of *The Antiquities of the Jews*, perhaps the most authoritative history of that period to survive down to modern times, written by the Jewish historian FLAVIUS JOSEPHUS.

While his father still ruled Judaea, John Hyrcanus had succeeded in defeating, albeit temporarily, the attempts of the Syrian ANTIOCHUS VII EUERGETES to resubjugate the Jewish people; however, shortly after Hyrcanus succeeded to Maccabean leadership, Antiochus surrounded the political and religious capital at JERUSALEM and starved the people into surrender. (Militating in the Syrian's favor was the ironical fact that his surrounding of the capital city came during the Festival of the SABBATICAL YEAR, a septennial festival year during the course of which the Jews were prohibited by the LEVITICAL CODE from harvesting crops.) Unaccountably, however, instead of sacking the city Antiochus merely exacted severe tribute from the Jews and went off, leaving John Hyrcanus in control of the ravaged land. (It is probable that ROME,

---

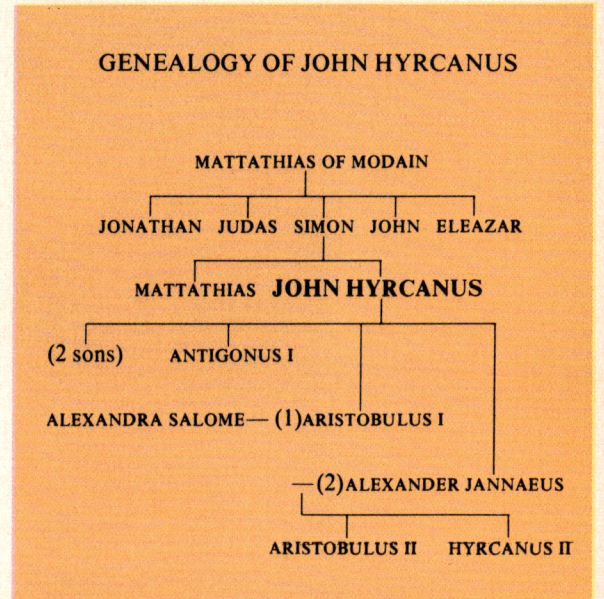

GENEALOGY OF JOHN HYRCANUS

```
                    MATTATHIAS OF MODAIN
          ┌──────┬──────┬──────┬──────┐
       JONATHAN JUDAS SIMON JOHN ELEAZAR
                ┌──────┴──────┐
             MATTATHIAS   JOHN HYRCANUS
          ┌──────┬──────────┬──────────┐
       (2 sons) ANTIGONUS I
       ALEXANDRA SALOME──(1) ARISTOBULUS I
                       └──(2) ALEXANDER JANNAEUS
                       ┌──────────┴──────────┐
                   ARISTOBULUS II        HYRCANUS II
```

John Hyrcanus was succeeded by Aristobulus I who imprisoned his mother and brothers with the exception of Antigonus I with whom he shared a brief rule; following Aristobulus' death his widow, Alexandra Salome, released Alexander Jannaeus from prison and married him, precipitating Jannaeus' long reign.

tied by treaty to Judaea through the prior efforts of Simon Maccabeus and antipathetic to the Syrians, brought pressure on Antiochus to make peace with the Jews, either through intervention or through the threat of intervention.)

Shortly thereafter, with the Jewish people in total despair, fortunes took a turn for the better when Antiochus was killed in a campaign against the PARTHIANS and was succeeded on the Syrian throne by the weak and ineffectual DEMETRIUS II NICATOR, who had been a captive of the Parthians. Hyrcanus took advantage of the internal chaos within the Syrian Empire, whose death throes now began under a succession of ineffectual monarchs—he even ceased paying the tribute that had been exacted by Antiochus Euergetes to reconstruct Judaea, bringing to his nation more than twenty years of stability. Undertaking a period of conquest on both sides of the JORDAN RIVER, he incorporated SAMARIA into his realm and conquered IDUMAEA, whose inhabitants (from which were descended the HERODS, successors to the Hasmonaeans) he forcibly converted to JUDAISM. Also, he broke with the PHARISEES, which party had evolved from the ASSIDEANS —the "Pious ones" who had supported his ancestors and who had been, in effect, the "government party"—and aligned himself with the SADDUCEES, of which alignment an ancillary perquisite or "fringe benefit" was the granting of the High Priesthood to that quasireligious party.

King in deed if not in name (his successor ARISTOBULUS I was to be the first Maccabee to assume that title) John Hyrcanus presided over a brilliant court; he even, in his dual capacity as temporal as well as religious leader, issued coins, the first of the Maccabees to be in a position to do so. (John Hyrcanus was also the first of the Maccabees to die in peace and from natural causes.) While bequeathing to his heirs a government viable both politically and economically, John Hyrcanus, for reasons unknown, fixed by will the line of succession: temporal powers were vested in the hands of his wife, but the High Priesthood went to the aforementioned Aristobulus, eldest of his five sons. This will was to prove unfortunate for all parties involved—including the people of the kingdom. (see HASMONAEAN DYNASTY.) M.A.B.

JOHN MACCABEUS (surnamed Caddis) (fl. 166-160 B.C.), eldest of the five sons of MATTATHIAS OF MODIN, initial leader of the revolt of the MACCABEES against the SELEUCID DYNASTY of the Syrian Empire; very little is known of John: his "history" is confined to two verses (9:36-37) of the First Book of the MACCABEES. Having been sent by his brother JONATHAN MACCABEUS, successor to their brother JUDAS MACCABEUS, to lead their cattle into the land of the friendly NABATHITES for safekeeping, John was murdered at MEDEBA by the Arab brigand JAMBRI, who took the cattle as booty. (It was while avenging his brother's murder that Jonathan suffered a serious defeat that threatened to result in the resumption of total hegemony over the Jews by the Syrians.)

JOHN MARK (Heb., *yohanan,* "the Lord has been gracious" or "the Lord's mercy"; Gr., *markos,* from the Lat. *marcus,* perhaps "polite" or "shining" or "large hammer"), nominal author of the second (but earliest written) of the FOUR GOSPELS, the GOSPEL ACCORDING TO ST. MARK. For the biography of John Mark, see MARK.

JOIADA (Heb., *yoyadha,* "the Lord knows" or "the Lord favors"), a HIGH PRIEST during the royal governorship of NEHEMIAH (Neh. 12:10) who was expelled from the PRIESTHOOD when one of his sons married the daughter of SANBALLAT, the Persian governor of SAMARIA (Neh. 13:28).

JOIAKIM (Heb., *yoiakim,* "the Lord will raise up"), a HIGH PRIEST who served in the TEMPLE during the royal governorship of NEHEMIAH (Neh. 12:10,26).

JOIARIB (Heb., *yoyoriv,* "the Lord will defend"), one who returned to JERUSALEM with EZRA following the PERIOD OF THE BABYLONIAN CAPTIVITY; Ezra sent him to the exiled Jews in CASIPHIA to recruit "ministers" who were to return to work in the TEMPLE (Ezra 8:16). Another Joiarib was the ancestor of a group who returned subsequently during the royal governorship of NEHEMIAH (Neh. 11:5).

JOKDEAM (Heb., *yoqedham,* "peopled" or "inhabited"), a town south of HEBRON which was included in the territory allotted to the TRIBE OF JUDAH (Josh. 15:56).

JOKIM (Heb., *yoqim,* "the Lord is exalted"), an early member of the TRIBE OF JUDAH (I Chron. 4:22).

JOKMEAM (Heb., *yoqmeam,* "gathered"), one of the LEVITICAL CITIES located within the territory of

Presumed site of the biblical city of Jokneam, in the vicinity of Beth-Shean (*Counsel Collection*).

the TRIBE OF EPHRAIM and allotted to those LEVITES of the clan of KOHATH (I Chron. 6:68); in the first account of the allotment of the PROMISED LAND among the TWELVE TRIBES OF ISRAEL, the place name is given as KIBZAIM (Josh. 21:22).

JOKNEAM (Heb., *yoqneam,* "gathered"), one of the LEVITICAL CITIES located within the territory of the TRIBE OF ZEBULUN, and set aside for those LEVITES descended from MERARI (Josh. 21:34); it has been identified as having been situated about fifteen miles northwest of JEZREEL, on the southern margin of the Jezreel plain. (The Jokneam mentioned in the First Book of the KINGS [4:12] is an error in the translation of the KING JAMES VERSION, and should read JOKMEAM [*see preceding entry*].)

JOKSHAN (Heb., *yoqshan,* "fowler"), a son of ABRAHAM by the Patriarch's second wife KETURAH (Gen. 25:2; I Chron. 1:32). From him descended DEDAN, ancestor of a tribe of Arabians (Isa. 21:13; Ezek. 38:13).

JOKTAN (Heb., *yoktan*), the youngest of the two sons of EBER, and the father of thirteen sons or races. His name appears in the genealogical tables in chapter ten of the Book of GENESIS and in chapter one of the First Book of the CHRONICLES. He was a descendant of SHEM through ARPHAXAD, and his sons became the heads of the ancient Arabic tribes (Gen. 10:25-30; I Chron. 19-23). Attempts have been made to identify the names of Joktan's sons with the names of geographic districts of ARABIA, but this has not borne fruit. Some of these names appear in other biblical genealogies. The ancient Hebrews used these tables to ascertain those peoples with whom they were willing to acknowledge a relationship. (*See also* GENEALOGY; GOVERNMENT.)

Ruins on the site of what may have been Joktheel in the Shephelah (*Counsel Collection*).

JOKTHEEL (Heb., *yoqetheel*, perhaps "God subdues"), a proper noun identifying two OLD TESTAMENT place names: a town of the SHEPHELAH allotted to the TRIBE OF JUDAH (Josh. 15:38), otherwise unknown; and the name given by AMAZIAH, eighth hereditary monarch of the Southern KINGDOM OF JUDAH, to a place he conquered in the land of the EDOMITES (II Kings 14:7), identified by most scholars as PETRA, the ancient Edomite capital.

JONA, a Greek variant of JONAH, the father of the Apostle PETER, found only in the KING JAMES VERSION of the NEW TESTAMENT (John 1:42).

JONADAB, see JEHONADAB.

JONAH (Heb., *yonah*, "dove"), one of the PROPHETS who flourished in the Northern KINGDOM OF ISRAEL, and nominal author of the thirty-second OLD TESTA-

JONAH 1691

Jonah, after having been cast onto dry land (*Counsel Collection*).

MENT book (*see following entry*). The son of AMITTAI from GATH-HEPHER, he lived during the reign of King JEROBOAM II (796-746 B.C.). According to the Second Book of the KINGS (14:25), Jonah prophesied that the boundaries of the Northern Kingdom would again extend from the entrance of HAMATH to the "sea of the plain" (i.e., the Mediterranean)—boundaries which were indeed restored under Jeroboam II.

The Prophet Jonah preaching to the citizens of Nineveh (*Counsel Collection*).

There is no definite historical data on Jonah (also known as "Jonas" or "Jona"). According to post-biblical rabbinical literature, he received his prophetic commission from the Prophet ELISHA, and served as adviser to the dynasty of King JEHU (fifth of the nine dynasties to rule in the Northern Kingdom).

Ancient Jewish and Christian commentators also believed him to be the author of the Book of JONAH, and believed that he actually lived through the adventures described in that text, but today these views are generally rejected. Historical discrepancies and the fantastic nature of his supposed adventures are the main reasons for this change of opinion.

The NEW TESTAMENT records that JESUS CHRIST drew a parallel between himself and Jonah. As narrated in the GOSPEL ACCORDING TO ST. MATTHEW (12:38-41), when some of the SCRIBES and PHARISEES asked Christ to give them "a sign" supporting his ministry, he replied, "there shall be no sign . . . but the sign of the prophet Jonas: For as Jonas was three days and three nights in the whale's belly; so shall the Son of man be three days and three nights in the heart of the earth" (cf. 16:4; Luke 11:29-32). H.G.G.

JONAH, THE BOOK OF, thirty-second book of the OLD TESTAMENT in the KING JAMES VERSION, and fifth of the Twelve Minor PROPHETS in the Hebrew Scriptures (*see* CANON OF THE OLD TESTAMENT); in four brief chapters (48 verses) it records the experiences of the Prophet JONAH, who presumably lived in the Northern KINGDOM OF ISRAEL in the eighth century B.C. The superscription of the book (1:1) tells us that it concerns Jonah the son of AMITTAI, who may be identified with a Prophet of the same name mentioned in the Second Book of the KINGS (14:25) who was active during the reign of JEROBOAM II. It is likely that Jonah was the last of the series of prophetic advisers to the house of King JEHU, founder of the fifth of the nine dynasties to rule in Israel. AMOS and the Prophets who followed him bore a different relationship to the kings and to the people. The book is unique among the prophetic writings (canonical books written by or attributed to the Prophets) in that it is not a collection of predictions or preachings, but tells the story of the Prophet's adventures, both physical and spiritual. Three of its four chapters are told in the third person and read like history; only chapter two, a psalm of thanksgiving, is written in the first person.

The book, which is relatively well preserved, tells of a Prophet who did not wish to carry out the command of GOD that he preach in NINEVEH, capital of the ASSYRIAN EMPIRE, a great city on the eastern bank of the TIGRIS River. The Assyrians, who were known as a cruel and violent people, were the most hated and feared of ancient conquerors. It is not surprising, then, that when "the word of God came unto [him], Jonah rose up to flee to Tarshish from the presence of the Lord, and he went down to Joppa [modern-day Jaffa]; and he found a ship [probably Phoenician], going to Tarshish" (1:3). But a wild storm came up, "so that the ship was like to be broken" (1:4). The sailors prayed and threw goods overboard to lighten the vessel, but to no avail. Finally they drew lots to find out "for whose cause this evil is upon us" (1:8). The lot fell upon Jonah, who told them his story and counseled them to throw him overboard. Reluctantly "they took up Jonah, and cast him forth into the sea: and the sea ceased from her raging" (1:15).

Jonah was swallowed by a great fish that God had prepared for the purpose, and three days later was disgorged on dry land (1:7-2:10). Knowing now that it was not possible to flee from the presence of the Lord, Jonah obeyed God's next call to go to Nineveh. There he proclaimed, "yet forty days and Nineveh shall be overthrown" (3:4). The people believed him: they went into mourning, fasted, and turned "everyone from his evil way, and from the violence that is in their hands" (3:8). Because they repented and changed their ways, God did not destroy them—much to Jonah's displeasure. Now he revealed the reason for his flight: he had not wished to save his people's enemy. "Therefore I fled before unto Tarshish; for I knew that thou art a gracious God, and merciful, slow to anger, and of great kindness, and repentest thee of the evil" (4:2).

Vexed beyond endurance, Jonah requested, "Therefore now, O Lord, take, I beseech Thee, my life from me, for it is better for me to die than to live" (4:3). Waiting on the east side of the city, Jonah sat in the shade of a booth he had made, but the leaves on the cut branches would have withered in the scorching sun. "And the Lord God prepared a gourd" (4:6), a fast-growing plant (perhaps a castor plant, whose huge leaves grow and wither rapidly), and Jonah was grateful for its shade. A worm cut down the plant, however, and when the sun rose, "God prepared a vehement east wind [probably the dreaded sirocco]; and the sun beat upon the head of Jonah, that he fainted" (4:8). Again he asked to die.

The Prophet Jonah, after being disgorged from the whale's belly (*Counsel Collection*).

JONAH, THE BOOK OF 1695

Then God made his purpose known: "Thou hast had pity on the gourd, for the which thou hast not laboured, neither madest it grow; which came up in a night, and perished in a night: and should I not spare Nineveh, that great city, wherein are more than sixscore thousand persons that cannot discern between their right hand and their left hand; and also much cattle?" (4:10-11). With this, the Book of Jonah ends. Its message is threefold: that repentance wins forgiveness; that God is supremely merciful; that His love and mercy should not be begrudged the heathens.

The ancient Jews and early Christians regarded the story of Jonah as historical. Although their view still has its adherents, most modern scholars consider the book either an allegory or a parable and have interpreted it in many different ways. As an allegory, Jonah is said to represent Israel, who flees from responsibility; the sea symbolizes the PERIOD OF THE BABYLONIAN CAPTIVITY; and the return to dry land the restoration of the Israelite nation. A basis for this interpretation may be found in the Book of the Prophet JEREMIAH (51:34,44). The fact that the fish was the symbol of Nineveh has given rise to another theory: that the two journeys described in the Book of Jonah are parallel versions of the same event; that the story of the three days inside the fish is a symbolic version of Jonah's three days in Nineveh. Some modern authorities declare that Jonah is a MIDRASH, a commentary, on chapter fourteen, verse twenty-five of the Second Book of the KINGS. It is addressed to the reader—in other words, the Jewish congregation. As such, once its point is made and its lesson received by Jonah, it comes to an end.

Still another theory holds that the author, wishing to teach a lesson, attached it to a series of well-known legends, centering them about the name of a popular Prophet: a folk origin would help to account for the homely, intimate, and even humorous terms in which the lesson is given. Similar stories are found in the folklore of many early peoples. Christians regard Jonah's escape from the fish as foreshadowing the RESURRECTION OF JESUS CHRIST, the three days in the fish's belly representing the three days in the tomb. The story of Jonah is alluded to in two of the FOUR GOSPELS (Matt. 12:39-41; 16:4 and Luke 11:29-30), and early Christians took great interest in it. For two millennia the Book of Jonah, with its message of repentance and forgiveness, has been read in the afternoon services of YOM KIPPUR, the Jewish Day of ATONEMENT.

There is no evidence that the Prophet Jonah wrote the book that bears his name. Although it may have been composed in the period it describes, as some scholars believe, it was put into writing several hundred years later, probably between 400 and 200 B.C. Chapters one, three, and four seem to be from the same pen. Only in chapter two is the Prophet given voice, and this chapter is mainly a psalm of thanksgiving, a form with which he would have been familiar and in which it would have been natural for him to express his thankfulness. Although the narrator refers to it as a prayer "out of the fish's belly" (2:1), the psalm appears to have been written after the Prophet had reached land. It makes no mention of a fish, but simply describes Jonah's rescue from drowning in the storm-tossed waters.

The fish is in no wise intrinsic to the story, although it is a whimsical device for suggesting that the ways of God transcend man's comprehension. It is miracle enough that Jonah survived the raging tempest, whatever the means; the point of the book lies elsewhere. Its message of repentance and forgiveness, its broad view of God, and its lofty concept of mercy for all living creatures are frequently overlooked.   H.G.G.

THE STORY OF JONAH

For Younger Readers

Jonah, the son of Amittai, was a Prophet of Israel, who lived not far from Nazareth. One day the Lord came to him and said, "Go to Nineveh, and tell the people that they have greatly offended me by their evil ways."

But Jonah was afraid. Instead of obeying, he fled to Joppa and boarded a ship for Tarshish. This was in the opposite direction to Nineveh.

The Lord was angry and sent mighty winds which terrified the sailors. They began to pray, each to his own god. They threw the cargo overboard to lighten the ship.

"*So they took up Jonah,*

JONAH, THE BOOK OF 1697

and cast him forth into the sea . . ." (Jonah 1:15).

Meantime, Jonah was sound asleep in the ship's hold. The captain came and woke him, crying, "How can you sleep at such a time? Get up and pray to your God to help us."

As the storm continued to rage, the sailors said, "One of us must be the cause of this misfortune. Let us cast lots to find out who he is."

The lot fell upon Jonah. "Who are you, and where do you come from?" the men asked him angrily. "What have you done to bring this calamity upon us?"

"I am a Hebrew," Jonah said. "I believe in the God of heaven, who made the earth and the sea."

He told them how he had disobeyed his Lord, and the sailors were afraid. "What shall we do to you so that the sea may be calm again?" they asked.

"Cast me into the water. Then the sea will be calm. It is my fault that the Lord sent this storm."

The men did not want to harm Jonah, so they tried to row the ship to shore. But the wind was too strong, and they began to pray again. "O Lord, do not destroy us all because of this one man."

Then they cast Jonah overboard, and immediately the sea became calm. They offered a sacrifice to the Lord and made promises to Him.

When Jonah sank beneath the waves a great fish, sent by the Lord, swallowed him up. For three days and nights he lived in its belly, praying for forgiveness. At last the Lord spoke to the fish, and it vomited Jonah out on to the shore.

For the second time, the Lord commanded Jonah to preach in Nineveh. This time he obeyed, and the king and people repented and did penance. Then the Lord forgave them, which angered Jonah because he had told them that they would be punished.

Jonah built a little shelter outside the city and waited to see what would happen. The Lord made a gourd spring up over his head to shield him from the burning sun.

But the next morning the Lord sent a worm, which attacked the gourd until it withered away. When the sun rose, it struck Jonah so fiercely that he fainted and longed to die. He complained because the gourd no longer sheltered him.

Then the Lord said to him, "You are concerned about the gourd, although you did not plant it nor water it. It grew up in a night, and it withered in a night. Should I not be concerned about the one hundred and twenty thousand people of Nineveh and the great city which they built?"

Jonah saw that the Lord was just and merciful. Later, the Book of Jonah was written to tell his story.

JONATHAN

JONAN (Gr., *Ionan*), an ancestor of JESUS CHRIST; he lived approximately two hundred years after the reign of King DAVID (Luke 3:30; *see also* GENEALOGY OF JESUS CHRIST).

JONAS, the Greek form of JONAH as it appears in the KING JAMES VERSION of the NEW TESTAMENT (Matt. 12:39-41; Luke 11:30-32; John 21:15-16). The first two references are to the Prophet Jonas, the third to the father of PETER.

JONATHAN (Heb., *yehonatan,* "Yahweh has given"), the eldest son of SAUL by his only wife, AHINOAM; though he was a glorious warrior-prince of great courage and daring, his name follows that of DAVID, who overshadowed him as the hero of his age. Thus, it is as the friend of David that his name has passed into legend; through the ages, the truest and most devoted companions have been proverbially called "David and Jonathan." He is first mentioned in chapter thirteen of the First Book of SAMUEL, as his father's second-in-command at GEBA, where the youth's courageous attack on the enemy garrison sparked a new spirit of revolt against the PHILISTINES: "And Saul blew the trumpet throughout all the land, saying, Let the Hebrews hear" (13:3). However, the Philistines heard too, and a great host of them gathered at MICHMASH to quell the rebellion.

Their might terrified the men of Israel, new to defiance, and they ran away or hid in the hills, until only six hundred were left to fight; but Jonathan, with only his armor-bearer, at great peril surprised an advance post of the enemy and killed about twenty of them, spreading panic and confusion among the Philistines. As they broke and ran, awed by the power of the Hebrew God, Saul fell upon their rear, and "the multitude melted away" (14:16); with the ARK OF THE COVENANT in the field beside them, the six hundred routed the swarming thousands. To keep up the pursuit, Saul unwisely forbade any man to pause to eat before evening, on pain of death. But Jonathan had not heard the order. Faint with the long chase, as he ran he scooped up a bit of wild honey, and it revived him. That evening, learning of his son's disobedience, Saul was ready to execute him in order to keep his oath; but the people loved Jonathan, and prevented it: "Shall Jonathan die, who hath wrought this great salvation in Israel? God forbid: as the Lord liveth, there shall not one hair of his head fall to the ground; for he hath wrought with God this day" (14:45).

Though Jonathan was his father's heir and the people's pride, his great heart went out to the intrepid young David who strode out to destroy the giant GOLIATH. From that day "the soul of Jonathan was knit with the soul of David" (18:1), and they made a covenant that endured as long as Jonathan lived. Far from being envious of the young hero's growing fame, the prince delighted in it, though it outshone his own popularity. But his father came to hate and fear David "because the Lord was with him, and was departed from Saul" (18:12). When the king planned to destroy his rival, Jonathan warned his friend, then "spake good of David unto Saul his father . . . Let not the king sin against his servant, against David; because he hath not sinned against thee . . . where-

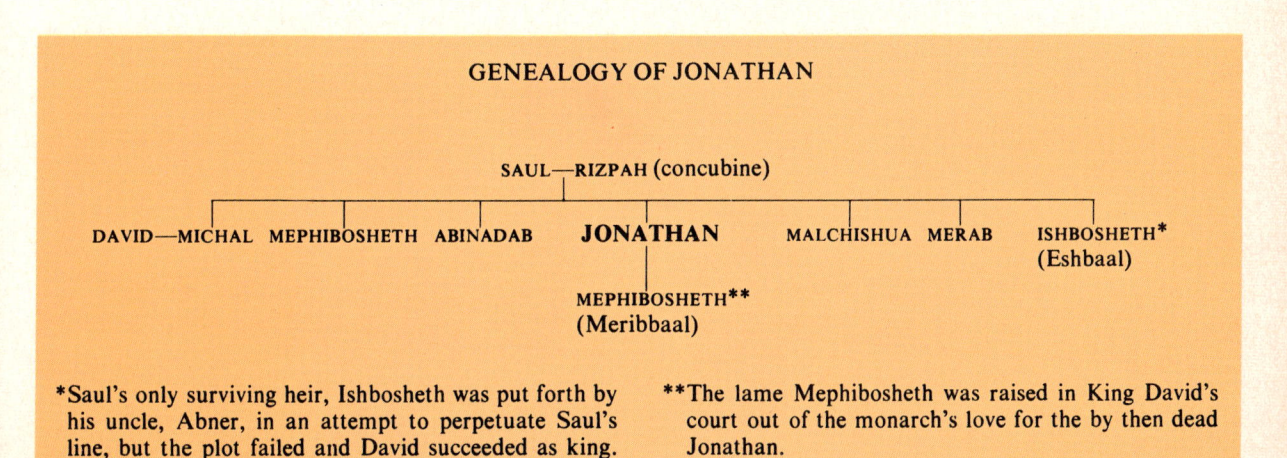

GENEALOGY OF JONATHAN

SAUL—RIZPAH (concubine)

| DAVID—MICHAL | MEPHIBOSHETH | ABINADAB | **JONATHAN** | MALCHISHUA | MERAB | ISHBOSHETH* (Eshbaal) |

JONATHAN
│
MEPHIBOSHETH** (Meribbaal)

*Saul's only surviving heir, Ishbosheth was put forth by his uncle, Abner, in an attempt to perpetuate Saul's line, but the plot failed and David succeeded as king.

**The lame Mephibosheth was raised in King David's court out of the monarch's love for the by then dead Jonathan.

Jonathan attempts to stop his father Saul from killing David who is hiding in the cave at the left; from a 1691 English Bible commentary (*Counsel Collection*).

fore then wilt thou sin against innocent blood...?" (19:4-5). But Saul could not long restrain his envy for the "man after [God's] own heart" (Acts 13:22).

After David escaped the king's assassins, the two friends had a final meeting at which David asked, "What is my sin before thy father, that he seeketh my life?" (I Sam. 20:1). They made a plan to discover whether the king still meant him harm. Jonathan sounded out his father, but only provoked Saul's jealous rage against himself: "Do not I know that thou hast chosen the son of Jesse [i.e., David] to thine own confusion... For as long as [he] liveth upon the ground, thou shalt not be established, nor thy kingdom... And Saul cast a javelin at him to smite him: whereby Jonathan knew that it was determined of his father to slay David" (20:30-33). Jonathan went to the field where David was hiding and by their prearranged signal warned him to flee. But the friends managed a private moment of farewell. "David arose out of a place toward the south... and they kissed one another, and wept one with another... And Jonathan said... Go in peace, for as much as we have sworn ... The Lord be between me and thee" (20:41-42). They never met again.

As David's renown grew during his years of outlawry, Jonathan's star waned. He is next heard of when, together with his father and two of his brothers, he fell on MOUNT GILBOA in futile battle against the Philistines. Their dishonored bodies were stolen out of BETH-SHAN and given burial by loyal men of JABESH-GILEAD; and their bones were eventually placed in the sepulcher of Saul's father, KISH, by David, who also raised Jonathan's lame son MEPHIBOSHETH for his father's sake. In one of the most moving elegies in all literature, David lamented his king and his friend with all the poetic passion of his soul. "The beauty of Israel is slain upon thy high places: how are the mighty fallen! . . . I am distressed for thee, my brother Jonathan . . . thy love to me was wonderful, passing the love of women" (II Sam. 1:19-26). Jonathan was the epitome of the true knight—intrepid and agile, resourceful and fearless in battle, devoted and selfless in friendship, and a leader who drew the hearts of men. Like England's Hotspur, "He was indeed the glass wherein the noble youth did dress themselves" (Shakespeare, *Henry IV*), a model to mankind of beauty of body and beauty of soul, a prototype both of the patriotic heroism of the ancient Hebrews and of Christian virtue and selflessness.

The name "Jonathan" was a fairly common one, borne by a number of biblical personages; perhaps the most noteworthy of the "minor Jonathans" was the son of the High Priest ABIATHAR. During the revolt against King David by his son ABSALOM, Jonathan was one of the two "messengers" instructed to remain behind in JERUSALEM in order to gather information following the precipitous flight by David to "tarry in the plain of the wilderness, until there come word . . . to certify me" (II Sam. 15:27-28 ff.); it was also this Jonathan who brought to Absalom the news that the latter's half-brother SOLOMON had been crowned as their father's successor, thus precipitating Absalom's attempt to usurp David's throne.

Other biblical Jonathans were: a descendant of MOSES through GERSHOM who established a branch of the PRIESTHOOD at LAISH which served the graven images stolen from the house of MICAH THE EPHRAIMITE (Judg. 18:30); a nephew of King David (II Sam. 21:21; referred to as David's "uncle" in I Chron. 27:32); one of David's "mighty men" (II Sam. 23:32); a descendant of JUDAH through JERAHMEEL (I Chron. 2:25-33); the father of EBED, one of the returnees from Babylonian EXILE (Ezra 8:6); one of those who opposed EZRA in the matter of taking foreign wives (Ezra 10:15); a Priest, a descendant of the JOIADA whose son had been expelled from the Priesthood by NEHEMIAH for having married the daughter of SANBALLAT (Neh. 12:11); a Priest at Jerusalem during the reign of JOIAKIM (Neh. 12:14); a descendant of ASAPH, and therefore one of the LEVITES (Neh. 12:35); one of those who warned GEDALIAH that his life was in danger (Jer. 40:8); the scribe in whose house the Prophet JEREMIAH was imprisoned (Jer. 37:15 ff.; he may have been the same as the Jonathan of Jer. 40:8); one of the Priests who led the prayer at the first sacrifice following the return from Babylonian Captivity under Nehemiah (II Macc. 1:23); the one sent by the High Priest SIMON MACCABEUS to secure JOPPA (I Macc. 13:11); one of the five sons of the Priest MATTATHIAS OF MODIN who sparked the revolt of the MACCABEES (*see following entry*). It should also be noted that the name "Jonathan" was applied as a cognomen to two of the subsequent Maccabees, ALEXANDER JANNAEUS and HYRCANUS II. *N.P.*

THE STORY OF JONATHAN

For Younger Readers

Jonathan, a brave soldier-prince, was the son of Saul, the first king of Israel. He was a man of great virtue, humble, unselfish, loyal, and honest. Above all, he was a faithful friend.

Jonathan began his military career when Saul fought the Philistines at Geba. He attacked the enemy garrison so bravely that, after the battle, Saul ordered trumpets to be blown in triumph throughout the land. The sound put new heart into the men of Israel.

But the Philistines also heard the trumpets, and gathered in a great host. Terrified at the sight of this mighty army, the men of Israel fled to the hills, leaving

1702 THE FAMILY BIBLE ENCYCLOPEDIA

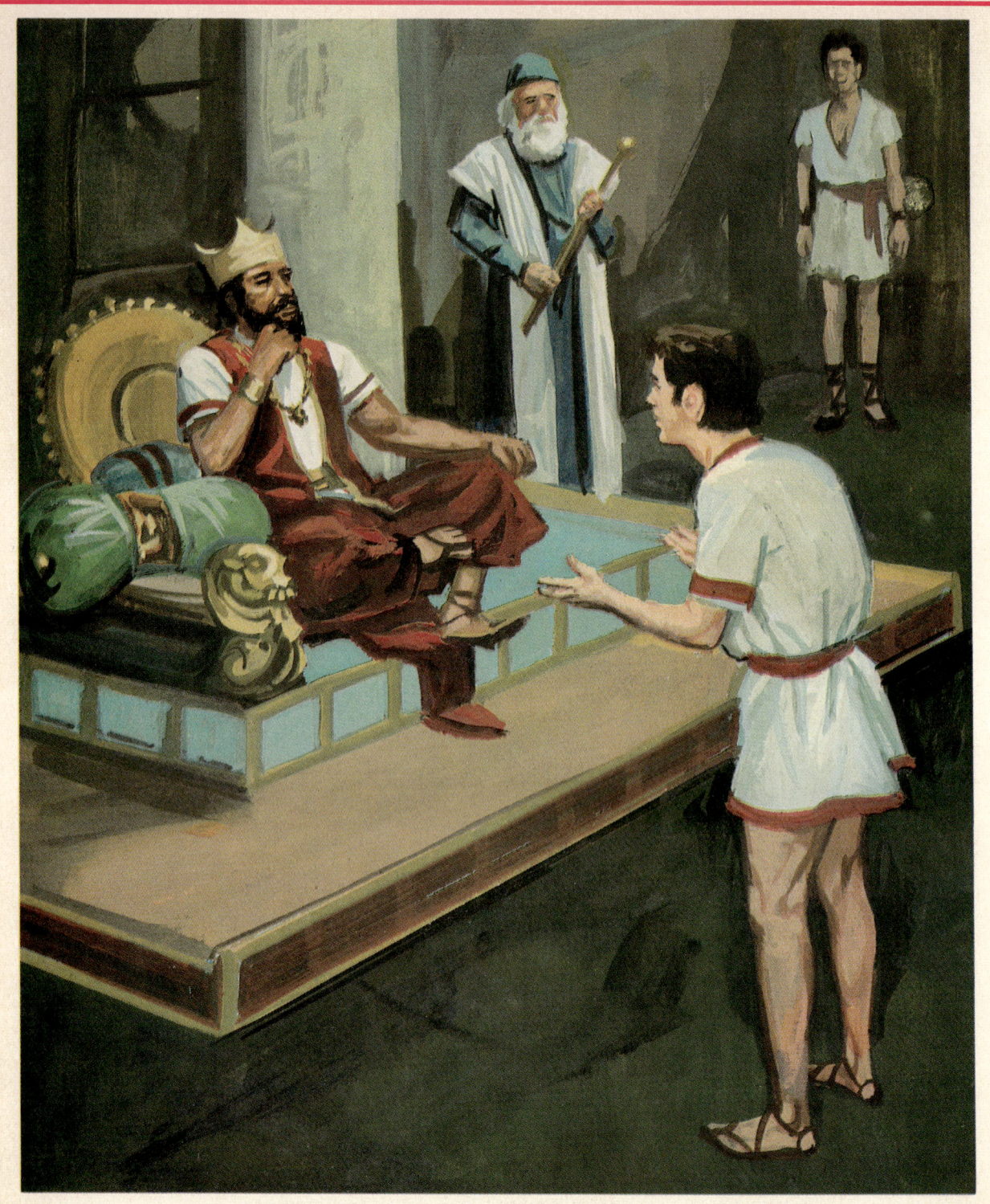

"*And Jonathan spake good of David unto Saul his father . . .*" (I Sam. 19:4).

behind only six hundred men. But Jonathan, with only his armor-bearer, caught the first of the Philistines off guard. They panicked and fled in confusion, and the great host began to run away, pursued by Saul's six hundred men.

Because he wanted his men to keep up the pursuit, Saul forbade them to stop and eat. "Cursed be any man who eats any food before evening," he said. Jonathan, however, did not hear his father. Weary and hungry, he scooped up some wild honey and ate it to refresh himself.

Although he was deeply grieved, Saul was ready to slay his son because of the curse he had sworn. But the people would not allow this. "Shall Jonathan be slain after saving us from our enemies?" they said. "As the Lord lives, not a hair of Jonathan's head shall be touched. For God has been with him on this day." So they rescued Jonathan and he did not die.

At that time, the young David, son of Jesse, slew Goliath, the Philistine giant. For this, Saul admired and loved him, and made him his armor-bearer. David came to live in the court, and often soothed Saul by playing upon the harp. He met Jonathan, and soon the pair loved each other and became as close as brothers.

But after a time Saul grew jealous of David because the people admired him. "If they think so much of him, he will soon want to have my kingdom," said Saul. And he began to look upon David with suspicion.

One day, while David was playing upon the harp, Saul hurled a spear at him. But David dodged the point of the weapon and escaped death.

Soon all Israel loved and trusted David. Saul became so jealous that he ordered Jonathan and his servants to kill the young man. But Jonathan warned David to hide. "Tomorrow I will talk to my father about you," he said, "and I will tell you what he says."

On the following day, Jonathan pleaded with Saul. "Do not harm David, for he has done you no wrong. Why should you sin against an innocent man?"

Saul promised not to harm David and sent for him to come back to court. For a time all went well. But after David fought again with the Philistines and slew many of them, Saul once more tried to kill him. So David went into hiding.

One day he came and spoke with Jonathan. They made a solemn pact of friendship, for they loved each other dearly. They also arranged that, on the next day, Jonathan would give David a signal to tell him whether it would be safe for him to return or whether he should flee.

On the next day, Jonathan went to the field where David was hiding. He gave him the signal to flee. But David wanted to say farewell to his friend, so he came forward and they embraced, weeping. "Go in peace," Jonathan said, for the Lord is with you and with me." After that, Jonathan never saw David again.

Jonathan was killed in battle when he and Saul fought the Philistines at Mount Tabor. David was filled with grief. He tore his clothes and fasted, and so did all his men. Then he composed one of the most beautiful mourning poems ever written. "How are the mighty fallen!" it said in part. "I am distressed for thee, my brother Jonathan . . . Thy love to me was wonderful."

Jonathan was survived by his five-year-old son Mephibosheth, who was lame. When David became king of Israel, he had the boy brought to his court and raised him as his own son, out of the love he had held for Jonathan.

1704 THE FAMILY BIBLE ENCYCLOPEDIA

JONATHAN MACCABEUS (surnamed Apphus) (fl. 160-142 B.C.), the youngest son of MATTATHIAS OF MODIN and successor to his older brother JUDAS MACCABEUS as leader of the MACCABEES; his history comprises over three chapters in the First Book of the MACCABEES (9:23-12:50). Though undoubtedly lacking his brother Judas' prowess as a military leader, Jonathan's knack for being able to exploit the dissensions among his enemies made him one of the most politically successful of the Maccabees; he was the first of the revolutionary group that evolved into the HASMONAEAN DYNASTY (regnal name of the Maccabees) to be recognized by Syria as HIGH PRIEST.

Shortly after assuming leadership of the Jewish revolt, Jonathan suffered a serious setback at MEDEBA, where he had gone to avenge the murder of his older brother JOHN MACCABEUS; indeed, but for the dynastic struggle going on within the Syrian Empire the Maccabee revolt may well have been completely put down at this point. Ironically, Jonathan's fortunes began to improve as he found himself being courted by the two rival claimants to the Syrian throne, ALEXANDER BALAS and DEMETRIUS I SOTER. Erroneously believing that he had succeeded completely in subjugating JUDAEA after having slain Judas Maccabeus, Demetrius Soter's military chieftain BAC-

19th-century engraving showing the death of Jonathan in battle against the Philistines atop Mount Gilboa (*Counsel Collection*).

GENEALOGY OF JONATHAN MACCABEUS

MATTATHIAS OF MODIN
```
*JONATHAN   JUDAS   SIMON   JOHN   ELEAZAR
```

*Succeeded to the leadership of the Maccabees following the death of his brother Judas, and was in turn succeeded by his brother Simon through whom the Hasmonaean line descended.

CHIDES had returned to Syria, most probably because his services were needed in maintaining Soter's succession as king following the death of ANTIOCHUS IV EPIPHANES.

However, in the midst of this internal conflict, Bacchides was forced to return to Judaea when he realized that the Syrian position there was still tenuous. Hoping to maintain order in Judaea, at least until the power play within Syria was resolved (hopefully, in favor of Demetrius Soter), Bacchides gave Jonathan the right to keep a fortress at MICHMASH. This put the Maccabee leader in the position of a licensed revolutionist, whereupon both Demetrius Soter and the usurper Alexander Balas sought him as an ally. Jonathan threw in his lot with Alexander Balas, and when Balas defeated his rival and grabbed the throne, Jonathan—eight years after assuming leadership of the Maccabees—won recognition as High Priest as well as governor of Judaea; he was also named by Balas to be a prince of Syria.

When, subsequently, the pendulum swung, with the defeat of Balas by Demetrius Soter's successor, DEMETRIUS II NICATOR, Jonathan became the latter's supporter, largely as a result of being "bought off" by Nicator when he was unable to raise Jonathan's siege of the Citadel at JERUSALEM. Taking further advantage of the chaos within Syria obtaining upon the attempts of the "Antiochan" and "Demetrian" parties to gain control, Jonathan went on to conquer a number of cities in and surrounding Judaea; strengthened the fortifications at Jerusalem (during the course of which he built a high wall to cut off the Syrian garrison stationed there); garrisoned and otherwise fortified JOPPA as well as a number of strategically important areas throughout Judaea; and negotiated treaties with the Romans and the Greek Spartans.

However, the rapid advance toward complete independence from Syria on the part of the Maccabees was halted with the downfall of Jonathan—precipitated by a sudden turn of events within the Syrian Empire. TRYPHON, an officer who had served under Alexander Balas, on the occasion of Balas' deposition and death took advantage of Demetrius Nicator's vast unpopularity by putting forward Balas' son (ANTIOCHUS VI EPIPHANES) as legitimate claimant to the throne, a candidacy which was merely a cover-up for Tryphon's ulterior motive: gaining the crown for himself. Tryphon succeeded, after killing both Jonathan and the young Antiochus. Ironically, Tryphon was himself deposed during the "reign" of Jonathan's successor.   M.A.B.

JONATHAS, the Greek form of the proper noun JONATHAN, found only in the APOCRYPHA (Tob. 5:13).

JONATH-ELEM-RECHOKIM (Heb., *yonath-elhem-rehoqim*, "a silent dove of distant places"), a phrase appearing in the superscription of Psalm 56, and probably indicating the title or tune of the melody with which this psalm was written (*see* PSALMS, BOOK OF).

JOPPA, JOPPE (Heb., *yapha*, "beauty" or "beautiful"), a seaport city approximately thirty-five miles from JERUSALEM which stands atop a rock hill about 116 feet in height; it is perhaps best known as the place where JONAH, attempting to escape his responsibilities to the LORD, boarded a ship bound for TARSHISH (Jonah 1:3); in the OLD TESTAMENT, the city is once rendered JAPHO (Josh. 19:46); in the APOCRYPHA, it is rendered "Joppe" (I Esd. 5:55). Though theoretically assigned to the TRIBE OF DAN (Josh. 19:46), the city was for a time firmly under PHILISTINE control. Subsequently, under King SOLOMON it became a major seaport from which the CEDARS OF LEBANON being imported for the construction of the TEMPLE were transported to Jerusalem (II Chron. 2:16).

In 164 B.C., in retaliation for the military successes of JUDAS MACCABEUS against the Syrian SELEUCID DYNASTY, the men of Joppa perpetrated "an ungodly deed" in luring "the Jews that dwelt among them to go with their wives and children into the boats which they had prepared, as though they had meant them no hurt . . . but when they were gone forth into the deep, they drowned no less than two hundred of them"; Judas struck back by burning Joppa's harbor and setting afire the boats that were moored there (II Macc. 12:3-7). In 147 B.C., his brothers JONATHAN and SIMON MACCABEUS occupied Joppa after defeating the Syrian general APOLLONIUS (I Macc. 10:69-85), and two years later Jonathan visited King PTOLEMEE there (I Macc. 11:1-6). In 143 B.C., fearing a conspiracy on the part of some of Joppa's citizens to turn the city over to the Syrian monarch DEMETRIUS II NICATOR, Simon Maccabeus "set a garrison there to keep it" (I Macc. 12:34), and a year later, fearing the possibility of a similar betrayal, Simon cast out Joppa's Greek inhabitants, thus rendering Joppa a Jewish city and "an entrance to the isles of the sea" for the new Jewish state (I Macc. 13:11; 14:5).

In NEW TESTAMENT times, TABITHA, a member of Joppa's Christian community who "was full of good works and almsdeeds," was raised from the dead by PETER, who "tarried many days in Joppa with one Simon a tanner" (Acts 9:36-43). The city survives as the present-day Jaffa.

JORAM

19th-century woodcut showing the ancient city of Joppa (*New York Public Library*).

JORAH (Heb., *yorah*, "rain"), the ancestor of a family who returned to JERUSALEM with ZERUBBABEL following the PERIOD OF THE BABYLONIAN CAPTIVITY (Ezra 2:18), and probably the HARIPH referred to in the Book of NEHEMIAH (7:24).

JORAI (Heb., *yoray*, "whom Yahweh teaches"), a minor member of the TRIBE OF GAD (I Chron. 5:13).

JORAM (Heb., *yoram*, "the Lord is exalted"), a name borne by two OLD TESTAMENT personages who flourished during the reign of King DAVID: one of the LEVITES (I Chron. 26:25), and the son of King TOI of HAMATH who congratulated David on the latter's stunning victory over HADADEZER (II Sam. 8:10).

"Joram" is also the short form of two Hebrew monarchs: JEHORAM, ninth monarch of the Northern KINGDOM OF ISRAEL (e.g., II Kings 8:16); and JEHORAM, fifth hereditary monarch of the Southern KINGDOM OF JUDAH (e.g., II Kings 8:21). The latter is thus identified as one of the ancestors of JESUS CHRIST (Matt. 1:8; *see also* GENEALOGY OF JESUS CHRIST).

Excavations of Crusader ruins at the seaport city of Joppa (*Counsel Collection*).

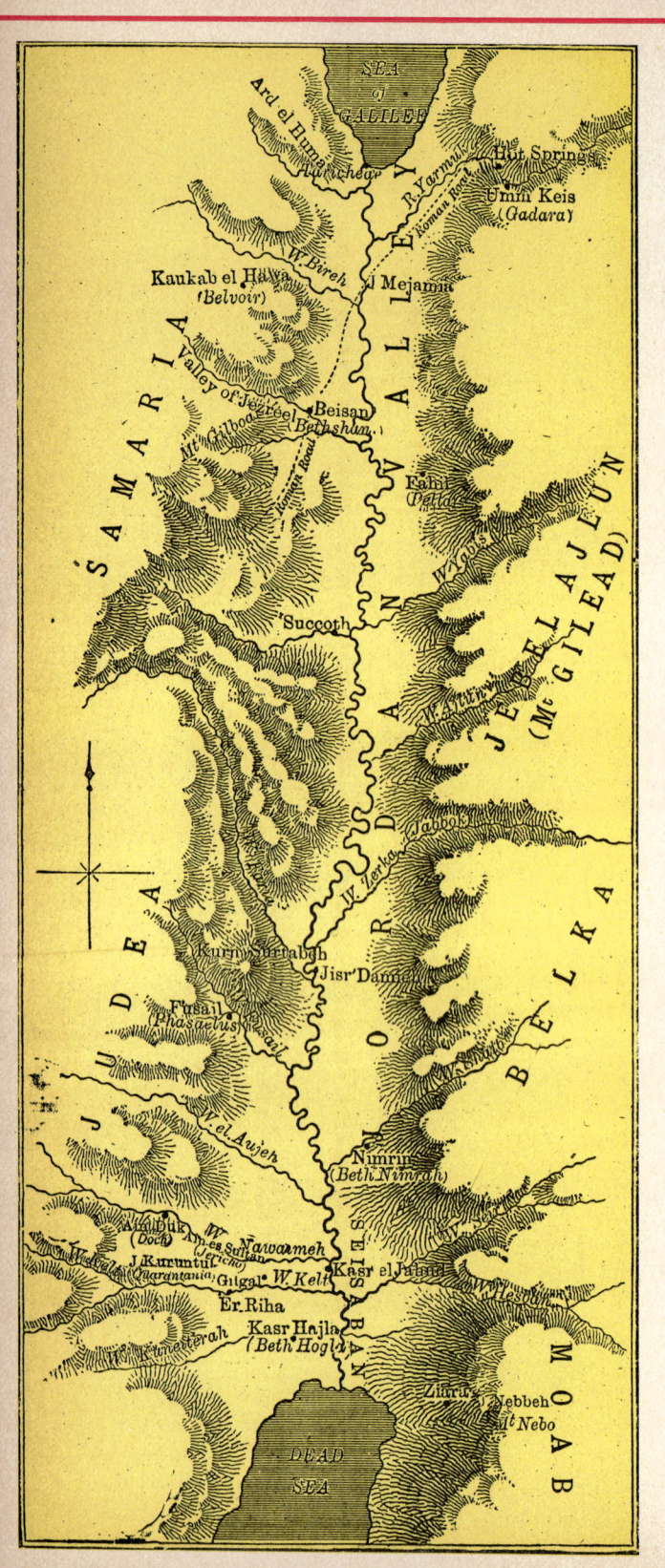

JORDAN RIVER (derived most probably from the Heb., *yarada,* "to descend," which forms the noun *yarden,* "the descender" or "the stream that descends rapidly"), the longest and by far the most important river in PALESTINE, remarkable both for its unique geology and natural character and for the prominent role it has played in biblical history. The four sources that unite to form the Jordan (the Banias, Leddan, Hasbani, and Bareighit) rise high up among the foothills of MOUNT HERMON in the parting of the watersheds there; then, following a tortuous, winding course (threading through a total of over two hundred miles) almost due south and descending rapidly en route, the Jordan flows about seven miles into Lake Huleh, about ten miles more from Lake Huleh to the SEA OF GALILEE (Chinnereth), and empties finally into the DEAD SEA, a total straight-line distance of only about one hundred miles, during which it undergoes a remarkable altitudinal fall of approximately three thousand feet.

The stretch of the Jordan from the Sea of Galilee to the Dead Sea, called the Lower Jordan, is the section that appears most frequently in the OLD TESTAMENT narratives; here, on either side of the river, grow impenetrable thickets of tamarisks, poplars, oleanders, thistles, and bushes of various kinds; it is this desolate, inhospitable area, inhabited mainly by wild animals, that is referred to in the Book of the Prophet JEREMIAH as "the swelling of Jordan" (12:5) and in the Book of ZECHARIAH as "the pride of Jordan" where "a voice of the roaring of young lions" can be heard (11:3). It is also in this stretch that the Jordan receives its tributaries; the Yarmuk, which enters the Jordan from the east about five miles south of the Sea of Galilee, bringing with it almost as much water as the Jordan itself; the Jalud, flowing in from the northwest about eight miles farther on; the Jurm, Yabis, Kufrinjeh, and Rajib; and the important JABBOK. Many important biblical cities arose near the points where these tributaries meet the Jordan, e.g., ADAM, BETH-SHEAN, GILGAL, JERICHO, SUCCOTH, ZAPHON, and ZARETHAN. The broad valley through which the Jordan descends is a long plain where, for the most part, grass and grain grow abundantly, an area the Hebrews called the ARABAH; the lowest level of the valley, near the approach to the Dead Sea, is

19th-century map of the Jordan Valley, showing Gilead and Moab on the east, and the Promised Land to the west (*Counsel Collection*).

JORDAN RIVER

One of the fords of the Jordan River (Counsel Collection).

the area referred to in the Book of JOSHUA as the place where the "Jordan overfloweth all his banks all the time of harvest" (3:15).

In Old Testament times, the Jordan was an important point of geographical reference and a natural geographical frontier; in the Book of NUMBERS it is given as the eastern boundary of the PROMISED LAND (34:12). The Jordan was also a formidable military obstacle. There is no mention of bridges in the Scriptures; when the river had to be crossed, the crossing was made at one of the numerous fords, where the water was shallow enough to permit wading (though according to a passage in the Second Book of SAMUEL, the rendering of which is greatly in doubt, DAVID and his household crossed by means of a "ferry boat" (19:18); to control these fords was to possess an extraordinary military and tactical advantage. Subsequently, during the PERIOD OF THE CONQUEST AND JUDGES, EHUD seized the fords of the Jordan, thereby cutting off a Moabite retreat and, according to the account in the BOOK OF JUDGES, "slew of Moab at that time about ten thousand men" (3:29).

When GIDEON attacked the MIDIANITE camp near the Hill of MOREH, the enemy force broke into two parts; one half fled across the river and into the hills on the opposite side, but the others, fleeing southward, were cut off at the fords by Gideon's allies from MOUNT EPHRAIM and were either killed or taken prisoner (Judg. 7:24-25). Similarly, JEPHTHAH seized the Jordan's fords against the Ephraimites, forcing all those attempting to cross the river to pronounce the word "Shibboleth"; when the fleeing Ephraimites gave themselves away by their inability to pronounce the word correctly, Jephthah's men slew them, "and there fell at that time of the Ephraimites forty and two thousand" (Judg. 12:6).

Earlier in history, during the PERIOD OF THE PATRIARCHY, LOT beheld all the plain of Jordan, and noting "that it was well watered everywhere," chose to travel there, pitching his tent finally near SODOM (Gen. 13:10-12). JACOB crossed the river with his

The Israelites carry the Ark of the Covenant across the Jordan (*Counsel Collection*).

Woodcut showing the Jordan River Valley looking toward the Dead Sea (*Counsel Collection*).

staff, perhaps indicating that he had used the staff for support while wading the ford. The last wish of MOSES was to be allowed to "go over, and see the good land that is beyond Jordan" (Deut. 3:25); when God denied this request, He instructed Moses to "charge Joshua, and encourage him, and strengthen him; for he shall go over before this people, and he shall cause them to inherit the land which thou shalt see" (Deut. 3:28). The Jordan is mentioned often in connection with the deeds of the Prophets ELIJAH and ELISHA; Elisha counseled NAAMAN, the Syrian commander, to bathe seven times in the Jordan to rid himself of his leprosy, advice which Naaman at first scorned but which afterward proved successful (II Kings 5:1-14). Later, Elisha caused an iron ax head to float in the Jordan's waters (II Kings 6:1-7). The Jordan figures in the New Testament as the place where JOHN THE BAPTIST preached and baptized; JESUS CHRIST himself was baptized in the waters of the Jordan, though the exact site of this event has never been ascertained. Since it was necessary for the Israelites to cross the Jordan River following the EXODUS from Egypt in order to enter the land of CANAAN promised them by God, the idea of "crossing the Jordan" has come to symbolize for oppressed people the idea of deliverance into a better life. Evidence of this is to be found in the numerous references that abound in the folk songs and spirituals of the American Negro. *M.L.F.*

JORIBUS, according to the APOCRYPHA (I Esd. 8:44), one of the LEVITES who flourished in JERUSALEM following the PERIOD OF THE BABYLONIAN CAPTIVITY.

JORIM (Gr., *Ioreim,* from the Heb. *yehoram,* "Yahweh is exalted"), an ancestor of JESUS CHRIST (Luke 3:29; *see also* GENEALOGY OF JESUS CHRIST).

JORKOAM, a member of, or town within, the TRIBE OF JUDAH (I Chron. 2:44). Many modern scholars believe that Jorkoam is the name of a place rather than the name of a person; thus, they believe that the appellation occurs in a Judahite genealogy not because it was borne by a member of that tribe, but rather because it was one of the areas settled by such an individual. If this hypothesis is correct, then Jorkoam is most probably a variant spelling for the geographical location known as JOKDEAM (Josh. 15:56).

JOSABAD (Heb., *yozavadh,* "the Lord has bestowed"), one of the men recruited by DAVID when the future monarch was at ZIKLAG during his period of outlawry (I Chron. 12:4).

JOSAPHAT, the Greek variant of JEHOSHAPHAT, fourth hereditary monarch of the Southern KINGDOM OF JUDAH, as it appears in the GENEALOGY OF JESUS CHRIST given in the GOSPEL ACCORDING TO ST. MATTHEW (1:8).

JOSAPHIAS, according to the APOCRYPHA (I Esd. 8:36), one who returned to JERUSALEM following the PERIOD OF THE BABYLONIAN CAPTIVITY.

JOSE, one of the ancestors of JESUS CHRIST, as given in the GOSPEL ACCORDING TO ST. LUKE (3:29; *see also* GENEALOGY OF JESUS CHRIST). "Jose" is a variant of the Greek "Jesus" which is, in turn, a translation of the Hebrew *yehoshua,* "Joshua."

JOSEDECH, a variant of the name JEHOZADAK (Hag. 1:1).

JOSEPH (Heb., *yosef,* "may he increase"), a name borne by a number of OLD TESTAMENT and NEW TESTAMENT personages. The major Josephs, each of which is treated within separate entries (*see below*), were JOSEPH, the Old Testament Patriarch; JOSEPH, the earthly father of JESUS CHRIST; JOSEPH BARSABAS; and JOSEPH OF ARIMATHAEA. Also named Joseph were: the father of IGAL, representative of the TRIBE OF ISSACHAR among the twelve SPIES sent out by MOSES to reconnoiter the PROMISED LAND (Num. 13:7); three men mentioned in the Lucan account (Luke 3:24,26,30) of the GENEALOGY OF JESUS CHRIST; and two LEVITES who returned following the PERIOD OF THE BABYLONIAN CAPTIVITY (Ezra 10:42; Neh. 12:14). A number of personages who bore the name "Joseph" are also mentioned in the APOCRYPHA: an ancestor of JUDITH (Jud. 8:1); and an officer who served under JUDAS MACCABEUS (I Macc. 5:18,56,60). Still another Joseph mentioned in the Apocrypha (II Macc. 8:22; 10:19) reflects either a scribal error or an error in the translation of the KING JAMES VERSION, as the "Joseph" mentioned in these passages refers to JOHN MACCABEUS.

JOSEPH, eleventh of the twelve sons of the Patriarch JACOB and the first by his second, and favorite, wife RACHEL. The name is derived from the hope voiced by his hitherto childless mother, "The Lord shall add to me another son" (Gen. 30:24); it has also been interpreted as being derived from the root *asaph,* "he takes away," symbolic of GOD having taken away the "reproach" of Rachel's barrenness (30:23). Joseph was the ancestor of two of the TWELVE TRIBES OF ISRAEL—the so-called "Joseph tribes"—descended from EPHRAIM and MANASSEH, the Patriarch's sons by his Egyptian wife ASENATH. The history of Joseph, in chapters 37-50 of the Book of GENESIS, is the longest and most complete patriarchal biography in the entire OLD TESTAMENT. One of the most skillfully wrought biblical stories, it is also one of the favorite tales of all time, dealing as it does with the most profound thoughts in simple, human terms; presenting the divine purpose expressed in the interaction of everyday events, it shows the triumph of moral and spiritual values over physical vicissitudes.

The biblical narrative goes into exceptional detail because of Joseph's influence on the destiny of the Hebrew people, and by extension, on Judaeo-Christian civilization. It was as a result of his having been sold, by his older brothers, into slavery in EGYPT that the Egyptian sojourn and the eventual enslavement of the Israelites came about, that MOSES arose as leader, that the LAW was given, and that the relationship of God to ISRAEL, and its unique religion—MONOTHEISM—came into being. In all of Joseph's experiences the Israelites saw the hand of God, as well as a deeper spiritual purpose, in the personal events of his life. Joseph emerges as one of the most attractive, fully dimensional characters in biblical literature, a person of physical beauty and grace of spirit, who was not embittered by his suffering but who displayed magnanimity to those who had wronged him. Humble in the face of good fortune, he credited all his achievements to God. He was devoted to and reverent of his father, protective and loving to his younger brother BENJAMIN, and compassionate to the erring. Though he

JOSEPH 1713

Joseph being cast into the pit by his envious elder brothers (*Counsel Collection*).

became viceroy of Egypt—a rank second only to that of the PHARAOH—he acknowledged his humble shepherd brothers and presented his aged father to the Egyptian king.

Born in the city of HARAN in MESOPOTAMIA, Joseph was about six years old when Jacob and his family migrated to CANAAN (on which journey Joseph's mother died in giving birth to Benjamin, his only full brother). Joseph is first mentioned in the Genesis text as a youth of around seventeen, living with his family near Jacob's aged father, ISAAC, at HEBRON. Favored by Jacob because he was "the son of his old age" and the child of his beloved Rachel, Joseph was so resented by his elder brothers (the sons of Jacob by his first wife, LEAH, and his concubines BILHAH and ZILPAH) that they "could not speak peaceably unto him." The "coat of many colours" that his father made for him also aroused the envy of the others, for it was the insignia of special rank, probably designating him as chief of the family on Jacob's death. Furthermore, Joseph's youthful behavior was not likely to endear him to his brothers—he carried tales to his father regarding the behavior of the other sons, and did not hesitate to tell of his dreams, in which he saw the entire family bowing down to him (37:2-11).

One day his elder half-brothers saw their opportunity. Their father had sent Joseph to inquire about the welfare of his brothers, who were tending the family herds in the vicinity of SCHECHEM. Joseph followed them to DOTHAN, a point on the great trade route to Egypt, where they had moved with the sheep. Seeing Joseph approach from afar, his brothers "conspired against him to slay him . . . [so that] we shall see what will become of his dreams" (37:18-20). REUBEN, the eldest, prevailed upon them not to kill Joseph: "Shed no blood, but cast him into this pit," he urged, secretly hoping to "deliver him to his father again" (37:22). They tore off Joseph's coat of many colors and threw him into a pit, a cistern at the time empty of water. Precisely what happened at this point is not clear. It seems that while Reuben was away, a caravan of Ishmaelites (descendants of ISHMAEL) came by "bearing spicery and balm and myrrh, going to carry it down to Egypt" (37:25); such spices, considered indispensable to religious ritual, the healing of the sick, and embalming, were in great demand in Egypt.

Here JUDAH is credited with saving Joseph's life, saying: "Come, and let us sell him to the Ishmeelites, and let not our hand be upon him; for he is our brother, and our flesh" (37:27). The next verse gives the impression that a party of MIDIANITE slave traders heard Joseph's cries, drew him out of the pit while the brothers were eating, and sold him to the Ishmaelites; it has also been suggested that "Ishmaelite" was a general term for "trader," while "Midianite" referred to the locality from which they came. When Reuben returned he was horrified to find that the boy was not in the pit. As the eldest of Jacob's sons, he felt responsible for Joseph's safety: "The child is not; and I, whither shall I go?" (37:30). The brothers dipped Joseph's coat into the blood of a kid and brought it to their father, who assumed that his son had been killed by a wild beast, whereupon the Patriarch rent his garments and mourned, and "refused to be comforted" (37:35).

Joseph was taken by the traders to Egypt (according to both Jewish and Arabic legend, while enroute he passed his mother's grave, upon which he threw

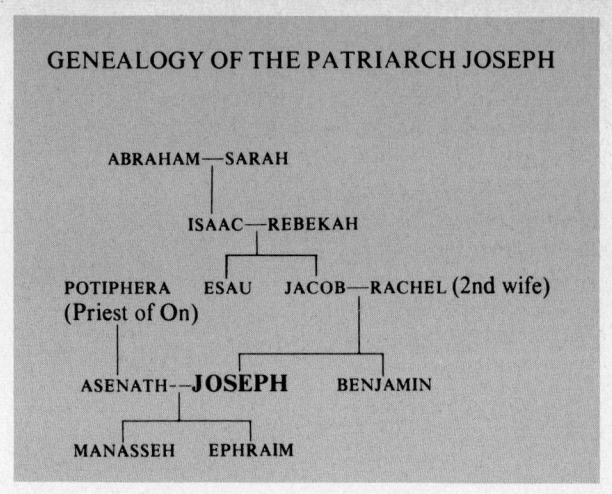

GENEALOGY OF THE PATRIARCH JOSEPH

```
            ABRAHAM—SARAH
                  |
            ISAAC—REBEKAH
                  |
POTIPHERA    ESAU    JACOB—RACHEL (2nd wife)
(Priest of On)              |
                  |
ASENATH—JOSEPH         BENJAMIN
        |
   MANASSEH  EPHRAIM
```

himself and wept bitterly), and there was sold to POTIPHAR, "an officer of Pharaoh, captain of the guard" (37:36). Joseph proved himself so able and reliable that he was made overseer of Potiphar's household and all his possessions. In this situation a new trouble arose: Potiphar's wanton wife attempted to seduce the young slave. Joseph replied that he could not betray his master's trust in him: "How then can I do this great wickedness, and sin against God?" (39:9). The infuriated woman obtained revenge by seizing Joseph's outer garment as he fled and showing it to her husband, explaining that his Hebrew slave had made an attempt on her virtue. Joseph was thrown into the prison in which the king's prisoners were kept, but here too his superior abilities soon became manifest, and he was put in charge of all the other prisoners.

Some time later, two of Pharaoh's officials, the chief baker and the chief CUPBEARER, were imprisoned and put in Joseph's ward. One night both of them had strange DREAMS they could not interpret. (Dreams play an important part in the story of Joseph, for the ancients believed that they were the deities' means of communicating with man; those who could interpret dreams were highly esteemed, in a class with magicians, soothsayers, and wise men. All the dreams in Joseph's story occurred twice, signifying that they were not idle dreams but messages of import.) Joseph interpreted the dreams of the two prisoners as foretelling that the baker would be executed, while the cupbearer would be pardoned. Events bore out the reliability of Joseph's interpretations, for on the king's birthday the baker was hanged, whereas the cupbearer was freed and restored to office.

Joseph had beseeched the cupbearer to intercede for him with Pharaoh, for he was innocent of any crime; unfortunately, once a free man, the officer promptly forgot Joseph, who languished in prison two years more—a total of twelve or thirteen in all. It was not until Pharaoh had two very troubling dreams which no one in the land could interpret that the cupbearer remembered the young Hebrew languishing in prison. Joseph was brought before Pharaoh, who remarked on the slave's purported ability to interpret dreams. "It is not in me: God shall give Pharoah an answer of peace" (41:16), Joseph answered. He explained the king's dreams as predicting that the cyclic seven years of plenty would be followed by seven years of FAMINE. The "dreamer of dreams" also proved to be a practical man. He recommended that "a man discreet and wise" (41:33) be appointed to store the grain during the period of abundance so as to provide for the years of shortage.

Knowing no one more discreet and wise than Joseph, Pharaoh appointed him to administer the program, a position of importance second only to that of the king himself. Joseph, then thirty years old, was arrayed in "vestures of fine linen" (41:42), given the king's signet ring (a symbol of royal authority) and all honors, and called by the Egyptian name ZAPHNATH-PAANEAH ("revealer of secrets"), a sign of his improved status. Also, the new viceroy was given as wife the high-born Asenath, a daughter of POTI-PHERA (not to be confused with Joseph's former master), the priest of HELIOPOLIS, the center of sun-worship in Egypt. (It was before the famine began that she bore

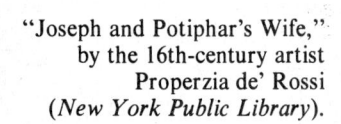

"Joseph and Potiphar's Wife," by the 16th-century artist Properzia de' Rossi (*New York Public Library*).

Joseph's brothers dip his coat into the blood of a kid to deceive their father, Jacob.

Medieval illuminated manuscript showing Joseph and his father Jacob (*right*) and (*left*) Joseph's envious brothers stripping him of his coat of many colors, the sign of his father's favor (*Mella, Milan*).

Joseph two sons, Manasseh and Ephraim.) The famine came, as Joseph had predicted, "and the dearth was in all lands; but in all the land of Egypt there was bread" (41:54). People from all the neighboring countries came to Egypt for corn—among them Joseph's half-brothers, the ten eldest sons of Jacob. (Benjamin, the youngest, and now doubly precious to his father because he was the only remaining child of Jacob's beloved wife Rachel, remained behind in Canaan.) The brothers bowed down before the viceroy, as had been foretold in Joseph's boyhood dreams (37:2-11)—unaware that the Egyptian viceroy was in fact their brother.

Though Joseph recognized them, he did not reveal his identity. Addressing them through an interpreter, he spoke roughly, accusing them of being spies,

1718 THE FAMILY BIBLE ENCYCLOPEDIA

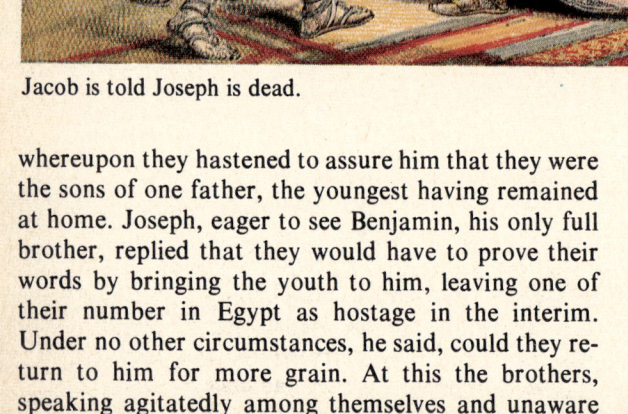

Joseph dreams as a youth.

Joseph cast into the pit by his brother

Jacob is told Joseph is dead.

Joseph cast into Egyptian prison.

whereupon they hastened to assure him that they were the sons of one father, the youngest having remained at home. Joseph, eager to see Benjamin, his only full brother, replied that they would have to prove their words by bringing the youth to him, leaving one of their number in Egypt as hostage in the interim. Under no other circumstances, he said, could they return to him for more grain. At this the brothers, speaking agitatedly among themselves and unaware that the viceroy understood Hebrew, expressed their sense of guilt: "We are verily guilty concerning our brother . . . therefore is this distress come upon us" (42:21). Hiding his emotion, Joseph took SIMEON as hostage "and bound him before their eyes" (41:24). Then he commanded his assistants to fill the brothers' sacks with corn, to put each man's money in his respective sack, and to give them provisions for the return trip to Canaan. The brothers were both fright-

JOSEPH 1719

Joseph sold into slavery.

Joseph in prison.

ened and dismayed when they found the silver in their sacks.

When the brothers told their father what had transpired, he flatly refused to let Benjamin leave: "my son shall not go down with you; for his brother is dead, and he is left alone: if mischief befall him by the way in which ye go, then shall ye bring down my gray hairs with sorrow to the grave" (42:38). But the famine was severe and starvation loomed for Jacob's family. Finally, Judah took command of the situation: "I will be surety for him," he declared; "if I bring him not unto thee . . . then let me bear the blame forever" (43:9). Jacob had no choice but to accede, and the brothers came before Joseph once more, this time with Benjamin. Joseph tested their behavior toward the boy, until he was satisfied that they were not mistreating his brother as they had once mistreated him.

The ultimate trial came when Benjamin was ac-

1720 THE FAMILY BIBLE ENCYCLOPEDIA

Joseph interprets Pharaoh's dreams.

Joseph becomes vizier of Egypt.

Joseph reveals himself to his brothers.

Joseph is reunited with his father.

cused of stealing Joseph's silver divining cup: as punishment, the boy was to remain in Egypt as Joseph's slave. The brothers were appalled at this development. Their behavior measured up to the severest test, showing that they were morally regenerated. As their spokesman, Judah proved faithful to the vow he had made to his father; he offered himself as a slave in Benjamin's stead: "For how shall I go up to my father, and the lad be not with me? lest peradventure I see the evil that shall come on my father" (44:34). It was then that Joseph, overcome with emotion, revealed himself: "I am Joseph your brother, whom ye sold into Egypt," and then he reassured them: "Now therefore be not grieved, nor angry with yourselves . . . for God did send me before you to preserve life" (45:4-5). He bade them return to their father and to bring Jacob and his family to Egypt, where they would be provided for.

JOSEPH 1721

Joseph's brothers arrive in Egypt.

Joseph presents Jacob to Pharaoh.

Joseph sent his brothers on their way, loaded down with provisions, money, and clothing as well as special gifts for their father. When Jacob learned the incredible news that Joseph was still alive and was governor over all Egypt, he was little concerned with his son's rank. "It is enough," he said, "Joseph my son is yet alive: I will go and see him before I die" (45:28). The point is repeatedly made that the Hebrew sojourn in Egypt was intended only as a temporary measure; it was, however, to last over four hundred years. On the way from Canaan to Egypt, Jacob stopped at BEERSHEBA, where he "offered sacrifices unto the God of his father Isaac" (46:1). There GOD spoke to him, saying: "I will go down with thee into Egypt; and I will also surely bring thee up again" (46:4). The divine message transforms the descent into Egypt from a family visit into an event of national significance, preordained by God.

Jacob's family—"all the souls of the house of Jacob . . . threescore and ten [counting Jacob himself, Joseph, and Joseph's two sons]" (46:27)—departed for Egypt" and "Joseph made ready his chariot, and went up to meet Israel his father, to Goshen . . .and he fell on his neck, and wept" (46:29). The family lived peaceably in GOSHEN and prospered. After seventeen years had passed, news came to Joseph that his father was ailing. He hastened to Jacob's side, bringing Ephraim and Manasseh with him—at which time Jacob adopted the two grandsons, giving them equal status with his own sons (as a result of which the tribes descended from Manasseh and Ephraim are ranked as two of the TWELVE TRIBES OF ISRAEL). Jacob also gave Joseph "one portion above thy brethren" in Shechem, where Joseph eventually was buried. (Some biblical commentators interpret the extra portion as symbolizing the fact that Joseph, through his sons, became the ancestor of two of the Twelve Tribes.) In his deathbed blessing, the Patriarch spoke with special tenderness of Joseph, and bestowed upon him the warmest of blessings (49:22-26). The esteem in which Joseph was held by the Pharaoh is indicated by the fact that when Jacob died "the Egyptians mourned for him threescore and ten days" (50:3). Joseph went up with the funeral cortege to Canaan to bury his father in the CAVE OF MACHPELAH, as Jacob had requested (such processions are frequently depicted on Egyptian tombs).

Now that their father was gone, the brothers feared that Joseph might take vengeance on them, but he reassured them: "Fear not: for am I in the place of God?. . . . I will nourish [sustain] you, and your little ones" (50:19-21); he realized that, however ill-intended their deeds, the brothers had been the unwitting agents of Providence. Joseph lived to the age of 110, an age described in Egyptian writings as the ideal life span; thus he "saw Ephraim's children of the third generation: the children also of Machir, the son of Manasseh [the leading clan of Manasseh], brought up upon Joseph's knees" (50-23). Before he died, Joseph requested that the Children of Israel carry his bones with them when the time came for their return to Canaan; he had faith that "God will surely . . . bring you out of this land unto the land which he sware to Abraham, to Isaac, and to Jacob." Joseph's body was embalmed and "he was put in a coffin in Egypt" (50:24-26). His quiet burial is in marked contrast to Jacob's elaborate state funeral fifty-four years previously and suggests that the situation of the Israelites may have already begun to deteriorate.

More than four hundred years later the Children of Israel kept their promise to Joseph. Following the EXODUS Joseph's coffin was borne to Canaan in the long journey through the WILDERNESS, and JOSHUA buried it in the parcel of ground that Jacob had long ago purchased from HAMOR at Shechem, "and it became the inheritance of the children of Joseph" (Josh. 24:32), i.e., part of the territory of the TRIBE OF EPHRAIM. Joseph's conviction that his people would eventually return to the land of their fathers is cited in the EPISTLE OF PAUL THE APOSTLE TO THE HEBREWS as an example of faith in the major Old Testament personages: "By faith Joseph, when he died, made mention of the departing of the children of Israel; and gave commandment concerning his bones" (11:22). The death of Joseph, with which the Book of Genesis closes, marks the end of the PERIOD OF THE PATRIARCHY.

It is the critical view that two strands, or "versions," are discernible in the Joseph narrative, a "J" (Jahwist) stratum and an "E" (Elohist) stratum, with a few additional details by "P" (the Priestly source) (see PENTATEUCH). According to the "J" narrative, for example, Joseph is rescued from death by Judah and is sold to the Ishmaelites, who then sell him to an unnamed Egyptian. In the "E" version Joseph is rescued by Reuben and purchased by the Midianites, who sell him to Potiphar, an officer of the king. Other details vary slightly, but the strands are closely parallel and both have been carefully preserved, showing that the biblical redactors, the later editors, considered themselves custodians of a sacred charge. The redactor might rearrange the material, but he was not free to suppress any of it. The "P" narrative adds a few statistics and lists the family members who migrated to Egypt.

Some biblical critics doubt the historicity of the Joseph story and regard its hero as a legendary ancestor of the tribes of Manasseh and Ephraim. Others cite recent archaeological evidence that Joseph was a real person who actually lived (see ARCHAEOLOGY; BIBLICAL CRITICISM). Two of the TEL EL-AMARNA tablets mention a Semite who held a high office in Egypt comparable to that attributed to Joseph. An ancient two-hundred-mile waterway that irrigated a district eighty miles south of Cairo is still known today as *Bahr Yusuf* ("Joseph's Canal"). Egyptians say that it was planned by the biblical Joseph, the "grand vizier" of Pharaoh. *The Tale of Two Brothers,* a popular story of Egypt's Nineteenth Dynasty, is based on a situation similiar to that of Joseph and Potiphar's wife, indicating that such a circumstance was not improbable.

Famines of long duration often occurred when the Nile failed to overflow: there is a record of a seven-year famine early in the third millennium B.C. Scholars point out that by reckoning from RAMESES II (who is believed to have been the "Pharaoh" of the Exodus account) back to the time of Joseph, one reaches the HYKSOS dynasty, in which period the Joseph story is entirely feasible. Under these foreign overlords, Semitic shepherd and nomad tribes from Canaan and Syria, Joseph could very well have risen to high office, whereas the Egyptians despised shepherds and nomads. Scarabs dating from the Hyksos period bear Semitic names—one of them, "Jacob-her." Altogether, the authenticity of the details in the story show a remarkable knowledge of the country and the court. Today the historicity of the biblical story is virtually unchallenged, although details may vary. The narrative could not have been recorded, however, before the ninth century B.C., according to scholars, for such names as "Potiphar" and "Zaphanah-paaneah" were not used in Egypt prior to that time.

The biblical text credits Joseph with centralization of landownership in the hands of the king, priestly holdings excepted. Some modern critics have professed shock at Joseph's apparent heartlessness in exploiting the hunger of the peasants to deprive them of their property. Scholars say this view betrays a lack of understanding of the era and of the historic process of social change. The pharaohs were absolute monarchs, and all property in Egypt was considered theirs by divine right. A sweeping economic change did take place after the expulsion of the Hyksos in the mid-sixteenth century B.C., but scholars say that it must have come about gradually over the lifetimes of several pharaohs, who reasserted their rights and tightened their hold on the country after evicting the foreign rulers. Crediting the change to Joseph, say the critics, is part of the idealization of his history, intended to show how ungrateful were the later pharaohs who "knew not Joseph." In the telling, however, the Bible again demonstrates an intimate knowledge of Egyptian affairs.

Joseph is a favorite subject of rabbinic literature. He is cited as a completely righteous man, as a model of filial respect, and as being modest about his lofty

Joseph, now vizier of Egypt, travels throughout the land to store the harvest of corn (Freedman Collection).

position. Supposedly the physical counterpart of his father, he was said to resemble Jacob in many aspects of his life. Both were born to mothers who had been barren; both were hated by their brothers, had to leave home, and were forced to labor for others; both encountered angels (*see* ANGELOGY). Conjectures on the "evil reports" Joseph brought to his father about his elder half-brothers range from the charge that they all "looked at the daughters of the land" to the accusation that Leah's sons slighted the sons of Jacob's CONCUBINAGE, referring to them as slaves (*see also* BILHAH; ZILPAH). The brothers were said to have received twenty pieces of silver for Joseph, which they divided, each taking two pieces with which they bought shoes. Potiphar, however, paid four hundred pieces of silver for his slave. The rabbinical literature also claims that Jacob never really believed Joseph was dead, because he could not forget him, whereas the dead are easily forgotten. Joseph meanwhile thought often of his family, and in the twenty-two years away from home never drank wine. Joseph was said to have been so efficient in the service of his master that Potiphar thought him to be a magician.

The Hebrew was unlike other slaves in that he was not rapacious but looked after his master's interests, and was not lustful but chaste. Some rabbis thought Joseph was too vain, believing that even before he left Canaan he was overly interested in his appearance. The *Sefer ha-Yashar* goes into considerable detail regarding Joseph and Zulaika (or Zulaikha), Potiphar's wife, drawing upon Arabic sources. In this version, Zulaika was so enamored of the slave that her health was impaired; her women friends cut their fingers peeling oranges because they could not take their eyes off him. According to the TESTAMENTS OF THE TWELVE PATRIARCHS she was ready to kill her husband so that she could marry his slave. Because Joseph had personally supervised Jacob's burial, Moses himself allegedly carried Joseph's bones back to Canaan, the coffin being carried side by side with the ARK OF THE COVENANT.

Joseph, or Yusaf as he is known to the Arabs, occupies an equally important place in Islamic literature; called "the Moon of Canaan," he is regarded as a model of manly beauty: "a second Joseph" is a familiar complimentary expression. The Koran devotes an entire chapter to him, and Mohammed called this narrative "the best of the stories." Many Egyptian public works are attributed to Joseph, including the city of Memphis and a number of obelisks and pyramids. Also in Islamic literature the story of Joseph and Zulaika is treated as a romance which ends happily years later, after Potiphar dies. The two are the subject of a favorite love song and of a Persian epic by the tenth-century poet Firdusi. Both Jewish and Arabic folklore have it that Joseph's sarcophagus was buried in the Nile and was raised at the time of the Exodus.

The story of Joseph has also left its mark on Western art and culture. In about the fifth century B.C., it was expanded into a Greek Apocrypha, basically Jewish with a Christian interpolation. *Poema de Jose* was written in Spanish with Arabic characters by a Morisco convert who had forgotten his ancestral language but remembered the ancient tradition. The sixteenth-century Renaissance artist Jacopo Carucci (Il Pontorio) painted the impressive canvas *Joseph in Egypt*. The great seventeenth-century Flemish master Rembrandt van Rijn painted two canvases on the subject, *Joseph Accused by Potiphar's Wife* (1654), now in Berlin's Royal Gallery, and the other (1655) in the Hermitage in Leningrad. The twentieth-century German-born author Thomas Mann made Joseph the subject of a massive literary work, the tetralogy *Joseph and His Brethren*. It is interesting to note that at the time of the 1962 Vatican Ecumenical Council, when Pope John XXIII received a delegation of Jews he greeted them with the words "I am Joseph your brother," symbolizing the common heritage shared by Jews and Christians alike. — H.G.G.

THE STORY OF JOSEPH AND HIS BROTHERS

For Younger Readers

Joseph, the eleventh son of Jacob, was born in Haran, in Mesopotamia, but later lived near Hebron, in the land of Canaan. His mother was Rachel. His older brothers were jealous of him because he was their father's favorite. Jacob even made Joseph a coat of many colors. Unlike the coats of that time, it had sleeves and was fashioned like the robes worn by young men of noble rank.

One morning Joseph said to his brothers: "Listen to the strange dream I had last night. We were all in the fields, binding corn. Suddenly my sheaf rose up and stood still while your sheaves bowed low before it."

"Perhaps you imagine that you are our lord and master!" his brothers said angrily.

Joseph had another dream in which the sun, moon, and eleven stars bowed down before him. This made his brothers angrier than ever. His father scolded him. "Can it mean that your brothers and even I must bow down before you?" he asked.

One day, Joseph's brothers went to look for fresh pastures in the neighborhood of Shechem, where Jacob owned fields. A few days after their departure Jacob sent Joseph to visit them. "Find out whether all is well with them," he said. At first Joseph could not find them, but a wayfarer told him that he had seen the young men farther north, in Dothan. He told Joseph how to get there.

When the brothers saw Joseph in the distance, they said, "Here comes the dreamer! Let us kill him and throw the body into a water hole. We can tell our father that a wild beast devoured him."

Reuben, the eldest, wanted to save Joseph's life. "We must not shed blood," he said. "Throw him into the water hole, but do not harm him." He meant to return later, pull Joseph out, and take him safely home.

When Joseph came up to the tent, his brothers seized him, stripped off his coat, and threw him into a water hole to die. At that time of year, the hole was dry. They covered it, and sat down to eat.

While they were eating, a caravan of merchants came along. They were on their way to Egypt to sell spices for use in medicines and in preparing the dead for burial. Judah suggested that they sell Joseph to the merchants. The others agreed, and they pulled Joseph out of the water hole and sold him for twenty pieces of silver. They dipped Joseph's coat in the blood of a goat, and later showed it to their father. "It is my son's robe," Jacob said, weeping. "A wild beast has devoured him."

Meanwhile Joseph went with the caravan to Egypt, where he was sold as a slave to Potiphar, the captain of the ruler of Egypt's guard. Potiphar soon made him the steward of his household and his personal servant.

Joseph grew into a handsome young man. Potiphar's wife admired him and asked him to make love to her. "That would be an evil thing," Joseph said. "I cannot sin against my God." The angry woman told lies about Joseph to her husband, who had him cast into prison.

God did not forsake him. He made the head keeper take a liking to Joseph. Soon the young man was put in charge of all the prisoners. Among them were Pharaoh's chief steward and baker, who were awaiting trial for crimes they were said to have committed.

These men had frightening dreams, which Joseph interpreted for them. He told the chief steward that his dream meant that he would be set free. But the baker's dream meant that he would be hanged. What Joseph said came true.

Two years later, Pharaoh himself had a dream that none of the wise men in the kingdom could explain. The chief steward told Pharaoh about Joseph, and the young man was sent for. Pharaoh told him: "I have heard it said that you have the power to explain dreams."

"I have no power of my own," Joseph said, "but God will give the power to explain your dream."

One of Pharaoh's dreams concerned seven fat cows who were devoured by seven thin cows. Another concerned seven thin ears of corn that were devoured by seven plump ones. Joseph told Pharaoh that both dreams meant the same thing. For seven years, Egypt would have rich harvests of grain. But these would be followed by seven years of terrible famine. Joseph advised Pharaoh to find a wise man and put him in charge of all Egypt. He should build great storehouses

"Reuben said unto them, Shed no blood,

JOSEPH 1727

but cast him into this pit . . ." (Gen. 37:22).

throughout the land and store in them enough grain for the years of famine.

"As your God has revealed all these things to you, there can be no man as wise and clever as you," Pharaoh told Joseph. He put his own ring on Joseph's finger as a symbol of authority and Joseph, at the age of thirty, became viceroy of Egypt. He was given the high-born Asenath as his wife and before the famine started he had two sons, Manasseh and Ephraim.

During the famine years, people came from all the neighboring countries to buy corn in Egypt. Among them were Jacob's ten eldest sons. Benjamin, the youngest, whom Jacob loved greatly, remained at home in Canaan.

His brothers bowed down before Joseph, not recognizing him. Thus his boyhood dream came true.

Although Joseph recognized his brothers, he did not reveal his identity. Through an interpreter, he accused them of being spies. They protested that they were all sons of the same man and that they had a younger brother at home. Keeping Simeon as a hostage, Joseph ordered the others to go and fetch Benjamin. But before they left, he told his servants to fill their sacks with corn, hide the purchase money in the sacks, and give them food for their journey.

When they found the silver in their sacks, the brothers were frightened. They told their father all that had happened and he, too, was afraid. He flatly refused to let them take Benjamin. "If anything happens to him," he said, "I will die of sorrow."

As they were close to starvation, Judah pleaded with his father. "I will be surety for Benjamin," he declared. "If I do not bring him safely home, let me bear the blame forever." Jacob then agreed to let Benjamin go.

When the brothers brought Benjamin to Joseph, he tested them to make sure that they did not mistreat Benjamin as they had once mistreated him. During one of the tests, Benjamin was accused of stealing a silver cup. The brothers were horrified. They showed by their concern that they had reformed since Joseph was a boy. Judah offered himself as a slave instead of Benjamin. "How can I return to my father without him?" he cried. "What would it do to him?"

Joseph was deeply touched, and told them who he was. "I am Joseph, whom you sold," he said. He made haste to reassure them. "Do not be grieved, or angry with yourselves, for God sent me before you to save lives."

Joseph sent his brothers home to Canaan with food, money, and special gifts for his father. Jacob, overjoyed that his son was alive, came to visit him. He adopted his grandsons and gave them equal standing with his own sons.

After their father's death, Joseph's brothers were afraid that he might now take vengeance on them. But Joseph told them, "Fear not. I will look after you and your little ones."

Joseph lived to the age of 110. He had had many sufferings, but he always believed that God was with him, watching over him. Everything that had happened to him was in accordance with God's plan.

Before he died, Joseph asked the Children of Israel to carry his bones with them when they returned to Canaan. His body was embalmed and lay in a coffin to await removal to the Promised Land. When the Israelites left Egypt, the coffin went with them on their long wanderings in the wildernesss. And when the Israelites reached Canaan, Joseph's body was at last buried in a piece of ground that Jacob had bought at Shechem.